Time in the Year of the Bluebird

Acknowledgments

I wish to dedicate this book to Dena A. Greenwood and her spirit with gratitude, in that she exemplified the human capacity to make a difference without blame or pause.

To Hanne, who took her first steps on the PCT ten minutes before me on March 19th, 2018. For six months of blistering trail and ever since, she's been speaking my language with more patience than I usually deserve. Ich bin ein Glücksfuchs.

Special thanks to Claudio Salguero for her beautiful hand-drawn cover. Her work can be found at www.claudiasalguero.com

To Randy: There was no trail without you.

Family, friends, and community: Thank you for sharing in this adventure.

Special note to the reader: There are no predictable paths.

Will R. P. IV
Zurich, CH
September 30th, 2019

December 12, 2018
Albuquerque, New Mexico

A series of memories. An extended moment. The kindness of strangers. Operating outside the comfort zone until comfort became a nuisance; when it became more important to sleep next to the lake than to make it into town. Two feet in two shoes. Pair after pair. Crumpled wet socks laid on a log next to a fire. Turn 'em over; steaming in the firelight. Tepid first steps turning into confident strides and somewhere, months later, twenty miles is a short day. Wake when you want…hike after sunset.

The tips of my toes are still numb sometimes and it hurts to run, but every day my mind wanders back. One step outside and I want to walk down the block, out to the main road, to the edge of town, and toward the mountains…

July 15, 2019
Zurich, Switzerland

...but the truth is, I don't know how to put anything from the past two years in a box. It's been one long year for me; a different kind of time that started in the autumn of 2017. To put the death of your mom and something like a thru-hike into a book, with words that actually mean something is almost insulting to the memory of both. It's bothered me since I started trying to put things in order.

The truth is that loved ones pass away. I don't claim novelty there and I don't claim novelty by walking the Pacific Crest Trail. After I got home in October 2018, I heard that the brother of a dear friend and bandmate I'd lost in 2013 had walked the Camino del Santiago the same summer to carry his ashes to some beautiful spot where he could honor his life. These stories are ubiquitous on the long trails. You *expect* homages and great silent gestures that help humans address what they couldn't address otherwise. We all have our reasons. Our own stories. This was mine. Some people write because they're writers; because writing helps them make sense of an experience. I needed the written word to communicate this as much as I needed a pair of Asics Kahanas to hike.

Hanne and I live in a "post-hike world" like a lot of other thru-hikers trying our best to navigate who we are after six months in the wild. The Alps are beautiful as much as a mandatory escape from Zurich. We bought a green converted Westy and each weekend we pack it full of the same bags, same clothes and gear that we took on the PCT and drive off to the mountains. We walk the trails, pitch the tent, cook the ramen, look at the stars, wake up, and keep walking.

An Email
June 9, 2019

Will:

" Sometimes it's amazing to see how much we actually had in common. Things I didn't even know. VWs and pictures of the Alps and old folk singers…can't believe it's been a year Tuesday. Everyone's in 2019 and I feel like my year started in October 2017. One long story…still trying to understand things that I'll never fully wrap my head around. Hanne and I watched The Big Year the other night as well. I was trying to tell her as much as I knew about birdwatchers and the community. I set up an Instagram account in honor of mom where I try to put up a bird a day with basic info, range, etc…just alphabetically. Still stuck in the "American…so and sos." American Dipper was last. Hope this Tuesday brings positivity in any way it can,
Take care,
W

Randy:

Reading this made me dig back through my old journals, something I had written after spending a few days alone out on the Navajo rez near the Little Colorado:

Walk alone
In the desert
Without other human voices
Then, finally you will once again hear yourself,
Hear the voices of the land
Deeper, older parts of yourself will surface and guide you
You will think more clearly, intuitively, creatively
You will see again
Your feet will learn the rhythms of the land
You will be inspired
You will remember who you are
And what is important
When you turn around and walk back
To the other parts of your life
You will laugh at the way you use to think things were.

June 7, 2019
A Dream

A.) Two tennis players stand opposite each other...suspended in a field of infinite white. As the first player lobs the ball we observe from a few meters away on the sidelines. The ball makes an arch. It comes toward us. Then it continues away from us. But we also have the ability to swiftly change our point of observation. Now we hover above the match. From this new vantage point the ball merely streaks below us in a straight line. If we observe from the position of the player, it forms a sort of phi half-spiral, leaving the right side of his body and flying over the net in to the left before abruptly dropping down. If we somehow maintain our proximity next to the ball itself like a tiny fly with a camera, the enormous ball merely rotates at various speeds while the court (should we have one) moves back and forth.

B.) A train flies past...but it hasn't gone *past* anything except the observer. It's still going toward something. The mind has the ability to play tricks on itself with these sorts of linguistic triggers. "There it goes..." as if the event is now suddenly a part of The Past, but nothing stopped. Everything is still in motion. Your past, made of occurrences that you happened to experience and observe from your own vantage point, is still in motion, still happening and unfolding. It just diverged from your position. When you choose in full awareness the opportunities for separate paths only appear to collapse into a single road. Your road. Yet the past is a perception that can only happen *now*. The question that actually bothers most people is "Ok then, *why* did I experience *that* in *my* past? What sort of former conditions did I allow to occur that gave me this current experience?"

What in the world is this thing we call "time"?

"I don't like either the word "hike" or the thing. People ought to saunter in the mountains - not "hike!" Do you know the origin of that word saunter? It's a beautiful word. Away back in the middle ages people used to go on pilgrimages to the Holy Land, and when people in the villages through which they passed asked where they were going they would reply, "A la Sainte Terre", "To the Holy Land." And so they became known as Sainte-Terre-ers or saunterers. Now these mountains are our Holy Land, and we ought to saunter through them reverently, not "hike" through them."

-John Muir

Number of times the word "hike" appears in this book: 244

November 2017
Four Months Before the Trail

    Nearly a month has gone by...some kind of dream. No music at all. Shifted gears. Sure. It's percolating I suppose. It always does. Right before bed often-times. But I haven't had any desire to tackle this right now. I did work on some album art and settled on a name. Another thing that came to me in a dream. I was worried that the word didn't actually mean anything when I woke with it, but it does. In Mandarin?
    I've been back to Arizona multiple times now. Checking in every day or so. Sending articles and essays and research about leukemia. A month in and one begins to accept the reality of the situation. A family member has cancer. The shock wears into frustration which wears into anger and emotions vacillate back and forth; the cartels that essentially run our institutions...and how someone you love is subjected to a degree of stupidity and misapprehension that any child can point out, but mostly it's just a desire to keep them from suffering. Someone that gave me so much...who honestly didn't want anything for me other than a sincere adventure. She lives to the fullest and always has. It's thrown a certain light on the fact that I've spent the last three years in a sort of self-imposed exile from society. I didn't know when I was younger that I'd be wringing my hands over tones and timbres etc. It seems so far from some core element I've forsaken along the road.
    A good time to me is nothing more than a decent challenge and I've spent the past few weeks climbing mountains, sand dunes, and rock walls; anything to push myself. Just for a clear head. Just to redeem something other than the whole subjective rabbit-hole of music.

If anything, I've only written music I like. I have no major influences. People I admire sure, but it's my music. I'm not going to put out anything I personally wouldn't listen to. I'll come back when it's time. Distance is healthy. Maybe obsession is healthy too. To an extent. But it's easy to get cross-eyed when you're in the middle of something. Right now, nature makes more sense. I pack a camera, drive a few hours to some place, and go exploring.

In about a month she goes down to Phoenix to begin the treatment process. It's this huge ordeal; not just emotionally but financially as well. I've helped raise thousands of dollars, yet I feel that it might be little more than a drop in the bucket. What an utter sham our health-care system is. An absolute joke. Treatment is one thing. Bankrupting people in the process is quite another. Shameless. There's nothing human about it.

I hear things. It's just part of falling asleep as long as I can remember. I wouldn't call it synesthesia. I think it might come under the chromesthesia definition but I'm not sure. It's just the auditory parallels between color and sound and texture which are already fairly established. It's there. It might be residue from the day working itself out. Who knows. I had a vision falling asleep the other night in relation to painting. It was very Pollock on the surface, but less random. It was feeling a color move to another color. Another shape; and layering instinctively on a canvass. It looked vaguely Pollockesque but there was very little Pollock in terms of how I experienced it. And I thought "…yeah, that's basically how sound should be done." It's a matter of paying attention is all…usually my biggest challenge. Either way, I couldn't care less right now.

January 2019
Three Months After the Trail

"Whence I walked among low fern and tallest pines…that wept
What heavens gifted
Through effortless spirit
In such a dance
That I praised the conductor
The molten texture of time
His black cloak. Her black womb.
Yet ever heralding and heralding
The ever-becoming and endless moment.
That glorious imperfection
And feeding of waves
By ever-drawn shorelines of the world
Who amongst you has read the Whole Book?
Who claims to know?
Yet that I were an autumn leaf
Sailing toward the brook."

January 3, 2018

Why do we hike, climb, and camp? What is that connection with source that we crave? Why do I crave it? What does it mean? It has its own quality - nature that is...
And we set ourselves amidst it to come closer to truth. Closer to the harmony that it shows us. It's difficult to describe. Even as someone raised around towering sandstone cathedrals and clouds of stars, I desire to walk deep and far to attain and reattain a sort of communion.
The PCT is 2,600 miles of desert, mountains, and forest spanning dozens of biological and geographical habitats.
Is there any way to feel truly prepared? My god. I have just over three months to get everything in order:

-To sell my car.
-To save the emergency funds.
-To pack boxes with correct shipping labels to go out at the correct times.
-To secure logistical support from friends and family.
-To purchase the last essentials.

Is this crazy? Can it be done? Yes and yes. I am all-too familiar with the way dreams quietly inch away for what authentic vision may lack. This time it's been wholly up to me to plan, save, and strategize from the ground up and when I can exercise that level of control I feel a little better...but anything could go wrong. Any number of things. Forty percent of hikers that set out with the best of intentions for a thru-hike will make it to Canada. Injury, lack of funds, mental exhaustion, etc. You name it. But right now...at this point my motivation is simple: I need to do it.

I have zero expectations of how it will fundamentally impact any level of my life nor do I see it as a panacea.

I also want to share the experience with my mom at this juncture. To send the pictures and words from the trail. But I don't do this *for* anyone. An undertaking of this class can't be done for anyone but one's self. Right? There's just no way to attach expectations to it.

Time will tell. If I set off with a good attitude and put one foot in front of the other; if I press on despite what feelings I'll undoubtedly encounter. I may spend entire weeks at my wit's end. Terrified. Alone. Short on water and food. All these things can happen, but on the other hand…I can see myself pushing through all that and quite possibly finding out something about myself that I've needed a reminder of.

At the end of the day I'm a proximity person. When I'm in the trees I'm in the trees. When I'm at work I'm at work. When I write music I'm writing music.

Circling into Silverton, Colorado at the end of a long drive. Summiting Wheeler Peak. Immersed in the moment.

Taking the best photographs I can. These things drive my heart and that is why I do it.

Outside of the logistics…there's very little I need to over-think. I need to walk. For five months I need to walk. This much I can do.

It doesn't need to be built up in my head. I don't need other people's opinions on how any of it should be done.

Yes, this thing looms. I'm already getting a few unwanted 'what ifs' but I've had them for awhile (since the day I started this thing) I don't fear death per se. There's something beyond all the immediate assumptions about the little life I've attained on this rock going around the sun.

On the other hand. Yeah, I'm just tired. Tired of being here. Tired of sharing an apartment. Tired of so many paradigms that I want an honest break from. Maybe I'll wind up back in Albuquerque after all. I don't know. I just don't want to attach some huge unnecessary level of meaning to all this. I kind of like my life honestly. It doesn't need to change *drastically*. I'd just rather have a little more inspiration in my pocket. It's been pretty humdrum and planning this thing has been a great big shot in the arm for focus, for clarity, for letting a lot of nonsense just slide to the side.

Wish someone was going with me though. Sometimes...other times I imagine the glory of watching stars high in the Sierras. I hope they lift that fire ban, though. What's an epic camping trip without campfires? In this case, still pretty epic.

I just want to do it. That's all. I want to finish it. I want to make it through the desert. Then the mountains. Then the forests. One by one.

*"Mysteries too unbelievable to entertain
We can't imagine what we can't imagine
Riding a thin frequency band
Arguing over breadcrumbs"*

December 17, 2018

There's a lot of synchronicity and different energy going around which is hard to pin down or appreciate logically sometimes. It's a feeling. A sort of clearing...a different sort of perspective on things.

For weeks after the PCT all I could do was stare at the accumulated photos and watch other people's videos and experiences coming in from the trail.

I didn't want anything but PCT on repeat. It was a sort of tunnel-vision that I couldn't (nor did I want to) escape. The trail had been a bubble of security and momentum and had become my entire way of dealing with the passing of my mom. It was one succinct package of experience that I didn't have to look past to appreciate. The only thing I worried about for those six months was how far to hike, what to eat, and who to share it with as our family transitioned through the experience. I won't say anything else on the post-hike world. I think it's all been said at this point and, although there's no way to truly tell where your perspective is at any given moment in life, I will say that the past two weeks held a remarkable set of experiences that helped in a big way.

Hanne came all the way back from Zurich and her can-do attitude helped knock some common sense back into me. We hiked the foothills of Albuquerque, the more challenging Laluz Trail high up into the freezing early winter snows that I'd trained on before the trail, and then took a two-day trip down to Silver City where the CDT actually crosses. I'd been reading about the Continental Divide Trail over Thanksgiving and my heart started racing every time I thought of planning another thru-hike. It just gave me old-fashioned butterflies looking at pictures of the mountain lakes and passes. Of course the CDT is a different beast altogether. It's not even officially finished as far as I can tell although this year the adjoined committees agreed on an official "best general route" that they've posted online. Also, this route was re-blazed this year so that's a plus.

 We drove down through smaller towns I hadn't seen in ages like Truth or Consequences and Deming; over some snowy passes in the southern mountains that I wouldn't have imagined in New Mexico, until we reached the sleepy town of Silver City and stopped at the Chamber of Commerce to inquire about the best way to get on the CDT.

 The woman behind the desk was extremely helpful as she'd hiked all the nearby trails herself and told us about the Walnut Rd access point just outside town so we hopped back in the car and took off until it turned to dirt and we started passing trailheads leading off into various sections of high-desert forest with lots of juniper and pine mixed with bright rocky brown earth.

 We made a quick lunch and sauntered off north with no idea how far we'd really get. For the first time we realized there was no prescribed distance we had to make, but boy did the pack feel good. It was maybe ten pounds lighter than it had been on the PCT, but it was the same Osprey Escalante and after a few hills and some huffing and puffing and a light shoulder ache on the left side I felt right at home. It was almost surreal watching Hanne's feet two meters ahead going back and forth and I lost myself in the old rhythm for awhile.

 When we came up to a gated property line we could see a Catholic monastery in the distance and every half hour or so the chime of bells came ringing over the hills. The terrain, for this short distance at least, was sort of like the southern California section had been. Similar flora and geology but no real passes or switchbacks like we'd encountered from the very first day onward back in March. Just rolling ups and downs...a distinct lack of animal sounds. A midday sun that was heading down fast with wisps of misty clouds moving about.

We only made five miles before we came upon a campsite; must have been used by plenty of thru-hikers. We stopped and looked about and realized this was as good as any other place. The ground was still wet from a good rain the day before and a decent fire-pit surrounded by sitting logs looked like the centerpiece of the deal, so we unpacked and after a few mistrials I remembered how my alpine tent actually worked. Hanne was laughing as I stuck wrong poles into wrong sections over and over. Of course, I'd only used it once before when I thought it was going to be my PCT tent. The thought now sounded ludicrous. The thing weighed about six pounds and spread out to what seemed like fourteen feet with the dual vestibules staked out. Thankfully, Randy had talked me out of it...to the point where he helped in the purchase of a Big Agnes one-person which stuffed into a pocket and weighed less than a pair of wet socks.

Either way it was great to be out there in the fresh air on the CDT of all places, trying to get a fire going with damp sticks and pine needles. I was about to give up, but Hanne wouldn't have it and after thirty minutes we got it hot enough to sustain a decent roar.

We set up the old stove, used the old sporks, inflated the old pads, and looked at the old stars under the old sky before putting out the fire and sneaking into our bags for a chilly December night.

Sleep was tough but it came, and we had no real schedule to keep the next day so we slept in and slowly made breakfast before heading back out to the trailhead.

Things felt different. The shock of civilization had worn off and the romance of the PCT had some perspective to it. Of course, you want to keep walking forever and you can...but life is a balancing act full of summits and valleys and right now was just the long plain before the next climb, but there were shapes and shadows emerging through the smoke and it brought me a sense of relief.

We rolled back into town just minutes away and stopped in at the Javalina Cafe for some coffee and sat on an old couch. Hanne spied a CDT log book and we opened it up to find no more than nine entries from 2018. All the towns and businesses along the PCT used to have them and I'd always sit there wondering what to write. At first we all left deep philosophical paragraphs, then logs became whimsical and at the Canadian border I remembered reading simply "I'm pretty tired. I think I'll go home now." (Forrest Gump) Pretty much. We're all home now. Wherever that is.

We share photos and information and check in on each other here and there. We're all either recovering or covertly working on the next adventure. My toes stopped going numb the week Hanne was here although it's still difficult to run. The knees will take some time. I had a few issues on the PCT with pain and stiffness like everyone but our little hikes were actually good rehab.

A couple days later we said goodbye at the Albuquerque Sunport and my heart dropped in a way it hadn't for a long time. It had been different in San Francisco back in October. The energy had been so relentless. I had no idea what was coming next in life and the reality of "saying goodbye" didn't register, but this time I sincerely didn't want her to leave.

So it's my turn to head to Switzerland after passports are renewed and flights are booked. Funny thing I never mentioned is that I've always had a romantic pull toward Switzerland; toward the Alps and the countries bordering them. So did my mom. We'd even talked about hiking a circuit around the base of Mont Blanc into France and staying in little cabins along the way.

The old house is quiet. I live upstairs in a room with a balcony overlooking the west side of town. It's warm up here. Rent is cheap and in some ways I'm in the exact same position I was over a year ago before this whole trail idea started; the little seeds being sown. The hints of possibility. Visions floating around. Life still out there...always on the horizon.

Journal
March 19, 2018

    Day one of the PCT. She dropped me at the southern terminus at about 7:00 am. Said goodbye. I don't know when I'll see her again. She heads to med school in San Mateo sometime in June. I felt sad, despite hitting the trail…something I'd been planning for close to four months. A man sat in a pickup truck and introduced himself as a PCT representative. Wished me luck. A few photos at the terminus monument. A girl from Switzerland showed up…left ten minutes before me. I caught up around noon so we finished the first stretch together. Hashed out our own anxieties about what we were about to undertake…pushed through to Lake Morena around 5:00 pm. Beautiful. Just Beautiful. Trail Angels offering snacks. A warm shower.

- Then I fell asleep
- Someone stole one of my water bottles!
- One of the kids from across camp I'm sure.
- 7:50 am. Bright sun. Clear sky. Ten miles to next camp.

Mostly flat. Kind of want to get away from people already. Anyway…"

What You Don't Know You Don't Know

A pack filled to the brim, contents jutting out the top, anchored by straps as best as possible. Pushing through the morning. Tripping over loose rocks and roots, trying to hold steady. Trying to keep up with the pace. Knowing I've got too much weight. Knowing I've got to adapt. Unwilling to let go of my 'grand resupply strategy'. I don't trust myself yet. I don't trust the woods. I don't trust the towns. I don't trust the other people on the trail. Why are complete strangers so enthusiastic, caring, curious, and supportive of *my* decision? I know there's more to this. I know my spirit is committed now. The beauty is too overwhelming. The silence is too exquisite. I know I've got to get through each day...get enough rest. Get enough calories. Enough water. Prepare for the next day. Try and keep a record through pictures and words. What's happening to me? How long will I be able to protect the Idea of Myself out here? How long before I accidentally forget the human having to pretend right now? How long until the animal reappears. Maybe the Dailo Tiger...the Mandarin word from my dream. Is it Mandarin? Waiting patiently behind the high grass, watching the world go by, slinking off under the moonlight to his den, only to reappear the next morning to watch again from behind the same grass.

Every night now, there's something else. I've never pushed this hard. Never asked so much of my body. It's only walking but it takes all of me every day. Every afternoon I'm nearly beyond words with exhaustion; an exhaustion that doesn't have a name and doesn't care what I think of it. It takes over and delegates access to primal energies on its own. It knows we're out here now. It knows all the high-brow mangled philosophies aren't going to cut it. It knows the nonsense is hovering over the butcher's block, waiting to be dropped and rendered into irrelevance, but right now I carry these packages of food in my pack. Exactly 5,000 calories each. Ten extra pounds that I don't want or need. Unable to let go because I don't trust anything anymore. Because I'm so self-sufficient I've forgotten the quiet importance of reaching out for the sake of reaching out and I'm so cynical that I don't need the soft smiles and encouragement of strangers to brighten my day. This was *my* plan. *My* idea. *My* trail.

Approaching the edge of the Salton Sea. The wind is beginning to pick up. We set our bags down and gather in little clumps, staring miles across an endless pastel valley dotted with the shadows of fast-moving clouds…revealing depth and dimension over an ocean of sand. Yellow, purple, green, grey and all colors in between. In the far distance, tapestries of virga that will never touch the ground. Brilliant flashes of lighting shatter the sky.

"Is this what you wanted? Is this why you're here?"

We pick up the bags. It's a long day. No time to lose. I'll leave a bit of nonsense right here on the edge of this cliff…

Be still. See what happens…

July 1, 2018

"Will – The memorial embodied and captured Dena. Her inspiration, enthusiasm, her love of learning and teaching and beauty and nature, her great sense of adventure, our immense gratitude, a too-short life fully lived, her courage / fortitude / creativity in overcoming distant parents, times of being a single mom short on finances, long on caring and creativity. There was universal appreciation for Randy; sorrowful but compassionate, receiving everyone...I was struck by his saying she was and *is* his best friend. Your, Aubrey and Lauren's words and stories were beautiful. I was one of many to mention mindfulness."

Peace, Tom

"Do you fear the force of the wind,
The slash of the rain?
Go face them and fight them,
Be savage again.
Go hungry and cold like the wolf,
Go wade like the crane:
The palms of your hands will thicken,
The skin of your cheek will tan,
You'll grow ragged and weary and swarthy,
But you'll walk like a man!"

-Hamlin Garland

March 19, 2018

Mom: Hey Will,

    The Spot is working. We can see you just made it to the I-5 in California. This is going to be fun! We also just read your blog. That was very sweet of you what you said. You have been so wonderful through this whole experience. Randy just sent Josh your blog site. I know they will be following you. So good to see Alana. Tell her thank you for me for taking you out there. Very sweet of her.
Sleep warm tonight.

Love, Mom & Ran

May 20, 2019

WOW! Congratulations on your big news. We are very happy for you two and wish you the very best as you continue to develop a plan for your lives together. Thanks so much for the card and letting us know of the big news. It means a lot to me.
    Things here are fine. We have nothing as earth shattering as your news. Just trying to get work done in anticipation of goofing off for much of the summer. The snow situation in CA may delay our planned start date by a couple of days for our Chester to South Lake Tahoe stretch. We went turkey hunting one day last week and found a couple of dump toms. Kris gets to shoot first then I get to improvise. Anyway, it was fun. We ate some last supper and it was good.

John and Kris

May 5, 2018

M: "Just got back from PHX. Another bone marrow biopsy. We'll talk tomorrow. Congrats on 700 miles! And Kennedy Meadows!" <B Mom
W: "Hey! So no phone service in Kennedy Meadows. Got your packages. Thank you so much! All the other stuff I was waiting for i.e. boots, axe, outer layer hasn't arrived yet so we're kinda stuck...waiting for a tracking number to find out where everything's at."
M: Oh, darn, do you know that your friend sent them in a timely manner? So you got our two packages? I hope you don't have to wait too long for the other packages to arrive. <B mom
W: Ya the food is looking great! It'll be a couple days...I just can't head into the Sierras without this stuff.
M.: Well, good time to recuperate. Sorry for the delay. But welcome to the Sierras! <B mom
W: Apparently everything was delivered and signed for but the guy at the store can't find them so we're headed over to figure it out.
W: Found it! Filed under wrong name again.
M: Yay!!! Now you can be on your way. When will be the first place you will have cell phone reception?
W: Getting everything together. Looks like we're heading out tomorrow.
W: They're saying 100 percent snow on ground above 9,000 feet.
W: I think it'll probably be Bishop unfortunately - eight days trek.
W: We're only the second group to go through this year aside from one other solo hiker and one person has already had to self-arrest with the axe apparently.

W: So it's looking like fifteen miles per day tops. Just have to take it slow and safe.
M: We'll send gaiters tomorrow. Maybe you should slow down a little and let some snow melt. Are you prepared to camp in snow?"
W: I think so. We're just going to share Hanne's Hilleberg if it gets super cold. I wish we could wait longer but it's food and money every time we exit the woods!
W: Thanks for the gators too!
M: When will you have to cross 9,000 foot passes?

W: All the way to northern Kennedy Meadows it's between 7-14k!
W: The highest stuff is this week around Whitney, etc.
W: Then pretty high for the duration of the Sierras.
W: We'll be in them for three to four weeks at the pace we're looking at.
M: Oh boy, that sounds treacherous.
W: Ya sounds like everyone's made it through - just been slow, cold, and tough.
W: Thanks so much for all this stuff. It really does help.
W: I think I'll probably be out of wifi / service for up to eight days here…might be able to contact if we get off the trail halfway or at a ranger station but I'll use the Spot when we're solid at camp sites.
M: I'm so glad. It looks like you have good weather for this next week. Look forward to your phone call.
W: Thank goodness! Love you - sorry I couldn't call from here. No one's got service at all and everything runs on solar and generators.
M: Congratulations on summiting Whitney!!! It must have been freezing cold up there. Was the snow bad? So proud of you!!!

Your Spot batteries are low. I hope you have replacements. <B Mom
M: Now that you're off that extremely cold mountain, batteries seem to be ok. <B mom
M: Hope you're ok. I see you haven't moved yet today. <B Mom
M: Your Spot just wasn't working. I think the cold on top of Whitney zapped it for awhile. Seems to be working fine now. <B Mom
W: Hello! I'm alive and well in Bishop. Spot has battery issues lately. I need to turn my cell service back on and will call as soon as I'm up and running. So much amazing to tell you ! <B
M: I'm so glad to hear from you!!! I can't wait to hear all about it. I'll be home all morning. Hope you are sleeping in a nice warm bed tonight. Did you bypass Independence? You know you have a pick up there. Talk to you soon. <B Mom
W: Hey my T-mobile is so weak. I'm having trouble connecting a call to you. Hanne will be back from the store in a few minutes and I'll use her Verizon!

Journal
March 4, 2018

    Everything becomes more and more pragmatic leading up to things like this. The romance wears thin...not thin per se, but it takes a back seat. Lists and lists checked and double-triple checked. Last minute things I think I'm forgetting. Last minute trips to REI. Last runs to Costco and Sprouts. Batches of homemade trail bars cooking nonstop making the house smell like a cookie factory. Where does the cat stay? Old friends offer to help. People ask more and more questions. It's the topic wherever I go, or "Oh hey man, I thought you already left!" Tonight I got: "So that'll take you what, like two or three weeks?" The look on his date's face. Things come in different contexts. A woman walks up and starts talking about how she always likes to have a song in her head when she's doing anything boring. My first thought goes to the trail. I always have songs in my head anyway. This week it's been the kids I recorded last week. A washed-out gothic something I can't quite define. Three chords that keep repeating. I'll catch myself and try to start a Boards of Canada riff instead. Those can drone on for days when they really sink in. Small things seems smaller. Basic bits of info that meant something relevant a few months before are relegated to some corner, usually discarded and forgotten and it gives me the sense that I'm forgetting something all the time. Music production is a thing that comes out of the head and heart and I've been in a world where remembering the most minute microseconds dominates the place I walk in. Working at my other job...doing what I do on a daily basis has been full of this 'thing' for ages. A parallel life. As in "Yes, go to work, work hard, hold things together...but the precious to-do lists and percolating ideas i.e. "what was that sample I heard the other week? What was that from? I wonder if the record shop has this...should I get another VCO? Why does that synth sound better at 24 than 96?" On and on. So, generally I think my mind is going "Wait a sec...what's going on here?" It's created a distinct blur and some people notice. I notice. My talking has dropped off considerably and new lists are appearing and re-wiring...maybe new connections going on. No idea.

On the one hand, walking is so profoundly simple. In all these training hikes I've come to appreciate the process such a great deal that I can't imagine leaving it behind, even after this. The simple act of walking does things to the brain, digestive system, all systems it seems. Time perception changes. Things that bother me incessantly sometimes...they all drop off and everything comes into crystal clear focus. I find myself in some ultra-lucid state where ideas make sense. I think it's the raw reality of walking in nature. Just being out there on the dirt with the trees. Fresh air. All the things I've already written about, but every time I go out I learn something new. About myself...about accumulated undigested data, etc. Either that or it gives me access to the reset button. What happens after five months of that?

There are fears present, of course. I've come to terms with most of them. Well, honestly with all the adventures I've already had, fear becomes mundane. It doesn't help either way and I wouldn't go out there if the anxiety outweighed the excitement. I say that now.

There's going to be a moment at those pillars in Campo and probably weeks afterward where I say "What the hell am I doing?" Again...God, how many times have I asked myself that?" What am I doing sleeping in this train station in Munich? What am I doing on this stranger's couch in Denver, San Francisco, Austin? What am I doing trying to make this summit in these conditions? Why am I jumping out of this plane? Look...

    Those are all adventures. Choices. The biggest questions in life are "Why am I still in this relationship? Why did I just move across the country to try and "fix" things? Why do I have the same patterns, habits, grudges, ad-nauseam. What are these belief systems? Is this inspiration, pure and simple - or is it something you're incessantly trying to prove? To whom? Is it both?

    I could stand to be more smug I suppose. It's easy when you can just hide behind the music. That's what it's for right? It's incredibly subjective and you're not accountable to anyone. So is the life I designed...I thought. But there's nothing to hide behind when it amounts to the most basic ideas of being and movement.

    At the end of the day I barely consider any of these things. It's easier to opt into when it's on paper. In a blog. Maybe. Self-deprecation? I don't know. Sometimes it's just another cop-out.

    Tomorrow I'm selling the car to a friend. I'll miss that car... I'll wake up slowly in a warm house. Turn faucets and flush things without thinking twice. Toss clothes in washers and dryers...Maybe cooking these trail bars is better if I just turn on that playlist I made...nah, the *other* playlist. Falling asleep...to this podcast I wanted to get to...maybe some more trail inspiration. Maybe this list of "trail dos don'ts" or "why I left the PCT" or what *not* to take or life-straw vs. sawyer or trail hunger or post-trail depression or caloriespermilefatsvscarbslabelyourdropboxes.

"You know...we weren't meant to consume information like this. We weren't meant to move at 75 MPH down paved highways. Not meant to do so many of the things that we do non-stop every day. But we do it anyway. Maybe on instinct. Maybe with the idea on some subconscious level that it amounts to furthering the genome. Fair enough. Maybe none of it is so bad at the end of the day. We have large brains and who wouldn't rather sleep on a down comforter instead of a wet freezing tent? Didn't we already do that for thousands of years? Don't we deserve better? Don't we get the slightest respite from slogging through creation fighting disease and each other at every turn? Seven billion people on islands on a ball made of 70 percent water. Mortality is at an all-time low despite what appears to be rampant stupidity every time a television flickers to life. Never before have so many had access to education, clean water, and information, but treks and adventures don't simply amount to 'western lifestyle choices'. It'd be easy to assume so, but there is a longing deep in the soul of mankind that exists in every generation of every culture around the globe. It isn't even really about adventure. It isn't about accolades. It isn't about escape or transcendence or fresh air.

It's about communion. I think this is why people do seemingly insane things like Annapurna, solo Antarctica, or test airplanes and swim the English Channel. Every single thing we attempt involves a level of risk, either physical or psychological, but we don't live like it. We seem to be singular, as far we know, in our ability hold a novel independent vision in our heads and experiment endlessly with our own experience. It seems so much safer in a warm home with a fire softly burning. It seems that way...but it isn't. When friends pass on the most stark perception is how unbelievably short this life is; how we're surrounded by what appears by all measurement to approximate infinity...yet here we are - for what amounts to an infinitesimally minute fraction of time."

The First Towns

The first towns leave such permanent impressions. Walking down out of the mountains, hitching your first ride and entering a coffee shop just as it opens. The smells. Oh, the spring-dawn-of-sun smells. From Julian to Idyllwild to Big Bear. From Big Bear to Wrightwood. Everything is new. Everything is being tested. All the little lessons and shortcuts are being calculated. How things work. What patterns emerge. How buses and post offices and laundromats and showers become a chain of events that you'll navigate for a day only to say goodbye, heading back to the same place you came from - usually an empty parking lot where the trail crossed a main road. Ten miles in. Ten miles out. Another hitch. Another conversation with a stranger. Another moment of such novelty that you've got to embrace it until it's done, shaking someone's hand and thanking them profusely. The selfless acts of ordinary humans begin to weave into your attention. The casual pretenses that served you so well becomes erroneous and plainly contrived; the little boundaries less relevant. The distance from your fellow man becomes a hindrance when you find yourself in need. I answer the same questions from different people on different journeys running parallel to mine. A woman breaks down in tears as she talks about the death of her dog. A man shyly approaches at a trailhead and asks everything he can, confessing that it's his dream to do the PCT someday. A man on a bus talks about nothing but losing his wife of 40 years. Our little hike means nothing to him. A woman asks us to pray with her in the back of her Jeep. A pair of cyclists fills their panniers while we fill our bags outside the store. The girl from the register comes out with a piece of string cheese and hands it to me. "Hey, you forgot this..." she winks. I didn't buy any string cheese. "Thanks."

I do nothing but walk. Conversation hasn't found its rhythm yet. I vacillate between worry and hunger; a sense of magic and a sense of the unknown. It's easy to hide on the trail. Easy to slow your pace just enough to create distance and stay there - rummaging through the past, wondering how you became the person the you became. Wondering who you are now just weeks into the trip, before it's even possible to get an answer. Wondering how you became someone willing to dig endlessly, compulsively, repetitively, sometimes mindlessly toward undefinable abstracts, trying to uncover "Cause"...trying to stitch together a narrative that finally works, that makes sense, that just...has...meaning.

I believe in a God. Not *that* God on the chair with a beard. I believe in a force; it doesn't matter what you call it. Some men call it God. Most men are too browbeaten to understand what they claim to believe, God or no God. Beliefs are easy...until they're not. My belief came through experience and the weight of simple odds under quiet observation; that there is a force which some men have called God and I don't care what theists, atheists, or pigeons have to say about it. I can see it in the rhythm of everything, the spiral flowers, the currents of cold wind, the icicles melting next to the spring on San Jacinto. I can see it everywhere and I feel most people will conceive any excuse and absurdist posture to avoid it.

Sometimes, I can take a blade of grass and wander in ecstatic prose about the sheer math that would even allow such a thing...who would I say it to? I'd say it to myself. I'd say it as a thing between me and the grass because nobody's listening. Maybe that's why I'm out here.

These are just first impressions and I'm all-too reflective now. I want to change the past for the first time in my life and the next moment I don't understand what was so bad about it. "I'm here and the past led here and here is pretty good." I want to communicate something I've never had words for and the only way I can do it seems to be through walking. Even music fails. At the same time I'm overwhelmed moment to moment by the language of nature which I'm becoming more familiar with as a timeless adverb that whispers here and there. It's something you don't see at first; blinded by hunger and drive, but one grueling hot day you become part of Her. You reintegrate. You allow yourself to return. (She takes you either way)

"As intellectualism suppresses belief in magic, the world's processes become disenchanted, lose the magical significance, and henceforth simply "are" and "happen" but no longer signify anything."

-Max Weber

March 13, 2019
Zurich, CH

This alternative narrative broke off in October and I followed it to the left through the woods. There are always three narratives in your life but we like the dualities. The idea of "choosing one road or the other". Maybe we like the moral liability of aiming higher, never suspecting the gears and programming of a western meritocracy or childhood are silently operating in the background.

Maybe some people just like fresh air and the smell of pines. I couldn't say for certain, only that different narratives appeared before me. There's always 'plod along, maintain, and stay afloat'. There's always victimhood if you want that route. It's more like a revolving door where you keep bumping into yourself and pretending to be frightened. The other option is to face your fears, go headlong into something that you haven't even got the proper language for, tie your shoes and figure it out. How do you do this without a solid vision though? So many times I've *wanted*. There's been a feeling in my chest that has propelled me forward and sideways, even backward on occasion, but it's been next to impossible to create something without a coherent vision...a little flame that I've protected, sometimes defiantly; sometimes defensively. This tiny little flame that illuminates and casts shadows and adds dimension to a flat world.

In October of 2017, the path split into three. I could see my options clear as day. The diagnosis wasn't good. At best, she had a thirty percent chance for a full recovery and what quality of life would she have after that? I saw the unknowns barreling down upon me. Here she was, one month from retirement. Fit, healthy, happy, ready to finally build her dream cottage up the highway with Randy. It's been nine months since I received the news in Chester, California and it's not her death that renders me so instantly. It's the moment I empathize with what she must have *felt* from the diagnosis to the end of her life. The shock, the hope, and the heartbreak. It still gives me nightmares and I'm still processing.

We're all still processing. The narrative split and I'm here in Switzerland after the trail instead of somewhere else. I'm sure I could have remained in the Sierras...somewhere along the trail. I'll probably return some day, walk down the grassy bank lined with trees and geese along on the edge of the Columbia River in Cascade Locks, sit on the rocky pier with the town on my left and face the Bridge of the Gods in the afternoon of some future summer.

My hair was longer. My skin was taught and tan. I felt contentment on a level I'd never known those six months, despite the fear I felt every time I got enough service to call home. Despite everything. In October 2017 I saw the three paths: Pretend that life events are completely out of one's control, that you just 'roll with the punches' and go along to get along. I could have capitulated to the horror of what we were all faced with, hidden in a corner and cursed the universe (and to be fair, there's always elements of the three) but without thinking I found myself mobilizing. I found a reserve of energy so unique and timeless; in fact one that had always been there - unguarded, unassuming, and completely unconcerned with how it might be perceived. Isn't that the great fear? You get out there and become yourself, find completion and wholeness...you claim your authenticity and your right to live on your own terms and then someone you admired greatly turns around and calls you an irresponsible hippy to your face. Woe is me. Woe are we to have such occasions before us. So, there I stood and there lie the trail. And on the trail, I became quite aware that there was no real turning back. I'd had enough. I'd had enough pretending for two lifetimes. I saw a woman who strove in the face of everything with three children for years. Who found herself and her calling, who put herself through school and gave back this knowledge through teaching...who, when there was virtually no support, created something out of nothing. I will never officially live down the teenage diatribes and tantrums, but we did have the trail as much as the trail had us and we had the time while time had us.

It's almost 11:00 am in Zurich. We've been on some long walks through the woods surrounding the city, changed phone plans, and figured out a few things at the US Consulate.

In contrast, the other day I found myself lost in the snow, perplexed by what I'd gotten myself into, wandered back on my own tracks, and asked strangers for help. I've been here nearly a week and things are settling. Jet lag is a mind / body experience and my stomach is still upset but my feet are on the ground.

In my pack is a small leather satchel that Randy made. It's soft and well-worked, tied at the top with another leather string and a Native bead. Inside are my mom's ashes and a lock of her hair. I am to take this little bag somewhere high in the mountains under a fine tree and say goodbye. Again. Somehow. Any time I'm faced with uncertainty I step back...all this beauty. This gift. These moments with other souls...experiencing some sort of separation just for the joy of identity in the middle of what we call light years. All those fridge-magnet cliches. "No really, life is PROFOUNDLY short. No, hang on. I don't think you're reading this fridge-magnet correctly: Do you know how short and unpredictable life really is? I'm saying the longest and not-so-long-lived among us have virtually the same experience."

And what do we remember? The fine-tuned aluminum / formica inlay of the office desk? The rounded edges of a new MacBook Air that perfectly appeals to my sense of natural aesthetics? Will I be so enchanted that an algorithm picked *me* out of one of thousands of potential consumers? Or will it be the musty smell of the Mountaineer's Lodge an Stevens Pass...or the last conversation I had with my mom? What do I create?

The Forests Have Always Been Waiting

"The forests have always been waiting...and mountains, gazing down beyond the autumn rains. Just here and over there the calls of an animal, ready to nest, ready to wake, ready to hunt. In less that a half-mile of trail, the world has changed again. Micro-habitats within ecosystems within the length of a small pond, a seasonal spring, or a single flower. It's the middle of August and I've seen so much, most of which I haven't got words for. Some seen and some felt. Only in the late hours toward autumn did I know anything and that something was less than a whisper. The whisper was all I needed. Later in the trail I become quiet enough to hear again, not the business of nature, but the silence itself. The silence overtook the trail like a blanket, like nourishment of some rare kind I'd never tasted. I didn't need words. I didn't need to express idle opinions about the quality of the day. I became so simple and this was the long silent simplicity I'd craved. It didn't matter who I was walking for by September. It only mattered that I walked because walking is what humans do. This was one of the whispers that met us along the way. We were designed to do this. It's in our DNA; the wandering spirit for whom anything but natural existence feels like poorly-disguised theater. Some live in vans and fringe communities and subcultures and fight tooth and nail to claim life as their own no matter what the cost. Some are desperate to be seen as capable of doing what others are doing on a daily basis. I don't know why I did the trail. I asked myself the same question over and over for six months and while I gave different people different answers, nothing really stuck. Nothing made enough sense to claim and I still don't know. I simply remember a series of small moments, always waiting for the golden hour, always delighting in the same things, refining and forgetting…struggling and standing each morning on two aching legs; feeling like I wouldn't trade it for the world."

Journal
March 26, 2018

So, we woke up early. Frost still covered my pack when I unzipped the tent. Put on gloves for the first time. Booked it up the mountain to the other side where the grass was growing. Yuccas sticking out of turnabouts in front of the morning sun. My ankle is killing me. I don't know if I can do 18 miles tomorrow. It's some stress-sprain up front on top of my left ankle. Swelling just a bit but painful all day. The goal is to get to Idyllwild in two days, but I hope this doesn't get worse. We made it to Warner Springs around 1:00 pm. Took stock of the Resource Center and headed for the post office for resupply - then over to a golf course restaurant for God knows what. Chips. Dips. Burritos. Etc. A glance in the bathroom mirror to make sure I was still me. My nose is burnt but that's about it. Hanne and I bid adieu to the crew and headed three miles to a great little campsite under some trees by a creek. A Czech couple were there and gave me ointment for my foot. The sun went down and I made a fire and we sipped wine 'till conversation went all about - both spiritual and otherwise. Hanne is tuned-in which is good to be around. These topics at once are impossible with some people and so casual with others so we drank the wine and opened that box and felt like we both finally got a real conversation in on this trip.

"Certainly we can say that the pace of modern life, increased and supported by our technology in general and our personal electronics in particular, has resulted in a short attention span and an addiction to the influx of information. A mind so conditioned has little opportunity to think critically, and even less chance to experience life deeply by being in the present moment. A complex life with complicated activities, relationships and commitments implies a reflexive busy-ness that supplants true thinking and feeling with knee-jerk reactions. It is a life high in stress and light on substance, at least in the spiritually meaningful dimensions of being."

-Arthur Rosenfeld

Journal
November 12, 2017

"The lucid dream always emanates from somewhere in the chest. It's some kind of projection process. I can feel myself leaving my physical body through my chest. There's a great deal of vibration when it happens. Deep tones. Physical sensations. I experienced what I've been trying to experience for some time, but when it happened I was so disturbed...I didn't quite know what to do...it's been some time...I believe I came in contact with a younger version of myself earlier in Rimrock. I said, "I need your help!" but it faded away. A young boy...maybe 12 to 13 years old? Still small. Mind-blowing...my younger self was in the back room. I lifted out of my body from a resting position and floated down the hallway where they currently have their study. Now trying to recall if I actually remember any sensations of that nature from that age? So long ago. So hard to tell. Certainly, a feeling like "you don't belong here" but I would go back in a heartbeat if I could find a way to overcome this illness. What would I actually tell myself at that age? "Love her more"? "Research cancer"? Originally, I thought I'd go in and destroy the cancer myself but the transplant has been done. I woke with dread, but it looks like she made it through the initial procedure."

June 20, 2019
Zurich, CH

"There is something going on with time. First, perhaps because there is no time as such. Time: the solar-based measurement between two objects. What would we say? Everything is happening NOW. There is only NOW. Simple. But there are in-between states. Somewhere between rest and movement, light and dark. The moment before waves collapse into something tangible. The all-important, magical "transition phase." Somewhere between spirit and matter…between archetypes, ideas, and form. There's something I can't wrap my head around…having experienced precognition before, sufficiently convincing in nature-objectively so. There's a timeline, right? And we're all on timelines…little consciousness creators…each with subjective experience. What is the veil here?"

Journal
April 1, 2018

Easter Sunday: Sometimes there aren't any words adequate to express being out here. The world as it is. When all is said and done and the sun goes down. The mountains stand immobile to perception. Pine trees sing together while the wind combs through high above. Birds and lizards and deer and ants - all busy being what they are with or without us. When you're out here - away from time and the innumerable distractions of civilization, you begin to see (and by seeing, understand). No matter how much we attempt to separate ourselves. No matter what ivory tower, however armed, with whatever motive, for however long. We are a part of this. This unfolding that never ends. And once you're out here for a few days, having walked and walked to the sound of your own footsteps and the breath of your own lungs and the beating of your own heart...to rest upon a boulder in the midday sun you see that the world is still rather empty of our presence. We tend to cram into cities for some reason. We tend to think we have it all under control but we're such a small part of this. This is beyond us. Sometimes the best we can become is stewards of the lands we walk...at best. People do this to reconnect. They use this term "getting grounded'. All I can imagine is how far we've gone off course to require those kinds of ideas. My own life comes into focus. What I've allowed. Where I've gone astray and why. How I, myself, disconnected like so many - assuming something greater than simply being alive. I don't know how I'll remember this...what I'll take with me. Already something renders. A kind of peace. A kind of humility...but I don't know what becomes of all of it. Every day is a singular challenge, but we sit around campfires describing it with reverence. The challenges are welcome. We rise with the sun. Stretch out sore muscles. Drink water. Load up. Put on the pack. Walk. Often in silence. Steps are deliberate. Everything becomes more deliberate. The way you eat, sleep, and breathe. With all this time, not a moment feels wasted.

Journal
April 7, 2018

Back on the trail today. After running around like mad trying to get laundry, post office, decent food in order for most of our stay in Big Bear we also managed some deep sleep which was much needed for healing. Long showers and red wine out of titanium mugs. Doesn't get better than that. I haven't written because I have this habit of losing pens apparently, but managed to jot down a few lines on the phone and update the blog while in town. So I'm doing my best to just keep records at least for my own sake and to send along to family when I can.

Notables: The six days out of Idyllwild were brutal. Rough on the knees and calves with sun burns. Exhaustion levels off the charts but have figured out that lack of protein is partially to blame.

Muscular stress plays such a big role out here. Must keep them well-fed and able to rebuild so new supplementing strategy with salami, cheese, Skyr, and more cheese. It's all the body craves at night. Not this carbo-fat-fluff from Costco. Learning to listen to my body. Listening to the pace; how much water and food I actually need to carry between sources, towns, etc. Hanne and I have been traveling together as a duo for over a week now. She's got that stoic German demeanor, but we get along and laugh easily. I think our philosophies and goals for this aren't entirely dissimilar. There's no need for bravado or forced conversation. We just talk when we feel like it, plan the next steps and tend to agree on strategy and food in town.

From what we've heard through the grapevine everyone in the previous group has injuries. We saw Karson in Big Bear and he was getting off the trail for a good week to recover. Fortunately, his family lives just up the road from here and we were invited to stop in once we made it to Mojave.

Mom left the out-patient facility and is back in Sedona. I only hope this is the last of it. We talk as often as I can, usually when the cell phone works in towns. She's just glad to be back in the Verde Valley. Hopefully the healing continues. Sometimes I imagine imparting my strength from the trail to her. Physically, I am doing excellent. Shin splints healed. A good night's rest gives me enough to keep going and I often sleep pretty well on the trail. The bag is warm and it's another thing I've noticed others are complaining about but I've avoided. Sleep equals healing. Healing equals getting down the trail without injury or being too foggy in the head to operate. Still no blisters and I'm fine sleeping twelve hours if I need to. I only focus on one day at a time and each stretch. The fact that I have to complete so many more miles doesn't enter into the equation. There's much more to think about and experience.

Alana called today. She cried for a bit. I miss her too. My ex. I don't know what to think or do about it. We'll try to meet in Northern California for a day or two. Sometimes you just keep people in your life. Sometimes you're just connected...

Notables: Gorged on breakfast and Mexican food in Big Bear. Had a good time, honestly. Hanne and I are kind of a cool little unit that just seems to work. Was it the Grizzly Cafe we went to? The one with the great pancakes? The terrain is rocky. Mountains. Switchbacks. Granite boulders. Towering pines. The wind is constant. Blowing us to and fro. Tents were a hassle but they held up. There's three distinct sounds in nature: Birds, wind and your own footsteps crunching over the earth. These three I've found, are the only constants. Maybe cars on some far-off road. A plane overhead. A dog in the distance. Your own words break the silence more than anything and walking quietly for hours is a meditative experience. It just clears out the bullshit. So many things that don't matter out here. Your accumulated 'gold stickers' in life. Your status...just doesn't matter. The trail levels everyone after fifteen miles. Everyone's human out here. Sore knees. Same water sources as everyone else. Same routines in turn to keep going. Nature can be ruthless, but in an almost whimsical way. I've found it has a great sense of humor and it plays fair.

Unpacking A Memory

It's been about a week. My ankle is throbbing nonstop at this point. One of the other guys is pretty sure he's got a stress fracture. The top of his foot has ballooned to the point where he can't lace his shoes. Karson is starting to experience issues beneath his feet as well. All of this happens in southern California. The body is breaking in. It has never experienced this sort of strain and each step compresses and flattens and forces imperceptible shock waves through the feet, knees, hips, and the rest of the muscular system. As long as I keep moving; as long as things are in some sort of motion the pain isn't so bad, but it's not making it any easier in the long run.

We've hitched from Scissor's Crossing with a woman who takes hikers into town regularly during the season. Five days out here and we're all starting to smell something fierce. She knows all about hiker trash and instinctively rolls all the windows down before the car has even started.

I shove myself in and immediately start going in and out of consciousness. My head leans forward and falls into the pack; held up by the front seat. This gear sandwich is the only thing keeping me upright. Some of the others engage with her and talk about the trip. I can only hear their voices like distant echoes alongside the drone of the car. I laugh occasionally. Barely audible. All I want is sleep. I don't even care about food at this point. I just want somewhere to lie down.

We are searching the town of Julian for a cheap place to stay and everything is booked. Tourists clog the small sidewalks and weekend warriors roll through with pipes chugging while they look for shops and restaurants. It's a tiny town but it's full of mid-spring enthusiasm and I know I've got another resupply package here...somewhere. Hikers are always conspicuous coming off the trails, especially the longer stretches: covered in a fine layer of dirt, smelling something atrocious...they roam in small packs hunting down food, laundromats, and lodging.

We walk toward the only hotel with a vacancy sign: an English Victorian-style building with a free breakfast. It's too expensive. Nobody cares. We split up into two rooms with three of us in each. The younger kids go for one room, excited to try a new strain of weed someone's come across. We take the other. Rock paper scissors for showers. I slump against the far wall and twist the top off a plastic airplane bottle of merlot and hand one to Hanne. "For the pain...cheers."

We've made it to the first town. Whereas Mt Laguna was more of a restaurant and post office on the side of the road, Julian is a little village with basic amenities and a few markets to stock up on essentials.

"We made it" She sighs, lying back on a fresh pillow. "I'm so hungry. I want the food to come to me."

"I seriously can't walk right now" I say. "I mean, I can. But it's bad. It better heal up tomorrow or this is going to get rough really quick."

"Get lots of protein for dinner and lots of water..." She says.

"I need one of those Emergen-C packets...but first, wine. Sweet, sweet wine." I unclip my titanium cup and pour it in."

"It's better this way."

I haven't had more than a few sips and I'm already drifting again. My mind grows silent and I imagine my blood thinning. The pain starts subsiding slowly and I crawl onto the other bed, hanging my muddy feet off the end.

Hanne sets her bottle on the table stand and looks out the window.

"So...I have been thinking. I want to tell you my plan from here."

I already know what she's going to say. I've been weighing my own options since Lake Morena too.

"About the group?" I ask.
"Yeah."
"You wanna go solo?"
"I think so. I feel like I can not have the right experience in a group situation...not yet at least."
"It's a lot of dynamics going on. I know what you mean" I say.
"Yeah, and I feel like I want to meet people and enjoy nature but right now it feels like we move too fast...and I feel stuck because of what everyone else wants to do" she says.
"I've been feeling out the group thing this week...just trying to get a better idea of things. I mean, they're all nice kids but yeah, it's like you're in this train that keeps moving."
"Yeah...and it's moving too fast. I don't know if it feels like competition but I don't like this feeling." She takes another sip.
"Everyone's getting injuries already." I'm thinking out loud now. "And I don't know if it's the pace or me but it's hard to get an intuitive feeling about everything when you're just going with the train." I say
"So, I think I decide on this but maybe we eat dinner and sleep and talk about it tomorrow..."
"Ok."
"...and I ask now if you wish to come with me because we have more of the same hiking style..."
"Oh. Ok. Yeah. So...I need a shower and dinner and some sleep. Let me think after that. I agree though...it's too much to deal with at the beginning. I really don't want to get trapped in a group this early in the trail."
"Do you think we meet other people though?" She asks.
"I have no idea. I know nothing right now...I didn't expect to meet anyone for awhile so everything's going different than how I imagined it already."
"Yeah, for me too. I feel this is not a desert we hike though?"

"No...I mean it's called "high desert" because it gets less rainfall but it's definitely not like the deserts I grew up around. To me this is all mountains and pines and squirrels."
"I mean...we are on the Pacific Crest Trail."
"We are! We are on the Pacific Crest Trail! Can you believe it?"
"It's nothing like I imagined so far. Nothing at all."
"I know...I had no idea what to expect. I guess I still don't."
"Do you know how lucky we are though? Just to be here?"
"I feel lucky yeah...I feel lots of things."
"Such as?"
"Just worried about my mom. I have to call her in the morning."
"Yeah, you must do this."

   It's my turn for the shower and I take my wine with me and turn the knobs and crumple to the floor, letting the warm water pull dirt and sweat from my hair. A pool of silt and mud starts forming and swirling down the drain. I angle my fingernails into the jets one by one and watch the water slowly erode the blackness from underneath. I push my legs out and rub my kneecaps and calves, gingerly touching my swollen left ankle. I massage the nerve in my neck and let my head pull forward and down toward the shower floor. Another sip of wine.

   "Almost heaven...western Cali...busted ankle...stranger to a burgerrr....Jesus Christ. I could fall asleep here. Right now. Like this."

May 20, 2017

MR: He also says there will be an illness in your family.
MR: And you'll want to stay here in Arizona a little longer than we intended.
W: Hmmm
W: Well...hmm
MR: And it will be a patching of a relationship with that person.
W: Ohh
W: Hmmm
MR: He's at the ashram right now and says he's super in tune.
W: This is all...lots of news.
MR: I know...
W: One moment
MR: Ok
W: One more sec, sending a file.
MR: No worries
W: Okay
W: Did he say anything else?
MR: I stopped him.
W: Hmm
MR: When he started talking about an illness in your family and that you would end up patching up a relationship etc.
I was like... ok.... ok...

January 3, 2018

Times are getting longer. I called the hospital in Phoenix somewhere out on the trail today. I check in as often as possible... until her immune system is in a place where it's safe for me to visit.

I'd rounded a corner and saw a granite spire in the middle of a field of yellow grass. Everything was getting the golden hour light. I climbed the little spire and sat on top with my pack drinking water with some powdered magnesium in it. I love the stuff. Phone rang a couple times and Randy answered and we talked for a moment. He handed me over to mom.

It was a "good day" because she was able to walk down the hall, get up for a shower, etc. Her voice has been weak since all of this but she was in good spirits. In the middle of the tough stuff something as simple as talking for a few minutes can be exhausting.

They'd had a scare a few days after the marrow transplant where she'd been troubled by blood in her esophagus from the burning that occurs when you get heavy doses of chemo. Her body went into shock and they saved her with a cocktail of antihistamines and more blood. Right now, her system is spent and the healing will be a long-term process full of good days and tough days. Today was a good day. Hopefully tomorrow is a little better. I've wondered how to talk about it.

Some people I barely know have approached me with hugs and words of encouragement and the whole "let me know if there's anything I can do" thing. I can't count how many times I've heard it. What else can you say? What can anyone actually do? I go between polite thank yous to feeling like "Get OFF me. I don't know you and you aren't part of this." I'm aware how easy it is to offer support when it's not your mom and I can empathize with the situation people find themselves in; trying to offer support vs. me craving anyone that has something real to say. It's just an automatic reaction and I am honestly grateful for anyone's words of encouragement. Then again...most things people say I've already said to myself. I've gone through the gambit. Meditated. Sent healing energy in any capacity I know how to send. I'm glad the Gofundme has collected so many donations from so many people. It's a small miracle.

    The best way I know how to deal with it is to be in nature. It was always our church as kids. It's where I always feel tuned in to something greater...some unfolding process. The trails get longer. The temperature is finally dropping, which is actually great for carrying a thirty-pound pack on my back. My legs are getting stronger each time. I blazed through twelve miles today without skipping a beat; without the nerve in my back acting up. Without my floating rib doing anything strange. Of course, this is barely over half of what I expect to come across on a daily basis on the PCT.

    Honestly though...I've been an endurance athlete for a good part of my life. I haven't had a big issue with cardio or exhaustion. I recover quickly. My legs are always moving one in front of the other. Thru-hikes and distance trips are often more matters of psychological endurance and that's just a fact of existence at extremes. Sierra snow I can handle. I'm well-equipped for both heat and cold. What tends to get me is a sense of isolation when I'm really out there. I mean, way out there. It's human, but knowing where the next food and water are going to be will ease any instinct to worry much. After all...I thrive on isolation too. I love getting away. Love being by myself and having a wide range of possibilities in front of me. How wide is too wide tho? I watched Seven Years in Tibet the other week and always remember the part where he says something like

"I've had a lot of time to think...too much" And I wonder what sort of hike I'll be hiking with myself. The great thing is that I'm good at talking to myself. If I'm alone in a car I'm usually talking to myself. I used to think it was an odd sort of tendency; something old men with dementia and questionable relationships with pigeons enjoy, but I tend to work through innumerable topics when I'm just idly chatting out loud to myself. There's the humbling aspect too of just going off on a tangent and then realizing: "Wait, I'm full of it on that one aren't I?"

Latest music has been very hands-off. Very minimal and conceptual. Ideas come in very basic shades like "I just want this saw to sound like it's about to erode from a broken chip / I want this drum to sound like it's coming out a boombox on a street with buildings on either side / I want this guitar to sound like someone's talking through it with each note." The broad strokes come in different forms. I've reached a point where, regardless of what I do (when I'm actually paying attention) it's got a contiguous feel. Everyone's got that "place" when they dig for it. It changes location over time. It only lets you hone in when you really want to.

January 2, 2018

M: Hi Will,
Sorry to stun you with this, but best to be prepared when you see me. This is the reality of chemo.
Pretty sad.
Love, mom

W: You are the most beautiful woman I've had in my life with or without hair, mom. Hair grows back. Your heart and kindness are always there and that's all I see.
Love,
Will

Journal
April 10, 2018

It was the best of days. It was the worst of days. It was winding, easy trails that dripped through high desert flowers and seasonal streams. It was also blazing hot and I didn't dress appropriately or that is, I took a chance and paid the price. Total physical exhaustion with five miles to go. Just utterly grueling. All because I walked in short sleeves, shorts, and no hat for a mere four hours before lunch. Sigh. Trail magic today: a wonderful couple with a pickup truck full of snacks and hot dogs about five miles after we broke camp. Delicious. We thanked them profusely over and over. The lady said, "I just think it's so interesting what you people do." Me too. By mile seventeen I was sure that "us people" were totally nuts. I just didn't want any more pain. Just wanted it to stop. I circled Silverwood Lake for what seemed like forever. Always thinking the campground was closer than it was. Finally (and I mean finally) made it down the short side-road that led to the day use picnic area where Hanne was waiting with a couple slices of pizza that some nice ladies had given her. I think the look on my face said it all. I was almost mentally lost at that point and it took another dinner and a lot of deliberate rehydration to get me together. Hanne was so helpful. She's pretty cool that one...
Notable: One more 3-foot rattlesnake.

    I try to write down random thoughts on the phone when I'm walking but I'll copy them down some other time. Tonight, I need sleep and healing more than anything. Today was rough to the point of being psychologically hard. Would like to avoid that in the future.

    Right now we're perched for the night just up from the shore beneath some acorn trees. Tiny bugs are going mad outside the tent because of my light but they can't get in!

Frogs singing in the background. Noticed my fingernails are growing way faster since the trail. Keep snagging them on stuff. Maybe get some clippers at the pass.

Tomorrow is thirteen miles to the junction at Cajon. We'll do lunch before and stop there to load up on Subway for dinner. Sounds strange huh? Also, about the tastiest thing we'll have had for the past five days.

It's been tough; not as tough as the San Jacinto stretch. Today was a lesson though: Don't test the effing sun. Two and a half more days to Wrightwood. Three hundred miles in. Feels like a dream. Some beautiful brutal dream.

Journal
April 11, 2018

Woke early again with dozens of twittering, warbling birds going mad over the rising of the sun. This ecstatic salutation. This praise. What is it that birds do in the morning? They sound excited. Like they're telling each other how amazing it is that the sun has risen again. I notice golden flowers on the trail; their little flower heads exuberant with the same recognition of the sun. Everything obeys the cycles out here. There's no other option. When the sun rises, they all start singing. When they start singing, they wake up exhausted campers who would rather cover their heads, roll over and go for one more dream. But the birds are in charge of the morning and soon we resign to wake with them...to curl into different stretches to release swollen static limbs. Unzip one thing. Unzip another. Peer outside. Begin deflating, re-zipping, re-packing, grabbing a few random things for breakfast to stuff into the pockets. Brush teeth. Dig for clean socks. Shake out shoes. Clip in. Give each other "the nod". Time to go. Climbing out of Silverwood Lake the left hip starts up again. This is what I feared but Hanne shows me a good yoga stretch and with a series of liberating pops my hip is free again. My stride opens back up. My gait normalizes. I move at a normal speed again. We climb and wind down toward Cajon. Only fourteen and a half miles today. The goal is lunch at the interstate junction. We hit a stride and make good time. Wind picks up, blowing sideways alongside sandy cliff edges. Through short grass and tumbleweeds we descend to 3,000 feet. A man in flip-flops and covered head keeps jogging by. We see him almost at the junction, belly-up in a wash. He's ok. We shrug our shoulders and make it to a dingy highway McDonald's. Two ladies (the ones that gave us pizza the night before) are there with big greetings. Consensus: In-n-Out wins hands down. It tasted like cardboard, but two Big Macs and fries after thirteen miles aren't something we're going to turn down either. Another couple of hikers enter. A man from England and a girl from Washington. They met early on the trail as well. Three little duos. We say goodbye and head for the campsite 1.7 miles away near the tracks. As I write the train blows its whistle in the distance. Still a lot of wind. We sat and shared some wine and talked about what happens after this…what we see our lives being like after something of this magnitude…and we spoke of the human ego: What it is. What it does. If it's necessarily "bad" or limiting. How one directs one's ego vs. being controlled by it. Tomorrow: Thirteen miles to get us up the mountain a bit. Then, it's into Wrightwood the next morning.

Thoughts along the trail:

The destination doesn't draw closer the more you suffer. The destination draws closer the more steps you take. Period.

It's always further than it feels.

Every day is completely new. The only constant is walking.

Everything returns to balance on the trail. Eat, drink, pace, weight, etc. Everything comes around.

February 10, 2019
Albuquerque

This time last year I was already in full PCT mode. Lists upon lists that I thought I needed. Training up in the foothills, putting water bottles in my pack and walking from the south side of the 365 trail to the tram and back. I remember the phone calls to the hospital I'd made when I crossed over the first ridge and walked down into a low grassy field with nothing but a few granite boulders in the middle. We'd update each other on where things were at, how far along I was in my planning and saving, and where her blood levels were currently at. I had to learn new medical jargon every week while she went from one process to the next. "Now we're looking at this. Now we're looking at that. Now *this* matters. Now *that* matters."

I still had my old Cutlass wagon with the reversible back seat that I'd taken everywhere looking for places to test my gear - thinking I was psychologically preparing for five months of impending isolation. Piles of bulk food had already begun filling the living room and I was still convinced I could get away with Nike gym shoes. All this…over a year ago now. A year of hope. Of loss. Of love. Of journeys and adventures like I'd never known.

It seems like a long time since the trail even though it's barely been four months. Each week a new matter of perspective coming to light. A different reason to exhale. Some days I wonder how long it stays with someone and sometimes I know it's fixed in my soul and that one path choice has irrevocably altered the course of events.

I've done what I came home to do. Things are wrapping up. The stunned quality of post-trail life has given way to lazy sleep-in mornings with the old French press and afternoons staring back at the laptop, referencing the trail journals and accumulating data, checking out PCT forums, answering a few questions from some of the "PCT Class of 2019" kids who are going through the exact same pre-hike over-planning hysterics I did. That's part of the fun isn't it? Sometimes I want to just write a ten-point list titled "How to Stop Worrying and Just Do It." And then I step back. In a few months they'll be in Campo and they'll be able to understand and claim it for themselves. That process is a magical thing that I don't want to interfere with.

    Lately I'm struck by timelines and narratives. How stories and ideas weave in and out and reappear in our lives. Things I started years ago coming to fruition and cycles that come to a quiet close. Moving on...

    What happens now? Different seeds being planted in different soil. Life is unreal sometimes. I've never been able to pin it down nor am I that interested in doing so. In recent conversations with friends this topic of vitality comes up: of all the ways you can live your life, all the Ted Talks and self-help books and get-rich-quick and hot-goat-yoga, etc...what are we aiming for? Vitality. Chi. Calm quiet confidence. Fearlessness. "The Call" or whatever it is that cannot be ignored. That which makes you vital has to be watered even as we encounter ourselves at different turns in life. That is what ultimately constitutes a lived life.

    I've put down the easy quotes and ideas that sustained me in the post-hike world for a few months. It was a fantastic and brutal blur of backward rehab. Endocrine changes, healing tendons, regular showers, paying attention to my diet again instead of grabbing the first burger in sight. The delicious red wine painkillers and frosty IPAs that met us in each town don't have nearly the same luster or ritual significance and it's all been on the shelf since December. Things change. Things rearrange, but The Path is still clearly marked.

I spend my most recent nights back in the same room where I spent hours stapling topo maps last year, listening to podcasts, learning German while I can...looking at the old poster of Switzerland on my wall. Talking to Hanne every day. Waiting for birth certificates and passports and tickets. 2019 has already shaped up to be completely different...and the trail goes on.

February 7, 2018
About a Month Before Campo

Spent the morning at Costco. Paid for the membership and took a leisurely stroll through gigantic isles with a gigantic cart checking things off the list I'd written up. High calorie / high fats. Some straight-up junk food just to fill the caloric needs of a thru-hike but also lots of nuts and other things. Two big boxes of Emergen-C packs and fruit snacks and whatnot. Spent around $250 and filled up the back of my old station wagon. Then over to Sprouts for bulk items needed to create my "high-calorie trail bricks". They're about 1,000 calories each. First batch was ruined when I thought "broil" might be a good setting. Next batch was hard as a rock but worked. Third batch I took out sooner and I think it'll work a lot better. All these little details. Lots of little calculations and basic math and calorie / price ratios vs. days on the trail. Eesh. I filled tons of Ziploc bags with various combinations of nuts and raisins and Cheezits, counting out tiny crackers one by one to get one serving just right. Overkill I'm sure, but it's easier that way. I finally got my first wave of anxiety about all this when I went outside into the cold to find a plastic bin to put everything in. "What if...what if...yes, but what *if*?" All those thoughts started swirling in my head. What if the trail bricks I've made don't work? What if I get stranded or lost and panic and wind up way off? I spoke with my mom and Randy in the midst of all this. The good news is that Randy offered to purchase an ultra-light tent after I sent pictures of the accumulated gear. I'd bought an Alps four-season tent when I thought this spring would be spent tackling fourteeners in the Rockies.

This whole thing started when I was back in Arizona trying to fall asleep to a documentary about Reinhold Messner. Funny. Instead, I stayed awake glued to the story. His accomplishments and records. His sheer drive. I was taken by his philosophical way of approaching each new challenge; the reasons why you'd sell everything to try and climb Everest without supplemental oxygen.

After I watched virtually every extreme mountaineering documentary and movie I could get my hands on, I decided it was time to get back into the real world for a bit. I'd spent too much time away as it was; holed up and working on music like a madman for years now. It's all given me a great deal of pause and a few moments of sober reflection about how it all came down to music in the first place.

It suddenly came one night I was looking for more content to watch and I stumbled across this thing called the Pacific Crest Trail. At first it felt like a compromise because I'd run out of mountaineering docs but a little seed took root in late November. By mid-December I'd accepted that I wanted a major challenge. A mental cleansing. With everything our family had confronted this year in terms of reality and mortality my heart went from sorrow to firm conviction on an hourly basis. The central theme, I felt, was that life is too short to even assume one can hide from it. I needed to know what role music was playing in that. Was it just "in me" or was it a cleverly-crafted coping mechanism. Maybe it was both? So, there it was and here I am, having no idea what hiking for five straight months is actually going to entail.

From everything I've read, most people abandon the trek because of emotional stress, not physical. There are various injuries that prevent one from continuing. A simple sprained ankle or blisters can derail the romance of a thru-hike without notice. Most people, however, simply find it too difficult to assume the role of a lone human on a desolate trail day in and day out. I wonder what I'll feel. A wave of anxiety crept up and it's not an unfamiliar feeling at all, but for all the treks and adventures and possibility therein, I'd hate to find myself more terrified than excited. A decent balance would suffice. There's honestly no way to approach something like this without a few old-fashioned human reservations. I'd watched videos about other people's mental approaches to the PCT. There's even a book written about the psychological aspects of all this but again, it's balance. Most of what you do on the PCT is put one foot in front of the other. Let it happen. At least that's what I gather.

 I haven't done an epic trip since...well, backpacking Europe was epic but in very different ways. Cycling across the country when I was thirteen...I didn't even know what I didn't know. I was a junior racer who'd been fixated on the idea of a long-distance tour since reading "Hey Mom, Can I Ride My Bike Across America?". The rest of the group I went with were students and teachers from Santa Barbara. It was all set up by the author of the book whom I'd contacted out of sheer enthusiasm to voice my praise.

 I've instinctively sought out extremes throughout my life or reveled in the possibility of goals and ideas that I couldn't find anywhere else but my imagination. It provides a solid identity at the end of the day, but the downside is that when you revel in the fringe; when you think you're out to protect your solitude and space all the time...ultimately, it's yourself that you end up dealing with more than anything else. There's a healthy level of fear that accompanies some of these things. The price of independence maybe.

I've tried and failed to convince two friends to go with me. It just sounds absurd on the surface. Needless to say, all my friends are musicians and the idea of spending five months consistently in the middle of nowhere sounds about as fun as learning how to farm porcupines. Most of my days, for the past ten or so years, were spent thinking about the acquisition of exotic keyboards and consoles. Tape-op comment boards. Festivals. A/B microphone comparisons and analog vs. digital debates. Wringing my hands over the nearly imperceptible and often irrelevant differences between pre-amp tones. And suddenly well...you get out into nature and nature doesn't give the slightest shit about any of that, which is good. Slightly terrifying and so good.

Forward in Time

Where was I? I didn't know which day of the week it was. Not by a long-shot. I'd come in and out of tiny towns, ski villages, and lakeside resorts. I'd been dodging fires and taking detours. I'd been stopping for supplies and sauntering down the trail. There hadn't been any need to motivate myself. Difficult days were just difficult days. The very occasional rain shower was a welcome change of weather. Food was still a good enough incentive to get from one point to another. I never suspected I was missing anything. It was total immersion and I wanted to be there. I lived "Here. In the woods." I woke with the birds. Life had become The Trail. Everyone I knew, everything I did, all my conversations, my daily struggles and small triumphs all revolved around occurrences on a thin line of dirt that we'd followed up and down through every kind of imaginable circumstance for nearly five months.

Even as we walked up to the ranger station in Stehekin to permit for the border and map out campsites along Ross Lake the bad days still felt good. The tough days felt good. The good days felt great and the great days felt beyond words.

In Stehekin I knew we still had another month to go. We hadn't decided whether or not we'd go north or south when we made it back to the Sierras and they still seemed like a world away. On the trail there's only so much you can do, only so many things that actually make sense to think about, and you've got plenty of time to work out the details. Right now we needed to take a detour nine miles to the west of the PCT which had closed due to another fire. We had to get to the East Bank Trailhead and walk that for three days to the border and two days back out, find our way to Seattle, and rent a car to return to the Sierras for the final stretch. Still one step at a time.

The rules were different for Ross Lake State National Recreation Area and we needed to decide beforehand exactly where we were going to camp each night. We browsed a big map and created an itinerary that doubled as a tag that we'd attach to our tent every night so that any ranger in the area could keep tabs on the hikers and sites being used. There were plenty of bears in the area as well so we'd have to hang the food. We'd done this off and on since northern California depending on the news and the rules. At that point we'd seen four bears, which was more that anyone we'd talked to so far. One Swiss fellow outside Mt Shasta had even gone so far as to declare that the whole bear thing was a myth: a story made up by locals to scare hikers.

 We wondered what it meant; making it to Canada after all this time. And yet, something happens to time out there. You're so saturated in each day that you forget a great many things your pre-hike-self swore he'd pay attention to. It's just that none of those things tend to matter much after the first month. You've got miles to make and that's it and somewhere in the midst of the journey, everything that doesn't fit into your daily routine gets discarded and forgotten just like the extra pair of "river-crossing shoes" I packed all the way to Kennedy Meadows. That is, a week before we weren't even thinking about the border. We'd been thinking about the Holden Village detour that we had to take because of the nonstop wildfires. We'd heard about the closure at Hart's Pass but trails opened and closed every day depending on factors like wind speed and direction and committed fire personnel that were already dispersed from Northern California to the border. It was a bad season; worse than most locals could remember and it got even worse after we left the trail. We got lucky numerous times and snuck through just before large stretches of the trail had to be closed, but sometimes we had to take small detours that would shoot us east or west and parallel for a few miles.

When we got to Holden Village we had fifteen hours to cram our faces with their homemade pizza and salad buffet, wash clothes, shower, sleep, grab some breakfast, and head out. You never officially stop on the trail. You rest and eat and sleep and zone-out as much as possible. You turn your body off but you plan on the go...not that there's much to plan but these detours caused some pause at first. Fire is unpredictable and spreads fast. A couple weeks before we'd squeezed through the Miriam Fire into White Pass just as another fire sprang up in the valley to the west of the trail. It'd been out of control for weeks and scores of firefighters had staged along the main road in rows of tents.

The News:

"The Miriam Fire was detected on July 30 at approximately 10:00 a.m. after lightning passed through the area on July 28. The fire is burning within the Goat Rocks Wilderness on the Naches Ranger District of the Okanogan-Wenatchee National Forest 32 miles southwest of Naches, Washington. The fire is east of the White Pass Ski Area, south of Highway 12, and west of the Tieton River.

The Clear Fork Fire is burning in the Goat Rocks Wilderness on the Gifford Pinchot National Forest. The fire is located southwest of Shoe Lake and approximately 2 miles west of the Miriam Fire. This fire was detected on August 8, likely the result of lightning in the area on August 4.

These fires are being managed with a combined contain, confine, and monitor strategy in order to protect public and firefighter safety; the White Pass Ski Resort and surrounding area; recreational cabins, camps and resorts on Clear and Rimrock Lakes; State Highway 12; Goat Rocks Wilderness; and fish and wildlife habitat."

Now a fire near Hart's Pass had closed the PCT for the last thirty miles of trail toward Canada. That meant no pictures with "The Holy Monument." I'd already heard of hikers bailing hundreds of miles earlier and driving up to get a picture with the wooden spires, to sit on top of it and throw their hands in the air with giant victory smiles. We all knew the real stories on the trail: people that skipped massive sections and magically wound up in the 2,650-miler list, but I'm no snitch. We came. We walked. We'd come this far and as we weighed our options in Stehekin, the little wooden spires seemed less important.

"This is a walk from Mexico to Canada" Hanne said.
"All we do is go nine miles west and keep walking north." I said. "It's not like we're *skipping* anything"
"We have to do the Sierras after this anyway."
"And...we don't have any other options except wait in Stehekin for who knows how long until it's under control."
"Ross Lake looks pretty awesome anyway, right? Just walking along the water for a few days?"
"Yeah...it'll be good."

So, we plotted our bid with a red marker and took the itinerary back to camp to compare with the other maps...

"We walk to here and come out here and hitch west to here. Then we walk three days north to the border and two days back."
"This last spot…"Nightmare Campground?"
"I know…"
"I can't believe it."
"Almost five months of this…"
"Five months."
"Yeah…five months."
"Five months…wow."
"It'll be six by the time we get out."
"Six months."
"Six months."
"Wow. Half a year."
"Half a year."
"Out here…"
"Out here…"
"It feels like we've been out here for at least a year."
"Longer…"

February 8, 2019

Dear Randy,

By unanimous consent, the committee for the upcoming Annual Native Plant Workshop voted to extend the honor of the Herkenham Award to Dena Greenwood. We had all hoped that she would be here with us to accept the award in person; however, that was not to be. We are hoping that you would be able to attend and accept the award in her stead. The event this year will be held at the Verde Valley School in the Village of Oak Creek on Saturday, April 6, 2019.

Please let me know as soon as possible if you will be able to attend and if you have any questions.

All the best

May 18, 2018

M: Quote: "Your body was designed to walk thirty miles a day and hunt animals the size of houses. It's just your mind that you have to convince"
W: Love this quote <B
M: You've done the hard part. You've already convinced your mind."
Love,
Mom

April 6, 2018
Back at the Beginning

We left Idyllwild after all the reloading was done. Last views of the town strung below us as we started climbing the steep side-streets toward the trailhead. We had four miles to go to reach San Jacinto's summit and a climb of at least 3,000 feet. Once off the main roads we ascended to mammoth pines and what I thought were sequoia, only I didn't expect them this far south. They don't have pine needles but flat thick leaves instead.

There were signs about the missing Irish hiker who'd disappeared somewhere outside Idyllwild a year before. The strange thing was that they'd found his backpack in pristine condition. It wasn't difficult to imagine getting lost on the San Jacinto trails though. For the first time we found ourselves turned around and consulting the maps more than once. There just weren't many blazes. Of course, all trails led somewhere toward civilization so we could only guess where a hiker might go astray. It's still a big mountain. Maybe he had just dipped out. Idyllwild has probably offered that allure to hundreds of travelers over the years. Still, it felt strange to speculate.

Going was slow and the trail was full of giant granite steps rising one after the other that you almost felt compelled to crawl over instead of walk. The whole ambience became very Tolkien as a nearly-full moon rose and we made our way to a small campsite overlooking the valley and Hammett Lake.

I pitched the tent and we sat on logs just rehashing the day. After a day of hiking, you can talk about anything or nothing. Sometimes silence is fine. Sometimes you or someone else opens up about topics they'd never consider back home. Nothing is off the table. Everyone listens. Everyone has fears, desires, hopes and reasons. We're just out here right now. For some there's a lot of processing going on. For others it's just another pre-college party. Others have planned for years to get here. Another guy who goes by the trail name Hurricane is only here to train till mid-April when he'll jump over to the CDT for his third (and final) go.

We tried to sleep in the next morning, but it was a little chilly. It makes sleeping and dreaming choppy and strange, but you get up and jam all your things into your pack and hit the trail. We only had eleven miles to go that day, but we started hitting patches of snow on the other side of the mountain and the downhill grades were unbearable on the knees at times. Little seasonal streams popped up here and there and we'd stop and filter some water and have a light snack and keep going.

At lunch we stopped at another water source and talked with a fellow that lived down on the other side of the I-10 who gave us advice about ticks and was meeting his wife at the bottom of the mountain. He'd come from Campo as well and like many others, did stretches of the PCT as time permitted.

The ice got worse that day and my stomach was feeling off. Maybe the elevation was getting to me. I was sluggish and slipped twice on the snow; once onto my backpack but the second time my elbow came down hard enough to make me check that everything was still in place and working before I got back up again. This was one day where the shoes I'd chosen to save me from blisters were not working at all. It was all sludge and snow and massive blocks to step down and blowdowns everywhere to navigate.

By the time we got to camp we were exhausted. Only eleven miles but the terrain and grade dictated everything. We set up in a small area in a clearing past a site that was occupied by a family with other tents scattered around. A few guys we'd seen over a week before ambled in and set up in the periphery while I got to work digging a tiny pit for a fire. I walked down and collected wood and we had a nice rock to sit while we ate dinner. Me and my pre-packed bars and whatnot and Hanne's Jet-boil Deluxe with dried soups that I pretended not to smell.

The moon came out again and when the fire rose a bit the three guys came over and we welcomed them into the warm glow.

Sometimes you can share a lot with people by just staring into a fire together for an hour. We talked about our experiences so far and how that snow had been. One guy had done the Appalachian Trail a couple years before. He'd been all smiles when I'd come up on him at a water source on day two. Now everyone was a bit more somber, myself included. It was going to be a lot of up and down every day for 2,300 more miles. Knees would hurt. Calves would hurt. You just had to try and get enough rest and food in between the hiking to heal and walk on. They all returned to their tents and we soon fell asleep too.

The next morning, we geared up for another short run of thirteen miles. All downhill, but I was full of energy and ready to go at around 9:00 am. I tore off down the trail for a day punctuated by a few new faces (a couple from Seattle) and a couple of guys that we leap-frogged with for a bit. I didn't know I was going too fast; just felt like I wanted to knock this day out and make camp early, but I pushed a little too hard. Downhills are more strenuous at the end of the day and once we hit camp, I was wiped out again. You have to be on top of your pace, your breaks, water, food, and sleep every day and I'd let a couple things slide. By that time my knees had had it and I could do little more than hobble around collected wood for another fire. This is how I got my trail name.

Just as we were getting ready to light our fire a young man with an African safari hat, pressed khaki shorts, and a bright red whistle around his neck strolled into camp and informed of his intentions to camp…until he saw the firewood in a neat stack next to the little pit I'd dug. He seemed to recoil in horror and stammered something about maybe looking for another site a few miles down. We said goodbye and laughed it off until a full forty-five minutes later when he returned with a fully-prepared lecture about the perils and moral ineptitude of enjoying a campfire. I listened. I told him we had permits for federal land and that we were responsible adults, but he kept persisting in a particularly nasal tone until I just told him off. He disappeared into the night and we enjoyed our small, responsible fire while little mice hopped around sniffing our food. The moon was now completely full and we knew we'd be off the steep grades the next day around noon. I fell asleep almost instantly. My trail name became Campfire two days later.

    We woke early and kept heading down. Winds were howling. Fifty mile per hour gusts pushing us every which way on shale and granite cliff edges that wound down to grassy fields where morning clouds were racing furiously and evaporation just as fast at eye level.

    We passed a group of PCT volunteers and chatted briefly. They were busy cutting weeds on the sides of the trail. By 10:00 am we'd made it to the bottom where the trail met a long water pipe that descended directly from a holding tank and straight to a fountain. To the left of the fountain was a shadow and as we walked further a safari hat came into view. What can you do. We spoke again and he apologized and we exchanged info and got our water and took off across the flat desert and creosote and washes to I-10.

    We'd heard rumors of an In-n-Out Burger down the road so when we hit the underpass we called an Uber and got dropped off. This is a big stop before L.A. for lots of people. It was right around noon and the place was packed. We claimed some seats and foisted the packs up while children stared and others asked questions and wished us luck. Everything's surreal when you come out of three days in the forest smelling like a roasted log with burnt, peeling noses and crazy hair, but we downed those burgers like they were the last burgers on earth. Hanne avoided fast food at all costs and had most meals meticulously planned but neither of us could've cared less just then. I had two double-doubles Animal Style and fries.

    We got another Uber back to the same spot and were back on the trail within an hour. We still had eight miles to go. It would take us behind windmills and up and down more maddening sets of switchbacks until we came over a grassy plane than wound down to the campsite at Whitewater Preserve. We could hear the hoots and hollers of hikers basking in one of the pools that had been made from incoming stream water and we soaked our feet and relaxed. Sweet relief. The campsite was wide and grassy and we had a bench to set our things on. Another hiker showed us the ropes and gave me a free Mountain Dew. It was gone in thirty seconds. The winds picked up and we staked the tents deep and tight and sat on the benches talking about childhood, previous adventures, anything that came to mind. There was a sign about a mountain lion spotted recently but that could mean anything in these hills. That's as good as spotting a raven. Who knows where animals go after they're "spotted".

    The next morning was blazing hot. Immediate uphills. Dusty dirty bits of ground granite. I was trying to keep a good pace but I kept feeling winded. It was a 17.5-mile day and my calves were cooked by 11:00 am. I hid by a bush and put on pants which just kind of clung to the leg hair and stung for a good hour. We lunched by a stream and carried very little water because we crisscrossed the same stream all day. It was pretty mucky. Lots of mud despite being in the middle of the high desert and lots of calculated hops and soaked shoes. We took a wrong turn that looked worn by lots of others and got off into some muddy reeds a good quarter mile off the trail 'till we stopped and realized it went nowhere. We consulted the maps again and I dropped my pack to scale a small ledge and get a better look. The trail was directly at the top of the ledge so we lugged the packs straight up and over and got back on course. The heat wouldn't let up and we both went through four to five liters of water each.

At the end of the day we finally hit camp. The older Asian couple were already making tea and humming away, laughing and having the time of their lives while we collapsed and tried to come to our senses.

We found out that they just did much shorter lengths and didn't stop in towns for more than a few hours. Another older man from England with an impeccable Attenborough quality to him idly perused a paperback while lying on a tarp in his old sleeping bag. He'd ask a few questions and go back to his business, nothing but amused at our answers. We sat with our backs against a rock and laid out a plan. The plan boiled down to more protein. The carbs and fats were good but we needed to rebuild muscles with all the constant up and downs. We decided to sleep in as much as possible to heal up and hit the last stretch to Big Bear around 8:00 am.

The first three miles had me out of breath with grades I'd never hiked before. Nowhere close. Right out of camp it went straight up for a gain of around three thousand feet in about three miles. Then it leveled out. It swept through burned forests, old horse pastures and soft layers of pine needles. For the first time in about a week we weren't going up or down. My legs began to feel normal again and the rest of the day went along a decent clip with a few rolling hills. We'd come across hikers resting, then they'd pass us when we rested. All day long. A few new names and new stories.

Hurricane passed us just before nightfall and told us some stories in his thick New Zealand accent. He didn't like carrying water. No one likes carrying anything out here but no water? He just didn't. He had a one-liter bottle with him and just filled up when he found it and drank primarily from streams. He never filtered and he never got sick. This level of trust gave me pause. He'd been doing thru-hikes for years and when I asked him what his advice was for first-timers he just shrugged: "Ya wheel...som days ah hahdeh then othas. Ya jos keep hoyken yeh?" And that's basically all you can do. If you overthink or complicate the reality of a thru-hike with conjecture, gadgets, and hubris these are ultimately unreliable tools to get you down the trail when the going gets tough.

So, we did a good steady eighteen miles to Onyx Pass with the lure of beds, showers, and hot food pulling us into Big Bear...and the lure is real. Six days in the wilderness leaves you feeling like a wild animal in some ways. Dirt and salt clinging to everything. All your clothes are mangled and smelly. You've eaten all the "good" food from your supply...then the rest. Your feet are swollen and you're just ready for a little break. These are called "zero days" by hikers and are part of the whole process. A zero day just means you're not lugging around a pack. You find a cheap place to shower, locate the hiker deals, run to laundromats, buy something at a convenience store to get dollar bills to get change for the bus to the other side of town to pick up your resupplies at the post office and try to furiously update pictures and blogs for family and friends while cramming down the biggest meals imaginable and planning some sort of strategy for the next stretch. And now...that's all done. That's one week on the trail and I'm fed, resupplied, and even got some good coffee. Tomorrow morning we set out for another six days to do the same thing all over again. Goodnight!

I Have to Keep Moving

A soft white line through a body of green hills
Over and down
Up and through
Carpets of white flowers reaching toward the sun...
Old weathered wooden post pointing north
Early morning humidity
The sound of my breath
The sound of my footsteps
Solitary black boulders lie silent in the distance
A water break at the top of a bluff
Five more miles...coming alongside a meandering stream
Through a forest of oak trees and bright moss
We reach a small gate at the main road
Outside Warner Springs
From here we can see the other hikers
Disheveled. Sunburned and exuberant in the late March afternoon
Bags unpacked and contents strewn here and there
A dozen different-colored tents around a great old tree fanning out Into the grass
Everything aches...
But there's more to do
Resupply, dinner, calling home
I have to keep moving
But I'll leave the pack here
For now
Another mile to the post office
Half a mile to the little store
"Back in half an hour."
We wait in a small group. We share our stories and injuries
Half a mile back to the tents

Hanne has another idea...
I've scarcely got my food sorted when she approaches

"Tonight I break from the group."

What is Food

The first bite of warm food. A restaurant, cafe, diner or food truck inching closer by the step. The first smells that waft through the summer air and hit your nose. What is that? Onion? Cheese? Fresh baked zucchini bread? The weight of the packs, finally leaning against a table instead of your spine. The sound of water pouring from a pitcher. A menu. A beer list. The weary smiles. The humble thanks for something other than trail bars and ramen. The body is craving protein. Craving sugar. Craving salt and savory. It must be fed. There will be two meals: an appetizer each to share and a main dish. A heaping plate of pasta. A burger filled with everything you can afford to add. Jalapeños, onions, cheese, mushrooms, bacon, green chile. Yes. Everyone has a different approach; different bodies with different cravings...but you *will* crave. Food fantasies are part of the romance and sometimes you're lucky enough to score the very item you spent half the daydreaming about when you finally walk into town, but you'll eat anything. Meals take on a sort of religious ritual tone from the day you start to the very last town. After depleting all your reserves and sweating out your last electrolytes, the mind switches to a different awareness: Biological Mode B. Long-forgotten instincts take over and the whole body begins scouting for solutions. My Achilles: A standard American breakfast. Eggs, potatoes, bacon, bread, and coffee. Add an extra egg. "A large milk with that if you have it please...oh, and we're going to split the short stack too." When we're getting into town the only thought is food. Maybe a shower first just to be polite, but then it's off to find that smell. Food is surrounded with wild tales that have become central to trail life. A pancake challenge, a free beer, an update on Guthook about the contents and condition half-eaten snacks left by Trail Angels up ahead. Our eyes widen and our mouths water uncontrollably the first couple months. Nothing in the world feels better than the moment a plate of nachos hits the table and this is how the small changes begin. The accumulated gratitude for the most simple things; things you took for granted most of your life. Electricity, fluffy beds, climate control, showers, and clean clothes...all within reach.

Suddenly, these are rarities and prizes that give simple substance and reward for all the grinding. A town is only a place to rest and recover for the night; a couple days at most if you're sincerely hurting, and then it's back to the road with thumbs in the air and a few minutes later you're walking back toward some of the most remote forests in North America. These moments are savored for what they are: A chance to connect and feel human again. To make calls to family and friends. To write. To unwind. To heal. To prepare for the next stretch. Towns can be glorious one minute and stressful the next because after you've resupplied and showered and washed a few clothes...well, then it just starts to encroach. It's less unfettered views and chance encounters with real life. It starts to fade quickly because it feels contrived; like a lot of people agreeing to behave within a set of parameters that don't line up with your current calling and that's a broad-stroke evaluation, exacerbated from a thru-hiker's point of view but oh, that first bite of food. That first sip of huckleberry milkshake in Trout Lake. That breakfast buffet at Timberline Lodge. A cold can of Sprite from a Trail Angel's ice chest. I feel as though I didn't understand that level of gratitude before the trail and I suppose I didn't understand that sort of selflessness until I needed it. We're all on this journey together, sharing our lives from different angles...giving and receiving without pause or expectation. Food, as always, is the glue that binds us as people; that old sacrament ringing in celebration and utility for the weary traveler.

Beginning in Groups

We came into Mt Laguna around 4:00 pm that day, walking up to a seasonal restaurant on the side of the road. A sign out front told us to leave our packs on the front porch and come inside for omelettes and coffee. Both sounded amazing and we gathered all around the large wooden tables and put our phone chargers in the wall. A couple guys from Denmark sat in the other corner nodding hellos and wolfing down food at the same time. I still hadn't had any reception and was getting a little worried that I wouldn't have any for days to come. There was one waitress and one cook and she apologized that it might take some time to get everyone's food out. No problem. It was warm and we got to sit down and take the weight off for awhile. A tiny post office was connected to the same building and held my first resupply package. I walked in and she sized me up after half a glance.

"Resupply?"
"Yeah, should be under Phillips"
"First name"
"Oh, Will"
"Oh yeah! I remember where I put yours. Came in just a couple days ago!"

I let out a sigh of relief as she turned and disappeared into another room. This would be my rations for the next few days until we got to Scissor's Crossing and hitched into Julian.
"Do I need to sign anything?"
"Nope! You're all set! You have a great trip ok?" She smiled so enthusiastically that it took me off guard. I tried to mumble a thank you in return but I was already tripping out the swinging door back toward the smell of coffee.

I sat the box by my backpack and went back inside, sitting at a tall table on a stool with Karson.
"How's it going so far?" he asked
"Pretty good. This nerve in my neck keeps giving me problems but I think it's getting better. What'd you get?"
"Denver omelet."
"Me too. Looked like the best bang for the buck."
"Yeah, so I missed why you said you wanted to do the PCT last night. What brought you out here?"
"Oh...well, I don't know if it's a long story or a short story but basically my mom is sick and I wanted to share this with her and I needed a big reset button in my life anyway I guess."
"Yeah...that's a good way to look at it. It is, isn't it? A big reset button. What did you do out *there*?"
"Just...music. Kind of holding other jobs to keep it all together."
"Oh sweet. I went to school for guitar." He said smiling.
"Oh! What style do you play?" I asked, feeling like I'd suddenly made a connection.
"Mostly blues and jazz but whatever...I just like to write songs."
"I was a jazz drummer in school but yeah...kind of the same. Just went my own way."
"You have any albums?"
"Yeah a few. Different bands and some solo stuff. I have a website where I keep everything together like music, blogs, photos, and stuff"
"Nice man. I was living in a van in L.A. just writing things...putting little videos online."

At that point I would have traded the studio for a working conversion van. I felt jealous but I was more excited to meet someone that lived in a van and didn't think twice about it. I wanted to meet more people like Karson on the trail. Vagabonds, adventurers, seekers, explorers young and old, from here and there. It was a tribe of like-minded folks that had something in their blood that didn't let up through school, careers, and relationships. They might often feel useless to society when attempting to lean into its corners but out here, miles from anywhere familiar...I think we felt most at home. Whereas some people might feel exposed in nature, I always felt more exposed in my attempts to convince society that I had any sincere interest in it. I'd learned through a quiet series of compromises, the measured dampening of my voice, partially with age, but mostly from an unconscious apathy engendered in the very narrative I held to. The spirit seems to know what you're trying to pull. It plays along but it pulls back, like a game of tug-o-war. The neurotics become normalized and sooner or later you can't hear the spirit at all. You only vaguely remember that you once had the patience to listen.

You Have Time

M: Nice Photos. Will, Is that snow-capped mountain San Jacinto or San Gorgonio? I'm glad you're seeing some wildflowers. I think CA got more rain than we did this winter. So when you are looking down into that desert. All of that is the Mojave Desert. You have been in the Mojave Desert (in and out) ever since you started the hike at Campo. Most of the desert in southern California is Mojave Desert. There is a little part of Sonoran Desert close to the Colorado River.

I like seeing all those windmills far off in the distance. There is a huge storm raging north of you across the Sierra Nevadas right now. I'm so glad it is north of you. You might get some wind from it but I don't think any rain. Plus it will really help with the fire potential this summer as you are hiking through. Maybe you won't have to detour.

Love the photos! Send more when you can. Enjoy your day off.

Love, Mom

W: That's looking back at San Jacinto in the picture I sent. San Gorgonio is on the other side of the valley - both highest peaks on north and south sides had snow.
Love, Will

"You're Wearing Pants"

I'm suddenly sitting in the back of a convertible covered in duffle bags and backpacks with world champion longboarder, Patrick Switzer at the wheel. My head is twisted into a corner watching the shadows of pine trees in front of stars fly by. The air is frigid but it smells like pines. I wrench my legs around trying to avoid the cramping. Wriggling toes and bending ankles all the way in.

We'd made it to the Paradise Cafe around 5:00 pm. Hanne waited for me at the highway while my ankle and I caught up and we walked on the hard pavement until the shape of a building came into view.

By this time I was having another sort of detached experience, looking down at my feet and laughing at the way they moved without any real intention on my part. The day had done me in completely and the ankle, while feeling much better, still called out here and there and made it an incredibly trying twenty two miles.

The restaurant looked like an apparition: one minute closer, the next minute as far as a restaurant can be. We imagined aloud what kind of food might be waiting there. It could be a standard highway diner or an historic outpost known for that "one thing" or a weary hiker's dream come true. Or perhaps it was all three.

We crossed the dirt lot and climbed up the wooden porch and opened the door.
"Welcome to paradise!" An invisible voice said.
"Yes! This is paradise!" I called back.
Our waitress appeared smiling with two menus.
"You're wearing pants!" She exclaimed.
I looked down confused, attempting to verify her claims.
"Yes. Apparently I am."

"You guys look hungry and tired! I'll take care of you right over here." She motioned to the far corner. "Set your packs anywhere and tell me what you wanna drink."

We obeyed and wrenched the packs down onto the floor next to a booth and two chairs.

"Water please..." Hanne whispered.

"Yeah for now, thanks" I added.

We felt dazed and grateful with a hunger beyond possession, directing every thought.

"Wine. Red wine."

"Yeah. Perfect."

"How's your ankle?"

"I don't know anymore. I'll know tomorrow."

I'm suddenly aware of two large hands massaging my shoulders with a high degree of purpose and care. Patrick towers above with a great smile.

"Don't worry. I know this is exactly what you want, right?"

Hanne is friends with his wife Tamara. They're both based in Zurich now; in the states for a competition outside San Diego. They're both fierce athletes and full of positive energy next to my "food and sleep, please." In a little over a year, I'll be helping Patrick in his startup kombucha factory and he'll be calling up instructions at the climbing gym. I don't know this yet, of course, and I've never been on a longboard in my life, but I won't turn down a free message. Ever.

"You have lost your reason and taken the wrong path. You have taken lies for truth, and hideousness for beauty. You would marvel if, owing to strange events of some sorts, frogs and lizards suddenly grew on apple and orange trees instead of fruit, or if roses began to smell like a sweating horse; so I marvel at you who exchange heaven for earth. I don't want to understand you."

-Anton Chekhov

Birds, Wind and Footsteps

Birds, wind and footsteps.
Birds, wind and footsteps.
Then it changes abruptly on the other side of a creek.
Where the wind carried embers in front of flames, devouring until it ran out of fuel.
Five miles of ash.
Sun bleached white trunks with blackened knots and limbs.
Small clumps of weeds and flowers.
Returning the moment they can.
Further down the path, two and three foot pines spread out, already claiming patches of earth.
They know what to do.
Whatever I think I have to say about it...
She knows better than I ever will.
She always has.
But her voice isn't so loud.
She speaks without the limits of words, syntax, and linear arguments, or paragraphs folded neatly with perfect arcs and conceits.
No big reveal.
No plot twist.
She says nothing.
For miles she says nothing.
And still nothing.
Until I became friends with the silence.
And learn to listen.
Learn to see.
And how to feel again.
Of course, I thought.
Thought I knew better.
Thought I had everything under control.

Thought I'd show up with the right shoes.
The right food.
The right technology.
Thought I'd show someone something.
Me?
Up until the moment.
That these sentiments become useless and slowly vaporize.
Until finally...
It's You.
And even then.
All she says is
"Grow."

Uphill. Downhill. Socal.

"The uphill: A confident approach. Heart in the chest. Lungs fill. Drops of sweat begin to fall in the dirt. Ten minutes. Twenty minutes. Half an hour. One more switchback. Then one more. Then just one more. A slow crest over the pass; the earth begins to level out. A ridge line…a rest. A view. An entirely different eco-strata. Looking toward the next pass. The downhill: Faster but more painful. Careful not to jam the knees. Letting the pack hang back. The weight wants to carry everything forward. It's a balancing act. Gating and guiding inertia. This is where the joints call out and tendons go counter to their typical function, flexing taught against bone, pulling upward, holding the knees straight, supporting you and the thing on your back. One false step and it's a rolled ankle. There will be many. One slip on the rubble and you might go down. There's no perfect steps. One second you're glad to finally take a rest on a log and the next your feet are pointed at the sky. That pack doesn't really act like a part of the body. It just adds forty pounds of extra force against your inclination.

The canyon: Maybe it's time for lunch. Creeks and snowmelt build in the shadowy canyons and the animals like being close to water as well. Deer, squirrel, snake, cougar, bear and birds all depend on the same sources. This trail is their trail too. Mornings often begin following hoof prints a good mile down the side of a mountain. Scare a feeding marmot and more often than not they go barreling away straight down the path; their homes built directly adjacent to the trail. In the valley a song is heard every day. The lilting dee-doo-doo of the mountain Chickadee or the cacophonic demands of the jay waiting for you to pick a lunch spot. Ravens are particularly good scavengers that can desecrate a bag of unattended snacks in minutes, but mice are the true bandits of the trail. I believe entire colonies have been set up according to the seasonal patterns of hikers that leave crumbs wherever they rest. If you've got a decent light during dinnertime, you'll catch them bravely hopping into your perimeter and back into the darkness. They gnaw through virtually any type of fabric including tents and the only way to keep them out of your pack is by hanging it and crossing your fingers.

Hanne scowls into the shadows: "I do *not like* such a creature as this."

Neither do I. But it's fun to watch them hop and I prefer them to bears.

The canyons make good camping due to their water, but they also make for cold currents of air drifting down the mountain at night and frost might settle overnight. If you sleep in a canyon, the first thing you do in the morning is climb, but it matters little. After a few weeks there's little preference for climbing over descending and flats are so infrequent that the idea is basically negligible. It all evens out. On the high mountain crests one downhill only means a corresponding uphill and so on. We learn quickly: Hope is futile. There's no secret strategy for the trail. No assumptions or grand declarations you offered before Campo that are going to amount to much.

You learn as you walk. You get there when you get there and predictions become unnecessary; even cumbersome in lieu of the very basics, that is; the challenge isn't the trail. The challenge is *you*.

Some days will feel like a discombobulated stumbling mess. The next day you're a lithe hunter, sprinting up a rocky pass to survey your lands. Others will feel like processing a million memories from a million angles. Some days a single song will take over your soul for ten hours. Some days you'll feel sick and you won't want to leave the tent. Some days you'll feel so thankful that you can't hold back the tears. Some days you'll

wish you could share it with everyone you've ever known. Some days you're ready for it to end and some days you know you can just keep walking...forever.
"How is it that we do the same thing every day...wake up, make coffee, pack it up, and walk for ten hours...but it never feels repetitive? Every day out here is like ten days back home."
"I know. I haven't felt bored once. There aren't any distractions out here. Nothing takes time away from what you've got to do."
"Every day the path is so clearly defined."
"...and nature has no copies. Every single step is something new. Back in society you see the same things and shapes and ideas a hundred times a day."
"It's funny...when you connect to what you really are...suddenly nothing's missing."
"Do you think we really used to live like this?"
"I don't know if it was exactly like *this*...but I feel it. It's like my body knows...like it's being used the right way for the first time."
"We just didn't get to hide in air-conditioned boxes under artificial light, staring at screens for most of human history."
"Pretty simple..."
"How do people complain about feeling disconnected when we're supposed to be more connected than ever?"
"It's just the way we do it now. It doesn't actually *engage* us anymore."

We Are Creatures of the Earth

"We are creatures of the earth. Strong and sensitive at the same time. Lifted from the trials of hunting, of darkness, and existential threats. But we still belong to the Earth. Maybe this has been our fatal mistake in the 20th Century; the one that might undo it all - accidentally eclipsing the very reasons to be here. We've sided with technological prowess and there's no going back. We demand it. We rail the moment the router blinks red and this generation will fight for the right to be monitored, governed, and controlled at every turn. It will be their solemn duty to plug in, scroll, copy, paste, code, consume, and sleep and their freedom will come from the "right" to sort and evaluate personalized entertainment. Truth will be seen as an infringement on one's right to conjecture. A liability. This human won't know how biological systems work in unison with a sun on one end and a wobbling watery planet on the other. Stars will be unheard of and our moon; the lyrical fluff of another pop song. This human not only won't care why they're here; they won't even have the ability to ask."

That's dark, man.

Yet out there it seems so evident: we're already living in an age of mass hypnosis and mass distraction; mass hijacking of imagination on a global scale one innovation, one target market, and one crisis at a time.

Out there on the trail I quickly forget what day of the week it is. Standard timekeeping is useless. Most of everything is useless...but we're told that primitive people had it rough.

All these symbolic rituals...what are they for? What do they mean when it comes down to food, shelter, and water?

Are we that lonely? That spoiled? That dull inside that we need all *this* on the outside?.

Maybe our story just keeps unfolding and it's neither here nor there.

After all, I'm covered in high-tech gear. I love this Patagonia windbreaker...

Maybe I'm the primitive. Maybe I'm the one hooting at shadows in the cave.

But I suddenly don't care. At all.

It's nothing compared to the taste of hot food after one hundred miles..."

Journal
April 21, 2018

    Yesterday we woke up in the hills outside Aqua Dulce. We'd walked for an hour through the night with headlamps until we found a nice little clearing. Woke up overlooking a large sort of trailer park / junkyard with half of a 747 jet on one side of the lot. Made it into the hills. I tried to call Alana but we only connected for a minute before reception went out. Sigh. So it goes out here. I don't know what to make of any of it.
    With my new hiking poles I was good to go for a brisk seventeen-mile stretch with some hellacious climbs but before we knew it the day was done and we found another little spot up a hill hidden in some bushes just past a couple of Austrians. Sometimes Hanne gets to speak more German than English out here.
    We laid out our things as the sun went down and poured some wine that another Swiss couple had given us at the KOA. It was a magical night. The kind of night you dream about when you plan these kinds of trips. So simple. Sharing some earbuds and listening to Phil Collins of all things. Staring at the stars in the middle of nowhere. It was the first night in weeks that was neither cold nor windy. Just us and little sparkling dots with the occasional airplane floating silently above. A crescent moon softly illuminated the tents and I felt a simple peace that I hadn't felt in awhile; perhaps the reconnection I'd been after. Just to enjoy music pure and simple. No judgments. No comparisons and evaluations.
    Today we slept in a bit. The cold didn't wake us as early and we hit the trail around 8:20 am. First stop was an old fire station with a spigot where we met "Papa Den" who was section hiking this year. He asked us every question in the book. I didn't mind though. I don't feel like I've got any part of myself to really

protect or hide out here. Everyone is open and exchanging information and that's a good thing.

    A few miles later, seven or so local ladies jogged by wishing us luck as they passed and a bit further down a couple more joggers asked another slew of questions. We always quickly explain that no, we're not both from Switzerland. Yes, we've been hiking together since the first day. No, we're not technically a couple. We tell people our last jobs, not the whole bobsledder / musician thing. It takes too long and just gets more questions…and it's hot out here.

    Today was a scorching nineteen miles. I came upon another rattlesnake that didn't want to rattle which is always a little unnerving. Hanne is terrified of these desert creatures. She's nearly stepped on one already. I've gone through what to do *if* you get bitten etc. Tie it off, hit your SOS button on the Spot and get to the nearest hospital if there's one to get to, but we usually spot the little guys first. I think we've now seen a total of six. Various spiders and bugs. Horned lizards. Dozens and dozens of other lizards. Ravens. A bobcat. Mule deer. Hummingbirds. Blue jays. Canyon wrens. Random dogs. Nasty gnats. A couple garter snakes which are tiny. I've been bitten by one mosquito and one fire ant so far. Hanne's only been stung by one bee on her hip coming out of the San Jacintos.

    My right knee is being weird again. Didn't want to bend toward the end of the day. Tomorrow is a twenty-four-miler. I hope I'm ready. We're starting to hear stories of kids doing twenty five to thirty miles regularly so tomorrow will be a big test. Who am I kidding…it's going to be exhausting, but we end up at "Hikertown" for some showers and H2O before the big L.A. Aqueduct desert stretch. The Sierras are two hundred miles away…starting to loom in my mind.

    I pray for my mom…to just get better. To heal. To get over this. Every day the thought of what she's enduring hits me…and

sometimes it seems unbelievable that she should be the one to endure something like this at all...
 Dreams come sporadically. Lots of dreams about the past. Former selves. Former loves. Former lives. A long process.
 Goodnight.

Journal
April 23, 2018
Assessment

We've passed five hundred miles. We've actually passed five hundred and thirty miles which means we've completed just over one fifth of this journey. Amazing! From planning to showing up at Campo full of nervous adrenaline, learning the basics, learning what twenty miles under the feet really feels like. We are one day from Tehachapi. The end of Section One. Less than two hundred miles to the Sierras.

This has all been so incredible. The exhaustion. The sweat. The nonstop daily, nightly morning pains in feet, ankles, calves, knees, hips, shoulders. Adjusting and readjusting. Finding out what the body really needs. Feeling the full pendulum of nature and its cycles. Rising with the sun. Sleeping under stars. Hitching rides from strangers. Making new friends and acquaintances; some only for one day. Some people we've seen for over a month now. It's a different world with different rules. Walking, eating, sleeping, repeat. There's a great cleansing process occurring. Something subtle; the mind and body - pushed to extremes, sweating liters of water every day, detoxing, pushing the heart rate, getting plenty of Vitamin D from the sun. These cumulative changes are barely noticed some days. Others, I think I understand why I'm here.

We left the mountains toward Hikertown around 7:30 am. I immediately felt the soreness in my right knee and left hip, so hiking wasn't physically the most pleasant thing on the 22nd, but I managed. Later a steep downhill did my knees in while I tried to prop myself on the trekking poles. They just need a good day's resting.

Filtered water from a guzzler at lunchtime and kept heading down the valley where we eventually caught a hitch from a young man on vacation named Hoi who was just taking the back roads to San Diego. He dropped us at the Neenach Cafe and even though the kitchen was closed we stocked up from the store and ate a sandwich and pizza before Richard showed up to shuttle us in.

The story of Hikertown unfolded as we sat in the truck cab. At one point I didn't know if it was a well-rehearsed story or if the whole thing was true, but Hikertown is a real place; built by him and his wife purely to accommodate PCT hikers. Showers, electricity, and tiny dorms sit in a row like an Old West movie set. It was pure Americana in the middle of a great lonely desert and Hanne and I pitched our tent on the edge of the large property, sipped wine and had dinner. A good night plus a shower equals double-plus-good. In the morning we woke and headed out around 7:30 am for the "Most Notorious Stretch" of the PCT. Nineteen miles following the old Los Angeles water system. Miles of canal, huge steel pipes, asphalt, and lots of Joshua trees that end in the middle of dozens of massive windmills and a bridge with water resupply in a great blue barrel. Again we met our Asian friends and learned a little more about them. Also, John and Kris have been passing us and vice-versa for some time. A nice retired couple; have invited us to stay at their place when we get to Oregon (they're only going to Kennedy Meadows this time). Another two older hikers we met today: Charley, a Chinese fellow going solo and Vlado, a former climber from Slovakia... "I am the only Slovak on the PCT!" Stuck in my mind. We decided to do seven extra miles that put our daily total around twenty four. We walked the final uphill with John and Kris until we dropped into a little canyon next to a stream with decent water. Tents up. Ramen noodles cooking. Drinking tons of water after that. Sunny stretch. Crickets chirping. Light cool breeze. Alana and I are trying to find a way to meet up around Kennedy Meadows. Would be nice to see her and just say hey after a month. She's headed up to look for housing for nursing school. Lots to do in Tehachapi. Checking snow reports, getting new shoes, submitting stories, starting a Go-Fund-Me, etc. Trying to do everything I can to insure the financial end of things while I'm out here. Seventeen miles in and a clean hotel for a couple nights. Sweet relief. Much needed, We've been in tents for well over a week now. Things are starting to smell. On that note...goodnight!

"With the hollowing out of community by the market system, with its loss of structure, articulation, and form, comes the concomitant hollowing out of personality itself. Just as the spiritual and institutional ties that linked human beings together into vibrant social relations are eroded by the mass market, so the sinews that make for subjectivity, character, and self-definition are divested of form and meaning. The isolated, seemingly autonomous ego that bourgeois society celebrated as the highest achievement of "modernity" turns out to be the mere husk of a once fairly rounded individual whose very completeness as an ego was responsible because he or she was rooted in a fairly rounded and complete community."

-Murray Bookchin

December 18, 2018

I'll start reflecting…I've had little more than three months to do so. I can't quite put my finger on post-trail life or what it means and where it's going lately. I know I'm headed for Switzerland. I know Hanne is there. I know the Alps are there…the great winding roads that will lead me up on the bicycle. I know there's more hikes in the future. More great stretches of fresh air and sunsets. But how could I ever recreate an adventure like the PCT? 2,650 miles. I write it. I hear it in my mind…the number. When I write I try to reminisce and hook a memory that triggers a set of parallel stories and visions. It always leads back there. You return to society and almost no one in your immediate world is concerned after about a week. There's a brief "window of interest". I appreciate whenever I get to talk about it for more than five minutes. I take it all in.

It's as if *inside* you've changed in ways you can't appreciate yet. Your worldview is both destroyed and augmented. Your sense of self…what you are capable of…what you can withstand and what really matters. All the small moments that brought a smile to your face and meaning back into your life…where did the meaning come from? Not only could I reconnect with a sense of the real world; the natural unfettered & uncluttered earth, but I was able to share it with my mom. It was one of the few things I did in my life that actually made sense in terms engendering a mutual understanding. I said goodbye to her, lying on a couch, her head covered in a soft silk scarf in Sedona. I said goodbye the only way I knew how…by thanking her. Thanking her for who she was. For the life and opportunities she'd given me through the innocent power of her own heart. For what she imagined and what she gave. Her natural kindnesses.

The day she passed away we'd made it into Chester, California. I made the call from a mom-n-pop burger joint and got the news. She'd left the world around noon, June 11th, 2018. I did what I could to indicate to Aubrey that I understood, hung up the phone…and as I did my mom's favorite singer John Denver came on the radio station and played twice in ten minutes. Maybe I've written about this in the journals…how I asked the fellow at the counter what station it was. He said "It says 'Singin' in the Shower' Radio". It wouldn't be the last time we heard John Denver. He's synonymous with the outdoors and followed us up and down the trail.

We hitched in to the North Shore Campground by Lake Almanor and paid for the night. The woman at the front desk was excited to see hikers and gave us free extra shower tokens and a great spot close to the water. On the hill directly behind us a thin stretch of asphalt lined with lanterns led down into the trees where most of the RVs and trailers sat with aluminum awnings, football flags, and summer decorations on display. These people are amazing.

There's so much to write that I'll never get it down…or maybe I'll have to keep writing forever until all the organic memories are replaced with millions of words all lined up in a row.

My uncle Kim did this. He lived off the grid outside Port Townsend and wrote for three hours every morning for decades. Every. Single. Morning. He had rows and shelves full of spiral notebooks lined up chronologically in the tiny wooden house he'd built for himself in the mid 80s. I never knew what he was writing about and I never asked. I imagined it was something close to the philosophical muse he'd carried about his whole life. People would say I reminded them of uncle Kim. I couldn't imagine what way that ought to mean, but as my beard grew around my glowing face over those months, I saw a sudden likeness. The fact that he passed away within a week of my mother has haunted the timeline. My mind looks at the puzzle compulsively trying to find clues...waiting for a key to unlock a narrative that makes sense. He was a writer. A thinker. An over-thinker. A stutterer. A sensitive, wizardly type. Blunt to a fault. A pothead. Maybe a genius...a sort of unassuming counter-culturalist who was less interested in marching to his own beat than drumming on pots and pans with wooden spoons and dancing around the kitchen when we visited. By Chester they were both gone...like their spirits made a pact to leave this world together. I didn't understand any of it. I kept walking.

A Passive Observer

For miles you watch the heels in front of you, appearing one at a time below the brim of your hat. You forget who they belong to and try to stay self-aware but it's virtually impossible. Sure and steady, crunching over the high desert. A measured march. Don't go too fast. Don't go too slow. Listen to the body. Listen to what it's telling you. How long has that pain in your ankle been bothering you now? When was the last time you stopped for water? Did you get enough protein the night before? What has recovered and what is still sore? Each day the configuration changes and takes a different shape. More weight on the hips today. Let's see how that works. Pulling the chest straps closer, but not so close as to affect my breathing. Big long breaths. How long until you relax and get in the flow? My breath was matching my steps, bound to some sort of rhythm that I couldn't escape. Walk, walk, walk. When a song came into my head as they invariably do, it always matched the tempo of my steps..."

I marvel at the memories flooding back. The fact that they're tempo-dependent as ever, as if my feet were the conductors and I, some passive observer in the cheap seats. They trigger long-forgotten memories; moments that I didn't know *still* occupied a space in my mind. Where do they come from? Everything's still there isn't it? The smell of the Tinker-Toys and Lincoln Logs in the Quaker Oats can at grandpa's in Riverside. The way the carpet on the stairs felt while I slid down face-first. The ocean wind traveling miles inland, dropping dew on the shrubs around the property. Granny Lynn doing calligraphy on the drafting board upstairs. Where did all these memories go? Why did I feel compelled to push them aside as if I had no connection to them? As if I wasn't made of them. I once imagined families like a great quilt, interconnected with different colors and threads;

each of us with our own stories...but I'd let that go completely. I detached. I hid.

Most of the family considered me a mystery; getting the occasional update and presence at holidays. When I'd finally left the house at seventeen my only concern was forging some kind of working identity. Something that I could use in the real world...but I'd forgotten that too. Life has a way of compelling the participant, willing or not, to move forward. To change with the seasons. To grow and survive and hopefully thrive...but what do you take with you? I was coming to the realization that it was all still there if I wanted to listen to it. Everything I'd ever experienced had been recorded with an emotional imprint attached: a reference code. What program was I running on? What sort of identity was I trying to concoct now? What would the trail mean in the end? A series of journals that I handed my grandkids? Would I even have grandkids? Would they get a stable home or would they move all over creation like we did in the early 80s? What constituted "stability" to begin with? I'd never actually sought it. It'd only happened here and there as if by chance. In the meantime, I'd been too busy writing, playing, traveling. It was too early to decide if this was a logical extension of myself or a line in the sand. When people asked why I wanted to do it I gave them different reasons depending on my own current understanding. "I needed to press the reset button." "I'm doing it for my mom." "I just wanted to do it." "I've never been to the Sierras."

On and on until I found reasons didn't matter anymore. The entire construct changed on its own. The days became single missions that required all of me and there wasn't time to have the sort of casual reflection I'd hoped for. It would scarcely appear on the zeros. It would come somewhere between consciousness and deep sleep cloaked in those last in-between states that dance for a moment and dissolve into darkness.

In the morning I'd wake, push myself upright, pull my legs in and lean forward to lengthen my spine. The first steps would be excruciating. Knees and calves begging me to stop. I'd go pee a few feet away and limp back toward the tent. "Ok. Ok. Get your shoes on. Ok. Good. Get your jacket on. Ok. Let's go." Stepping out into the cold again, pulling the bag and pad and lanterns and journals and pens out and setting them on the closest log or tree branch, popping the tent-poles out one by one and yanking the spikes from the ground, slapping them on a rock and thumbing the mud out. Everything smashes together. Sleeping bag. Tent. Food. Clothes. Whatever's left. Poles on the side. Pad strapped down. Breakfast is extracted before-hand and left on a rock or log to consume when I'm done packing everything up.
"I don't know about this instant coffee."
"Yeah...that ain't coffee."
"I'll get some honey in town."

The pack goes up. Yank the shoulder straps down. Pull the other straps until you've got it snug...not tight. Just snug. Nod at the others if there are others. Thumbs up. We all turn toward the trail and start moving.
Who's feet are in front of me today? I can't remember this guy's name...we're spreading out over the hills and bunching up in the valleys. Some people are stronger climbers. Some are stronger on the downhills. All day from sunup to five or so. Walk. Get three miles in. Break. Water. Grab a snack. Walk three more. Break. Grab a snack. Refill at a cistern, a well, a pipe-spring or the jugs left by the Trail Angels. Try to take pictures. I've got service for a moment at the top of a pass. Send photos home to mom...still at the hospital. Wait for a reply. Try to get a call in. Signal is too weak. I text, giving coordinates and an ETA where I'll call from.

We come to an overlook above a long red valley...strewn with Ocotillo and volcanic rock. It looks dead compared to the mountains of the last few days. Like the surface of Mars. "That down there...that's Scissors Crossing." We've got to make it to the main road, still ten miles in the distance, to hitch a ride in. Fifteen minute break before the final push. We discuss options...where to stay. The packs go back up. Little hops to let everything settle. Straps down. Moving.

"Live a life worth living."
"Live before you die."
"Waste not a moment in bitterness."
"Live."
"Live."
"Live."

We begin descending fast and on my third switchback something finally gives and sends a jolt through my foot like someone stabbing it with a hot knife. "Arghhh no!" I know it's bad. I've been injured plenty of times before. *That* feeling. Something's been pushed too far. Some muscle or bone couldn't take the strain and broke down. A wave of panic hits me and I imagine myself out of the running. Off the trail, limping back home and saying "Hey, I tried but that's life huh?" Less than one hundred miles in. I can't believe it. It's the dreaded shin splints or something. I had them in track and field. I had them in cycling. I've broken this ankle twice...sprained it God knows how many times...I remember this feeling. The ankle swells and travels up your shin. Walking becomes nearly impossible without severe pain, but once it has happened it's like any other sprain. Nothing makes it better and nothing makes it worse. It's just there until it heals. Hanne comes up behind me.

"What's wrong?"
"Something's bad with my ankle. Not sure. Just gotta make it to Julian. We've got a zero there, right?"
"Yeah, I take a zero for sure. Can you make it to Scissor's Crossing?"
"Guess I don't have a choice."
"You'll be ok. When we get there you can put ice on it."
"Yeah, maybe something to stabilize it. A wrap or something."
"I'm so hungry...I've never been this hungry before." She looks up, pleading to the sky.
"I want a burger...I don't care what kind of burger. No. I want Mexican food. Enchiladas. A combo plate. Enchiladas with cheese and red sauce...onions, then a taco and a tamale on the side. And I want there to be a salsa bar. You know about Mexican food?" I ask, hopefully.
"Only a little...I had it a few times before when I visited."
"Oh man. I hope there's Mexican food down there...you know, if a Mexican restaurant has a salsa bar it's a good sign. This means they know what's up."
"Salsa bar?"
"You know...chips and salsa?"
"Yeah, yeah. Chips and salsa."
"So you have an entire salsa bar and get to choose different salsas. Spicy, not-so-spicy, maybe some guacamole."
"With avocados? I love this thing."
"Pray for Mexican food."
"Ok I pray for this. I will manifest this for us."
"Thank you."

We walk down into the long valley. Every one hundred steps or so the pain comes back in deep nauseating bursts. I'm worried, but now I have something to focus on: Food.

Journal
April 26, 2018
The PCT Organism

We pulled off the PCT at Willow Springs Road in the middle of hundreds of windmills. The very first car we thumbed for pulled over. She tearfully told us about her prize Doberman pinchers, of loving Tehachapi and working for the school district for years until she was forced into retirement due to injury. We listened in the back of her '97 4-Runner while she careened toward town, dropping us a quarter mile from the hotel.

We grabbed some quick coffee and headed in. Got the keys, dropped the bags, took showers and just relaxed for the first time in days. Later, went out for burgers at Jake's Steak House. I'd had enough of the Nikes. I didn't know it but the cumulative effects were close to becoming debilitating. We slept like babies and woke for a pillaging of the continental breakfast. Eggs, sausage, cereal, melons, yogurt, milk, OJ, coffee, bagels, everything in sight and seconds. We needed to figure out Hanne's resupply, a visit to the Post Office, more coffee, shoes, and more food in no particular order. We made it no further than fifty feet down the road until we were offered a ride by a passing Trail Angel who dropped us in the center of things. We sat in the Tehachapi Cafe with more coffee and planned the next stretch. Then it was over to Big 5 where I found a sturdy pair of Asics Kahana trail shoes. I almost cried when I put them on. The difference was night and day. Couldn't believe I'd just walked 560 miles in a flimsy pair of gym shoes. I was elated. Hopefully this would cure my joint issues and give my body some respite. Was I trying to be tough before? I just didn't know. I met Hanne in Albertson's and a fellow walked up and offered us yet *another* ride to the Post Office. He just waited in the parking lot until Hanne was done. He dropped us off and I got my resupply.

A squirrel had eaten through the side of the box! Haha. It wasn't too bad. Just a few nibbles off the side of a couple trail bars. I helped Hanne pack her bounce box to Lake Isabella and Kennedy Meadows. A few other hikers were getting their food too. An old veteran told me about the best fishing spots by Bishop and the best restaurants in Kern. Damn…Tehachapi was friendly. We barely stuck our thumbs out again when "Butterscotch" pulled over, gave us a ride back in and offered to take us to the trail the next day. We were becoming mesmerized by the nonstop generosity and thanked him.

    We went to the German bakery so Hanne could get some real German bread. I got a croissant and a minute later The Howdies, (John and Kris) showed up. They sat with us and we spent half an hour or so telling our best tales from the trail and other adventures in the Andes they'd been on with their kids. A real genuine couple we've been leap-frogging for days since the Mojave Rover. They left and we headed back soon after. I wrote a little and we went out once more for sushi. As usual we got "The Hiker Deal" with free miso and rice and another discount. Just amazing. Afterward I was seriously spent. Still had to finish writing, updating bank info, and a dozen other details before bed. I was out like a light in a deep sleep with one passing dream about fishing. Woke up. More continental breakfast. More planning. More arranging. Butterscotch got us to the same spot we left at Willow Springs Road around 1:00 pm. Nice guy; mandatory picture with his Mogwai stuffed animal and hugs and well-wishes to us both.

    "How are we going to adjust to society when people don't treat us so amazing every day?" I asked.
"I wondered the same." said Hanne.
    We climbed over some hills, waited for a train, and went over the interstate and climbed some more until we reached a perch overlooking the highway, windmills, Mojave, and other small

towns in the distance. A cool breeze and a bright moon that will be full again in a few days.
"Has it been that long?" I asked. "Yeah. 38 days." she replied.
"Wow. We were just coming down out of San Jacinto with the last full moon."

Rewind and Repeat
Letters Home #1

 We left Wrightwood in an Uber to bring us back to the trail for a short day up Mt Baden-Powell and back down to Little Jimmy campground.
 Our driver was a huge gregarious guy from Los Angeles, covered in tattoos. The car gently expelled cannabis from the windows the whole way. We gave the usual rundown of distance and resupply but the topic quickly turned to the statistical lethality of bears and mountain lions and things that go bump in the night.
"Aw, hell no!" He'd say after every story.
"I mean, it's usually just lizards and birds you hear in the leaves" I said…"but then, sometimes late at night you're sitting around the fire and you just hear this one big CRUNCH a few feet away in the darkness..."
"Oh hell no! Hell. No! Uh-uh!"
 At the trail we took our packs out of the trunk and he wanted to see how much they weighed.
"Aw, hell no!!! No way!"
 He wished us luck and we waved goodbye. Sometimes you're reminded that what you consider to be a reasonable way to spend a summer is the literal definition of crazy to someone else...
 We climbed Baden-Powell for a few hours. Plenty of other hikers on the trail. It's the big packs and unkept look or something. People pass and offer a "Good luck guys!" every so often.
 Another man approached quietly and after some small talk tells us it's his life goal to do the PCT. I don't know what to do with this kind of info sometimes. Hanne says "Yeah you should

do it!" I say "It's more challenging and more amazing at the same time then I ever imagined." But, I'm not sure if this sentiment translates well. We snap pictures at the summit and descend to Little Jimmy Campground where numerous campers have already set up in the dusk light under a canopy of giant pines. I start a fire in the metal pit and we cook our new favorite: Marunchan ramen noodles. Two packs equals six hundred and fifty or so calories of monosodium glutamate and stock flavor that is simply the most psychologically satisfying non-town thing you can eat after a long, cold day of hiking. We add Cholula and hot pepper seeds and then get busy with the "healthy stuff" from the bottom of the bags.

We lock our remaining food in a bear vault and fall asleep full and tired.

We wake up and put things into the packs. Mornings are sore. You feel like your feet are forty years older than the rest of your body. The pads of my feet always swell during the night, sometimes to the point of waking me up. The knees feel spent and it's a slow process hobbling around the campsite, breaking things down, walking far enough away to do your business, coming back, sorting out something for breakfast, etc.

The first mile is a bit awkward as limbs come to life and already-abused ligaments and tendons warm up. Just as this is getting going a man with a great red beard under a stocking camp is calling his two yellow labs back from the trail, smiling ear to ear, asking all about the trip, offering whiskey to warm us up (it's about 35 F) and we're politely declining and trying our best to be thankful and communicative.

I can't believe how incredible people have been on this trail and every day it gets to me, even if it's a little forward. You know people are just genuinely curious and I try my best to share all my best stories and give detailed information about my own experience i.e. how I got my trail name, what my favorite town is so far - what it's really like. I honestly love these interactions but this morning my brain is on autopilot and it's freezing and ten minutes later we've got to summit Mt Williams just to get the day started. So, we climb. And climb.

You sweat...and when you stop, you're suddenly soaked in the middle of a wind-chill, so you just keep walking.

We come down the other side to cross a paved road and run into another couple of Trail Angels who met on the PCT in 2016, fell in love, married, have a child on the way and decided to fly in from Luxembourg this year just to give snacks and cold sodas to hikers.

I can't process this level of sincerity sometimes. I see things like this every day now. Random acts of kindness yes, but the whole-hearted dedication from so many people to this adventure is beyond words. Anonymous people spend hundreds of dollars on water caches just to make sure we're ok in the long stretches without streams or springs. I don't know who these people are. I just thank them in the logbooks signed: "Campfire".

Hanne talks with the couple for awhile in German while I talk to Ned from Portland about pants, jobs and sugar intake. We thank them for the potato chips and ham slices and cheese and make our way toward another paved detour a few miles down.

There's an endangered frog around here so we've got to spend four to five miles on a paved road until we meet back up with the trail. I don't mind. It's easy on my feet. We kick pinecones back and forth while motorcycles and Corvettes zip by every so often out on leisure cruises outside LA.

"Do you like cars?" Hanne suddenly asks.

No one's put it to me like that before. This could be a test question.

"Yeah, I guess. I've only had a few though."

We pass under ski lifts dangling in the air. Out of season. White billowing mists form and evaporate on all sides and shroud around the pines in seconds, bending under huge gusts of wind.

We find shelter next to a log and eat lunch on the side of the road before heading further down. The temperature doesn't let up one degree and we pull up our collars and hoods until we reach a scout camp with an outhouse, bunkhouse, bench, and a kiosk that offers hikers free post-cards to send home.

We sit down and write short thank you notes to family and friends and deposit them in a slot at the kiosk without any idea of when they'll be sent or if they'll pay postage for a letter going overseas.

This is where we also met Ginger Tiger from Great Britain who has noted, along with us, the astounding number of working outhouses and port-a-jons along this stretch of Angeles National forest.

"He called them "privies". I said to Hanne: 'I thought the Brits called them a "loo".

"In German you can say loo-loo" she said.

"Hmm."

We walked on. Little white rocks lined up showed us mile four hundred in three official places within a half mile of each other.

The cold was relentless. We finally reached a campsite by a small stream where some of the hikers from Little Jimmy had already made camp. Another fire. Another group with Ginger Tiger leading came in thirty minutes later. They got a fire going as well. It was cold no doubt, but this was the first time in four hundred miles I'd seen anyone besides myself make a fire. I'd only made a few but people seemed fire-phobic. It made sense, especially in certain conditions and we generally avoided it altogether, but it made me happy and we could hear them laughing and telling jokes into the night next to their own warm glow.

    Hanne and I sat by ours in silence for a long time, slowly remembering interesting things that had happened so far...how our perspectives had changed...but we found ourselves in hysterics over the sheer amount of strange and hilarious things that had already occurred. Nature, I think, has a sense of humor. Here you are: this bumbling animal trying to find places to eat and sleep and find temporary relief from the elements and suddenly you trip on a pine cone, a bee stings your hip, a fire ant bites your thigh just before bed, a gust of wind blows your solar panel so hard it flies over your backpack and smacks you in the face. Or you go to squeeze water through a filter and get a mouthful of everything you tried to filter out the day before...but it's all punctuated by a sense of raw experience that I've never been a part of like this. It is brutal and beautiful at same time. It is the epitome of balance as I know it.

    The next day I tried trekking poles for the first time. It is now officially a new PCT. Poles essentially give you extra limbs, allowing you to drag yourself up steep inclines and brace yourself on the downhills and water crossings. At the beginning of my preparations I'd been skeptical of the idea. The thought of carrying anything extra at *all* sounded cumbersome at best and outside the Whitewater Preserve by Cajon Pass I'd given Hanne's a five-minute evaluation before handing them back, but on this day the rhythm suddenly clicked and I was converted. We wound down through shrubs until we found a spot next to an old industrial side road with broken telephone poles scattered about. It wasn't pretty but it worked.

    The next day we planned to pass through the Acton KOA and get a little closer to Agua Dulce, but after twenty miles the lure of a shower and soft grass was too much. We made it in around 5:00 pm, just before their little convenience shop closed and bought sausage links and snacks for dinner and got hot showers and laundry done too.

Another couple, John and Kris, had taken a kindly interest in us about a week back. We saw them pitched across the field and while I got my shower Hanne had a long conversation with them.

John is a retired engineer and Kris is a retired science teacher and there aren't many places they haven't been. We'd met them at the base of the Mojave River before Silverwood Lake and called them "The Howdies" at first because John's greeting was invariably "Howdy Howdy!" But as usual, getting to know people unraveled stories and fostered connections previously unthought of. By Tehachapi we'd become regular trail buddies, passing each other routinely throughout the day.

We spent the next morning in the lobby of the KOA trying to plan the next stretch under a television blaring Bewitched reruns until a couple ambled in at 10:00 am on the dot, switched the channel to The Price is Right and turned the TV up ten more decibels, discussing with another fellow what sort of taxes were actually taken out of your winnings, should you actually win on The Price is Right. It turned into a full-on debate and I realized things were getting strange. The milk I'd bought smelled expired. Very expired. The coffee was so watered-down that I threw it away.

We had to get out of this RV oasis fast, so we threw our things into the packs, checked water levels and headed for the hills toward Agua Dulce. This turned into a beautiful albeit short eight-miler through grassy hills and eventually a sort of county park that labeled various geological and floral features as we went.

Great silhouetted sandstone spires fanned out across the desert and we strode past farmlands and haystacks with our thumbs out in the late afternoon sun until a woman in a white pickup gave us a ride to Hiker Heaven up the street.

Hiker Heaven is a private sort of collective run by the person who greeted us (I presume) because she gave us the full rundown.

Dogs circled and barked passively as we came onto the site. It looked like a strategic PCT headquarters with rows of resupply boxes, computers flickering with Sierra snow reports, dome shelters, and rows of overflowing hiker boxes. This is where I found a sturdy pair of aluminum trekking poles for free - just sitting there. I double-checked to make sure they were in working order. Score. Just in time. We knew we could stay at Hiker Heaven if we wanted to. It was a great spot, but we weighed our options.

A lot of other hikers we'd seen earlier had begun to trickle in but we were keen on Tehachapi and finishing Section One so we hit a Mexican restaurant, a small market, caught a hitch from a guy with a van to the trail and put on our headlamps to hike about two miles in the dark until we found what looked like a decent flat place just off the trail.

The wind picked up and smashed our tents every which way for about two hours but then suddenly died completely like someone had flipped a switch. When I woke up I got a view of the valley below and what appeared to be multiple trailers surrounding one half of a Boeing 747 in the middle of a field; the front half to be precise. I shrugged my shoulders and brushed my teeth. Now that I had the poles, we set off at a solid pace that didn't let up for seventeen miles. It was hot with some crazy inclines but we pushed through, taking short breaks until we came to a little hill with two Austrians at the bottom. They nodded as we approached which is sufficient in hiker-speak to say "Hi. Respect. Too tired to talk," and we moved up to a little clearing above them.

    The night moved in a magical sort of way. At first, we just had dinner and went through the motions, but I didn't put the rain fly on my tent so I could see the stars. Hanne lent me her iPod for a moment and I realized it'd been weeks since I'd just listened to any kind of music. I'd cleared my own phone of all music hoping to get some sort of perspective on things after years of production and project, but now the music came through in the most innocent way and for the first time in years...I just enjoyed it.

    We split the headphones and spent the rest of the evening listening to Phil Collins just staring at the stars and singing along and it was just perfect somehow; one of those moments you imagine having when you imagine doing this to begin with. I slept deep that night. I realized I was becoming acclimated to everything. The trail was starting to sink in and I felt more at ease with the wind, dirt, owls, and stars than the towns we passed every week or so. It was just so much simpler out here. Walk, eat, drink, sleep. Repeat. Just keep going until you reach your campground. Change, amend, and adapt as needed. Cover three mountain passes, three climate zones, talk to total strangers for any length of time, make new acquaintances daily with no knowledge of the duration of your relationship; only that you're in this together on *some* level; that you both decided to do this for whatever reason and now you're all doing the best you can to sort it out on a daily basis.

    The next day we followed the footprints of the Austrians up and down until we caught up around noon. One of them was so into the local flowers he was leaping across the switchbacks with his camera for miles. I watched this for an hour or so:

running past us, letting us pass, over and over. I understood what he was feeling. It's a sort of energetic rapture I've experienced on my own short photo expeditions. You feel mesmerized by nature, moving with the light, willing to do almost anything to capture the right moment if it takes a thousand shots to get it.

Eventually we all wound up in some pine trees above the great desert stretch below. The 'Notorious L.A. Aqueduct Stretch' according to Guthook. We found a sandy area with hummingbirds buzzing around under a great orange / pink sunset and I tried to eat as much as I could to repair the cumulative aches in my left hip and knees. It was the shoes honestly...a pair of Nikes that were designed to do stair masters in climate-controlled places but the thousands of tiny shocks where finally getting to me. I hadn't had a single blister in almost five hundred miles, but I had no sole support and needed a change soon.

The next morning we headed out over the crest for ten or so miles before heading straight down toward Hikertown. Straight down. Knees began killing me and by the time we hit eighteen miles I was in serious pain. My left hip had been tight for a week since the Mojave ridges and I constantly needed to stop and stretch it. The good thing was that since the beginning of the trail I'd become more conscious of exactly what my body needed. Now it needed new shoes. ASAP. The Nike soles were so thin I could feel every little pebble beneath every step. It was decided that in Tehachapi I'd find a good pair. First, we had to get to Hikertown and before Hikertown we had to get a hitch to the Neenach Cafe to resupply. The moment our thumbs went out a car stopped and we caught a quick ride in from "Hoi" who was on vacation, taking back routes from St Louis to San Diego on vacation.

When we stepped in the property gates a low voice behind a cap and a cigarette in the corner told us the diner was closed, but we could still get food from the adjoined market. I didn't realize he was a hiker just then but thanked him for the info and walked in.

Sandwiches, pizza, jerky, Gatorade. We sat at an outdoor table and devoured it. Richard, who ran Hikertown, showed up and drove us back to the property where we ended up staying that evening. Hikertown is hard to describe...only it's wonderfully strange and beyond that, a great service to the PCT community. There are free showers, toilets, and charging stations but most notably the property is surrounded by small dorm rooms with single beds all done with exterior facades resembling the Old West. One dorm is the "Sheriff's Office". Another is "The School". Another is "The Mercantile" etc. Here we met up again with John and Kris as well as our Asian friends Cherry and Leo who we hadn't seen since a few days before Wrightwood. Everyone was in good spirits and preparing for the nineteen-mile desert stretch in the morning.

The great challenge with the L.A. Aqueduct stretch is that there isn't any real shade or shelter. There's also no water so you've got to fill every bottle you've got (which is heavy). In the mountains I'll barely go through one liter for every ten miles but in the heat it feels like it's impossible to get enough. Liters disappear in great gulps just to cool the body on top of rehydration. I had three and a half liters. I knew I could make it. Just had to keep the sun hat on, keep the sleeves down and walk steady.

So, we started out at 7:30 am and passed a few people. Then we'd stop for water and they'd pass us. Through the canals, over the huge iron waterworks flumes, and over miles of dirt road and cement. At one point I just decided to try walking a mile with my eyes closed and told Hanne to make sure I didn't walk into a ditch or something. She'd push my shoulder to get me back on course and twenty-five minutes later that was over...and we kept walking. And walking.

Then it was mile 530 and I drew it in the sand with my foot. One-fifth done. What does that even mean? It meant something...but we kept walking. Under the massive windmills to Cottonwood Bridge where we met John and Kris again. They'd left Hikertown at 3:00 am, walked through the night to beat the heat and hiked up under the bridge until the worst part of the day was over.

We were all at nineteen miles. Charley, Smoker, Cherry and Leo, Jon and Kris, and now Vlado who had decided to take it easy that day. He'd camp at the bridge with the Smoker. Charley looked like he'd stay too. He was pretty beat. Cherry and Leo would head to the wind farm headquarters a mile down the road where there was supposed to be a running spigot. They'd said they'd probably camp there. John, Kris, Hanne and I decided to do six more miles to the end of the wind farm and camp by another seasonal stream. I knew it'd be no problem even at twenty-four miles because we'd been on flat ground all day, so we wound up through more flowered hills, past more windmills groaning in the light breeze and dipped down into a little dark valley with a perfect flat spot by the water.

We lost John and Kris but figured they just called it a little sooner and camped above. Ramen noodles never tasted so good. The water from the stream was silty and full of algae but I dug down a little to make a shallow pond where we could fill up our bottles for filtering. The next morning we headed over two passes and more windmills straight for Tehachapi: The gateway to the Sierra Nevadas. We caught a ride from a Doberman Pincher breeder who was driving an old 4-runner like the one I

used to have. She broke down into tears talking about her sixteen-year-old dog who'd just passed away and we talked for about twenty minutes till she dropped us off. We walked about a quarter mile to a Best Western and...
  Sleep. Showers. Resupply. Post Office. Laundry. Continental Breakfast. New Shoes. Hiking pants. Socks. Calling home. Calling friends. More food. Coffee. Blog. It's taken me about four hours to write about the past week...I'm spent. Who knows how many typos this has. My apologies! Tomorrow we make for Lake Isabella. Then three more to Kennedy Meadows. Then the Sierras. Section Two. Central California. Same length as the desert section we just finished-just more like 10-13k feet now. Time for sleep!

Journal
April 29, 2018
Mental or Physical

The night we left Tehachapi we climbed high above HW 58 looking out over Mojave and hundreds of windmills; the shadows of entire mountains drifted while we set up camp on the side of the trail on the 26th. It got windy. Then it got windier. Then it got so windy that neither of us could sleep. The tent felt like it was tearing apart and the sides came in from every angle. For hours; through the night until the morning. No sleep. Next day was sluggish. Tired obviously. No energy for hiking. Lunch break was also a nap break and by the look of the other hikers we passed, they'd all endured the same night. Nods and blank faces.

Sometimes the trail just takes it out of you. We made camp out of a small spot down a ravine where it wasn't too windy and both passed out immediately after dinner. I slept for ten hours. So much needed. Woke rejuvenated. Headed out into a misty morning that had us walking through clouds for five or six hours. It looked more like Oregon autumn than anywhere in California. Eventually another break, refilled at a spring and a couple more miles to the campground. Young Buck and Yoga Bae were there. I lent Yoga Bae my ankle stabilizer for his own shin splint. Made a fire. Stars and pines. Some other campers with trucks and motorbikes down the way. Woke early but slow to get going. Hanne in a mood on the trail starting off. Upset about some childhood thing she's still processing. Apparently so mad she broke one of her trekking poles. Some of her family has been pretty distant through this I guess.

We've gone into lots of details about families and growing up. Lots to ruminate sometimes. The trail is ideal for it. I don't judge. Sometimes you gotta break stuff. Trail magic soon after though, with ice-cold Pepsi and other sugar-foods. Met a nice older guy from Israel who had retired and now backpacked around the world. We wanted to pick his brain a little more but going at a different pace today.

    Winds picked up again like never before at the crest of a long sandy stretch. Insane hurricane-force seventy mph. Knocking us off our feet. Hours like this. At one point the wind was so strong I leaned into it and ran down a super-steep section with my arms open. Almost like flying. Total exhaustion. Total beauty. The scenes today are foreshadowing what's to come. The mood is changing. In the distance, silhouettes of massive 13-14 k peaks.

    Tomorrow: Twenty-one miles to Lake Isabella for resupply and food. A day "off" meaning no backpack but plenty to get in line for Kennedy Meadows.

    So, so tired. We shared tea and chocolate. Jerky and peanut M&Ms. Wind still blowing outside but we're protected in a little spot beneath a tree. G'night. Oh, also: Shoes! Finally healing and getting stronger with correct pair. So good!

September 20, 2017

Hi mom,

    I'd recommend that, but also Manuka honey. Not cheap but better than any antibiotic out there. Glad you got to check out the peaks. Is it cooling off and becoming autumn up there? Ya. Albuquerque is something. There are nice areas for sure but the infrastructure is ridiculous and not put together a lot of the time. It is affordable but sometimes that's all it has going for it unless you're working in very specific sectors. I personally love Colorado. I wonder if you've looked at the Pecos, NM area though. It's just east of Santa Fe. I see a lot of cabins there. It's very much a Rocky Mountain vibe even though I think it's nestled in the Sangre De Christo mountain range. I love it up there. Beautiful hikes and a little river and plenty of secluded areas. I have not seen the documentary. I don't have regular TV but can look it up online. I'll check it out. What does Randy think of it? I am considering Thanksgiving in Arizona as money permits so that's on the table. Hope everything is going well. Definitely look into the Manuka honey. I've heard some positive things about it.

Love
W

September 27, 2017

Hi Will,

    Bad news. I just went in two days ago for a regular check up to do blood work. The doctor called me right away to have me repeat the blood work because all my blood levels were off. Then they had me go see an oncologist today. The oncologist took a bone marrow sample and results came back that I have a very aggressive form of bone marrow leukemia. They want to start treatments right away. We are going down to a cancer center tomorrow where I will talk to a leukemia specialist and she will discuss the treatments. Apparently, there is not time for alternative treatments. This is a very aggressive form of cancer. It came on very suddenly and they said there is not time to try anything else and if I don't do the treatments the cancer will kill me. I'm sorry to have to give you this information via email. I wish I could talk to you. But here we go. Another chapter in our lives. You know your mom is a fighter. I feel confident we can beat this. I am otherwise a very strong, healthy person. The doctor so far feels I have a good chance.
We will email when I find out more information. I may be in Scottsdale at the cancer center for at least a week. But we will have email.

I love you very much,

Mom

"The fear of death follows from the fear of life. A man who lives fully is prepared to die at any time."

-Mark Twain

October 2, 2017

Mom:

Wow Will, you are amazing too! You have been working so hard for me with all your research. I don't know how you have the time to do this.
You should be a naturopathic physician. You have such a passion for this. I feel like I have my own personal events coordinator, my own private medical researcher and my sweet emotional support therapist. You are all so amazing. I can't thank you enough for all you three are doing for me.
You brought up a lot of good ideas. The CBD oil sounds like a great idea for the nausea. We'll pick some up next time we go to Flagstaff.
The vitamin C sounds like a good idea too. My only concern with Vitamin C is I have such a low platelet count, which aids in blood clotting.
And vitamin C thins the blood. I'm already at risk for bruising and internal bleeding. But I'll ask about that.
Aubrey, You know that naturopath you recommended in Flagstaff? I wonder if I could work in tandem with her through this process? She could monitor all the supplemental natural cures while I'm undergoing treatment. I just don't feel qualified to do it myself when we are introducing so many drugs and I don't know the interactions.
Will, the doctors say that I can't eat raw foods. I know how cleansing raw foods are. They say my white blood cell count is so low that I can't risk any bacteria in my food, in crowed spaces, around kids or dogs. If I get an infection of any kind it will hugely complicate this process not to mention potentially kill me because I have no resistance to infection. But if I

sterilize the raw foods, like use a tiny bit of Clorox bleach in a bath of water and rinse the vegetables then they should be fine.

    I'll check on the colloidal silver, apricot extract and baking soda water for alkalizing and see if they will allow that. I'm totally staying off sugars and refined foods. Even breads, but I am eating whole grains like oatmeal. I can't have raw milk anymore. But I'm thinking about pasteurizing my own raw milk, because I think it has better nutritive value.

    Thank you so much for all your research. I really appreciate it. I will certainly do what I can.

I start Chemo today at 1:15 pm. Wish me well.

Love, Mom

October 4, 2017
Cousin Kristin

My dear sweet Annie...
  I absolutely want to start biofeedback on you asap....I am so glad you are open to that! I do have it...I do use it! But not nearly enough! We can test you every 3 days but we can run therapies daily! I did it for Sheryl when she was in the hospital and even from a distance it was so accurate and amazing! I believe our world is extremely organized and everything that is came from energy first and foremost...I believe it is the intelligence of God and we are directed here on this earth to that knowledge energy and understanding! My doubts at times make it hard to create a business in biofeedback...I go back and forth and back and forth! I have done the exact same thing in my religious beliefs but as of late I have felt and witnessed some miraculous things which leaves me with a knowing that there is indeed a higher power of love truth and light...doesn't matter what one calls it...I know it absolutely exists! And I know that any and every way that we can tap into that good energy is time well spent on your road to recovery! For myself I do not utilize it enough! In my case it is easy to be complacent but in your case that is not an option! We will DO IT...you have so much love backing you! I read the post from your boss...was so beautiful...you are so beautiful and loved!
  I will start biofeedback today...Annie, I would love to get William going on this if he is interested! Rob made some really good points to bring up; mainly the fact that you are going to make your own choices and so it is nothing but helpful all the way around for William to be participating and researching! I am so glad he is! There are so many good things to be open to! I

am glad you are open within sound reason! When I do biofeedback for people, I feel I am helping and feels really good to DO something positive! That is the best thing for Will too! When I come there, I will bring it and show William the ins and outs! I'd hate to just send it without working together a bit simply because I have learned so much from Carol over the past few years and there is so much more to it than those basic protocols...I am training on it currently to finally get certified, but I am open to whatever we can work out to get you as much help from every resource possible! I will talk to William...there is a music called "Wholetones" that works with frequency too. Do you have a good DVD player? I'm guessing William knows a lot about it...there are also rife machines that are very easy to run...and not too expensive! We will look at that too...remember I told you about the gal that used that for scabies! It's all very fascinating! Sorry you got so very sick already on day one! I am so glad the meds helped day 2 and thrilled that you have another doctor to talk to that can work with some natural things! I wish medicine weren't so left/right extreme! I wish that of all people because there is so much good that comes from meeting in the middle! You can only benefit from more knowledge! Forward HO my dear auntie! I love you so much and my heart is with you every step of the way! Is there a best time today to start biofeedback? When you are back from treatment? All my love to Randy too!

I love you.

Kristin

October 4, 2017

W:

Tommy reminded me also about two specific mushrooms some of his clients have used for immune regulation. Chaga mushroom and Reishi mushroom. Pretty standard in Asia as far as treatments for any type of cancer. During chemo the organs needs detoxing as much as possible to avoid any current / future compromise in ability to function in tip-top shape and these are fantastic.
He also sends all his love and was so grateful for your advice and help back in the day. You actually got him in a much better place just from that one visit you know...

October 5, 2017

M:

Ahhh...that is so sweet of Tommy. Tell him thank you very much.
We'll get some mushrooms. Making a whole list of supplements and foods you are recommending. We just learned the cost of some of these medications. The weeks cycle of Chemo is going to cost $2000. Of which we pay $400. One shot they gave me yesterday to help stimulate my RBC production cost $1500 of which we pay $400. The anti-nausea medication cost $300 of which we pay $90. Anti-fungal, Anti-viral medication costs $200 of which we paid $50. The Naturopath / Oncologist first time fee is $500 of which insurance pays nothing. Not to mention all the expenses incurred during that 2-day hospital stay

which we have no idea yet how much that will be. And this is just the first week...

It's just criminal when people are at their most vulnerable and the Drug Co. charge these outrageous prices. You can see how a year long's worth of illness can bankrupt people.

We are going to apply for medical disability, and when on disability I may be able to get Medicare. Medicare with the VA insurance might help cover some of this. Talked to the financial person in the Dr. office today and they are going to try to get some financial assistance. Also through the state may be able to get Unemployment. Every little bit helps.

What a racket. If I didn't have VA insurance it would be over for us financially. We count our blessings that we have that. Most of my life I didn't have insurance. We are so fortunate.

Today I started CBD oil + anti-nausea med. After I get enough CBD oil in my system I may try to go without the anti-nausea med. That's the goal.

Josh sent all the comments by JBB customers today from Facebook that we can't get. So sweet of people. Some of them I don't even remember. Very sweet of Bill Phillips to say Randy is in his prayers too. And Dianne also said very nice things. Aubrey your comments were so sweet. Made me cry.

Kristin is going to give me a Biofeedback treatment in a few minutes, so better go...Love to you, Mom

October 5, 2017

W:

I have set up a Gofundme account. Please review and tell me if you'd like me to edit any of the information. You can share this link with anyone including Facebook. Gofundme will take 5 percent of the accumulated funds for their services. I've set the current goal at $50,000. If I've left anything important out or typos or said something inaccurate etc please tell me asap.

M:

I just looked at the page and am overwhelmed at the generosity of people. Kei Miura - $400. Unbelievable!
   People I don't even know. How can I thank these people? Are some of these your friends? Or Aubrey's friends?
   And anonymous people. How will I know who to thank?
   Now I can go to the naturopath / oncologist and won't have to worry about the money.
Thank you so, so much.
   I'm home every day next week, except for Dr. visits, but you can go with us. I'm retired!!! So, I am free as a bird :)

Love, Mom

October 10, 2017

M:

Hi kids,
Yesterday we went to the naturopath / oncologist hoping he could answer a lot of the questions we had regarding natural remedies, immune support and alternative therapies. He essentially said there are no natural therapies for the leukemia I have. My only course of action is to go through with the bone marrow transplant. After that process is over he can then begin to work with me and start to rebuild my body from all the toxins that have been pouring into me which can destroy the digestive tract, kidneys, liver, skin, etc...he also said for me to stop taking reishi mushrooms, astragalus, essiac herbs, and bone broth. His reasoning is that all those products boost the immune system.

The immune system is composed of white blood cells. My WBC are misfiring / non-functioning so I don't want to encourage the proliferation of these erratic cells. I guess that makes sense.

I guess I'm glad I went to him. I didn't really care for him. He seemed to know his stuff. He knew all the medical terms. But he talked without compassion or trying to help me understand. He just talked and talked fast. William and Randy were there so between the three of us we seemed to sort it all out.

Today we got another blood draw. Then met with a Dr. who I like very much; the oncologist in Sedona. She said the white blood cells had stabilized with that first round of chemo. That's a good thing. They are held in check for the moment. It buys me time waiting for the bone marrow donor. They had given me a shot to boost RBC last week and she said that is working because my hemoglobin counts are a little better. That should give me a little more energy. As they are killing WBC with the chemo they are also killing RBC - which they don't want to do because the RBC are healthy. They're just getting pushed out by the WBC. Does this make sense?

So now I get a blood draw once a week to see if the WBC are still held in check. I have to do another round of chemo at the end of the month if we don't have a donor by then. This was the protocol set up by the leukemia doctor from Scottsdale.

I feel fine, no nausea, no pain. Just a little weakness. Today I got over 50 cards, books, gifts, gift cards that Randy picked up at Jay's Bird Barn...amazing! I feel like it's the biggest birthday I've ever had. It makes me feel sad in a way too for all the people who are not in the public eye like I was who are going through the same thing but don't have near the love and support that I have. I count my blessings every day and you three are at the top of the list.

Love, Mom

October 13, 2017

W:

    Your entire body is replete with cannabinoid receptors. It's called the Endocannabinoid system.
    You've got lots of time on your hands, mom! I'll keep sending info and you need to take a little time to actually read / watch things and use this window extremely wisely whether you end up having the transfusion or not. I would be doing everything humanly possible to get yourself in a place where these upcoming blood tests show significant positive changes. There is no risk in helping yourself, doing your own research and having an actual treatment protocol as long as it doesn't make your immune system reproduce too many white cells or flush the anti-viral / fungal stuff out. You need to be on top of this. There's at least FIVE treatment protocols I've found and I've sent them all and you can use any number or amount of them. There are thousands of testimonials online about how people's leukemia has reacted to different methods. You asked "Why aren't there places we know of if someone's found a better method?" There are: everywhere from Mexico to Sweden and hundreds of thousands of people treating and curing on their own. The fact is that most people who get diagnosed get rail-roaded into the accepted treatments. Either way you need to be doing more than just
"eating healthy". You can also just go on Youtube and search "cbd oil leukemia" or "cannabis oil leukemia" for this specific topic.
    Love, Will

October 14, 2017

T:

Will - Thanks. Excellent analysis. I'm convinced you're on the right path - continual researching, understanding the various levels / systems at play (e.g., cell-level interactions, different approaches), passing on for decision...
 Our seniors yoga class has a member who had a bone marrow transplant that cured leukemia and inexplicably her Crohn's disease as well. One of the success stories.
 Tough to sort through the counter-intuitive. Go easy on alkalizing and veggie / fruit drinks to maximize nutritional intake because they would excessively boost the immune system? No need to answer. Her doctors undoubtedly address such. Also brilliant was the Go Fund Me page. I turn to it next. Where are you now? Still in Albuquerque?
 T

October 25, 2017

M:

Hi Kids,
 I did a blood draw yesterday to find that my CBC came out a little worse than the week before. Nothing alarming. Just not any better. However, I feel good. I don't know how a body can function so well with such off numbers.
 We talked to the nurse working with the bone marrow donor. She was very helpful and explained the whole process.
 She said out of an initial scan of 101 people that met my blood criteria they have narrowed it down to three. Those three

are all international and are now in the process of sending a vial of blood to the cancer center in Scottsdale. (Actually, the hospital where they have the blood drawn will send it overnight). The doctors will compare their blood to my blood looking at all the microscopic detail to see which one matches mine the best. Once that person has been selected, they go through a vetting process. They have to be screened for everything to make sure they are not carriers of any disease. They are given a daily injection of something that stimulates their WBC production. Then when everything is given the O.K. they go into a hospital where they draw their blood out (like a blood transfusion) they spin out the stem cells' and put their blood back in. Their body instantly replaces their WBC so they are not without. The timing all depends on the person's timing. They will have to take off work, they might have just planned a vacation….so we are at their mercy. Whenever they get to all that is required of them.

    Once the person commits and they are starting the procedures over there (wherever "there" is). That is when they call me back to the cancer center and I start going through all kinds of testing to check my fitness level. EKGs, stress tests, CT Scans, etc, etc. And that's when they start the heavy duty chemo to ready myself to receive the new stem cells. So this whole process could still take a month. Meantime I start back on the 30th for a week of chemo while we wait….

    Lauren, feel free to add as much of this detail as you want on the Caringbridge site. I think people are curious how this whole procedure works. Thank you so much for all your sweet phone calls. I really feel loved.

    Love, Mom

Journal
May 2, 2018

The 30th found us at a rapid clip-passing people on the trail one after another. The shoes have my body and joints healed and I'm so grateful. I had no idea what was going on as I slowed down more and more over the 1st month. Since Tehachapi only minimal pains here and there. Hints of blisters but I've mostly kept them at bay. It's a new trail. Thank goodness. Sam the Israeli passed us close to Walker Pass and told us he had a car down at the day-use area and we could all pile in to go to Lake Isabella with him. He had two other Israeli friends driving who were on the trail but taking a week off for sickness; SloMo and Dodo. SloMo and I talked about all the great places to visit in the southwest after his PCT trip. Hanne and Dodo talked about bobsledding, and Freebird and I also talked about photography and the presentation he wants to do when he gets back to Austria. It involves a talking back-pack. Right on. Red Flower is from Germany and his English is not as good but he's a very nice guy. He and Freebird look like a team. There's also Tom the younger German who is sometimes with the other two and sometimes solo. Do what you feel. In the minivan we had three Israelis, one Swiss, two Germans, one Austrian and two Americans; myself and a girl from Dallas named Snow White. We all unloaded at the RV park where Young Buck and Yoga Bae were already posted up. Cherry and Leo would arrive later that night. Hanne and I walked into town one mile thinking we'd find a big dinner. Ended up at a Burger King after one false lead after another. We both got this very odd vibe from the town, but I was too tired to care. I like it in a very Steven King sort of way. We scarfed the burgers and fries, bought some wine at Von's and head back to camp. Hot showers. Talked with some of the guys in the community house about plans for the Sierras.

Who's going to team up etc. I think the general consensus is we'll all hike our own hikes but keep everyone in the loop of our whereabouts and generally camp at the same spots. Love stuff...oh man...what is going on here? It is what it is. I think we just get along really well. Conversations with Alana back home have been strange. I don't know what her deal is. Maybe I'm just not interested in Albuquerque or any narratives going on there. Sigh. I'm on the trail now and I want to be here in the moment, which is very easy to do when you do nothing but hard physical exertion all day. Woke up. Errands. Post office. Figured out Hanne's bounce box situation and got everything re-routed from Mojave to Kennedy Meadows. Groceries and resupply. Heavy protein. Got these 40 MG protein Cliff Bars, cheese and meats. Good to go. Plus, more instant coffee for these cold mornings that are surely on the way. Listened to music. Talked about how life is looking over Mexican Food. Came back...another shower. Took the bus back to Walker Pass and hiked thirteen miles up and then down to Joshua Tree Springs. Tomorrow is seventeen, then into Kennedy Meadows. Starting to hang our food in case of bears but who knows with that. Just the usual precautions. Dinner was ramen and cheese slices with salami. Delicious. Something so satisfying about ramen noodles after a day of hiking. G'night.

Journal
May 3, 2018

Late start due to abundance of snuggles. No prob though. Only seventeen miles today but it was hard. Left the cement holding tank for Joshua Tree Springs which had Guthook warnings about Uranium content. I had to have a little. Woke dehydrated and stayed dehydrated all day. Consumed mass quantities of little oranges. Cravings on the verge of hypoglycemia but couldn't drink enough water. Winding trail that almost looked like it doubled back on itself multiple times. Good and sunny, but took it out of us. Strange unsettled scores courtesy of dehydration and ego. Scars from decades ago; floating through my head. Old arguments. Old miscommunications evaporating with food. I wonder what's actually being processed. Things come up so randomly. Usually, it's music all day but I think recent convos with Alana left a bitter taste in my mouth. Anyway…good camp. Hanne crashed after lunch and was down for sleep as soon as dinner was done. Small fire. Millions of stars. Tomorrow we reach Kennedy Meadows. Wow! Boxes with new gear waiting. We'll do a night there to prepare for nine days ahead. Can't believe we'll finally be in the Sierras.

Journal
May 8, 2018

Left Kennedy meadows and Grumpy Bears (the only place happening) with Scott and Kendra, Yogi's little resupply shop across the way and the general store (who initially misplaced my box, forcing us to stay another day longer) while Red Flower and the rest of the group headed out. We were on a search to locate the box with tracking info, time stamps etc. Turned out it was filed under "Wozenstein" again. Tad decided he didn't need to send my ice axe because it would cost too much...another (?). I was baffled. It weighs three pounds tops. Yeah, yeah. He forgot. Finally got it sorted. Spent another $140.00 on an ice axe and micro spikes plus loads of heavy food. Time to get out! Kendra said she liked us so much we got a free breakfast our last morning! Wow.

    Freebird left with Snakebite from Quebec and we met them an hour later at the trailhead. I was so loaded down I could barely walk. Must have been pushing fifty pounds. Bear canister (another $80) and eight to nine days of food to get us to Bishop and an extra day figured in for the Whitney ascent. I felt like garbage...nausea most of the day but we ended up at a great spot sixteen miles in by a bridge with hundreds of starlings flying about.

    An hour after we hit camp a woman came back down from the opposite direction and walked into our camp all flustered. She was supposed to be heading north so we were confused. She'd had an encounter with another hiker who'd summoned her off the main trail complaining of stomach issues, but at some point, she got a bad vibe and hightailed it back down the trail. Details were vague. The guy didn't actually *do* anything. He just seemed "off" to her. She conceded she might have let her paranoia get to her. Understandable. Solo hiking woman. She wanted to alert someone to help if he was indeed in need of assistance. Apparently, he was in too much pain to walk. She wanted to go two or three more miles further south to find a house we'd passed. We said we'd set up her tent and she could leave her pack. She took off and we went about our business. Hot ramen and anything I could dig out of the bear canister. Sunset was great by our little stream. She made it back well after dark and I poked my head out the tent to make sure all was ok. She'd been unable to locate the house and, having done over twenty miles already, called it quits. We'd get more details in the morning.

Hanne and I took forever to get going this morning. Just a slow day. Lots of uphill. Everyone broke camp before us. First instant coffee though! So glad to have the propane mount finally. Three miles in we found the guy's campsite. Nothing but an SOS sign made from rocks pointing toward the site, an old phone camera tripod in the dirt, and the lid to a bear canister, chewed and scraped up…by what we could only assume was a bear.

We thought the plot had thickened but soon came upon everyone and the fellow, an actor from L.A. who was still having problems. It seemed legit. Freebird and Snakebite were going to escort him back to his car six miles off another trail and return-maybe camp at the same spot. Tara, Hanne and I would make it to Death Canyon Creek ten more miles and wait for them the following morning. Still slow going. Patches of snow - more climbing to 10k feet and first good views of the Sierras. I think we can see Whitney twenty or more miles by crow in the distance. Back down to camp.

Fire. Invited Tara over. Little chat. Everyone's tired. Two other campers down the trail we heard but don't know who they are. Maybe the Czechs or Cherry and Leo. Sleeping in tomorrow to wait for Freebird and Snakebite.

Journal
May 12, 2018

    Took off early to hit the exit for Independence. Freebird and Snakebite showed up at noon. We'd sat around wondering what to do and leaned against the trees listening to the wind and nature sounds. That was the day we'd truly get into the Sierras.
    We'd heard Spiderman was on the trail and thought he'd pass any moment. A super-fast kid from South Korea. We'd finally met him at Kennedy Meadows.
    Still no snow. We were starting to feel like we'd been sold a bunch of gear from exaggerations and hearsay. Truth is: no one knew.
    Around 3-4 pm Freebird caught up with us; said Snakebite had all of a sudden decided to head back to the Independence trail exit like Tara. No real explanation. We'd only hiked with him since Kennedy Meadows. We wound up at Dutch Meadows mile 743 that night. Millions of stars - never seen so many. Just clouds of clusters of stars. We talked long into the night. Next day: made it deep into the Sierra. Snow-capped mountains looming. Spiderman caught up and replaced Snakebite. It was Hanne's 34th birthday and the views were unbelievable. At first she was sad that she had no cell service to talk to anyone but she said the Sierras were "The best birthday ever."
    We walked well past 8 pm in the dark to Rock Creek Camp next to the first sizeable river crossing. In the morning, Cherry and Leo passed by, waving as they crossed. Another group came through led by a guy named Jumanji from Alabama. Freebird and Spiderman came through around 8 am and we took it slow, had coffee, packed it up, crossed the stream and headed for Guitar Lake on the Mt Whitney Trail. Beautiful meandering streams. A new kind of nature after this. A different type of

sunlight. Everything more clear and bold. Raw alpine nature. We crossed into the trail and passed another lake before camp.

We saw the Czech couple again at Crabtree Camp and got some info on the Whitney ascent. Hiked further in, set up in the big shadows of Whitney on the west side of the lake.

We all decided for a 4:30 am ascent and tried to sleep early. Wasn't great sleep but got everything together quickly; headlamps and gear. I'm so exhausted I'm going to do another separate entry for Whitney tomorrow before we take off. Needless to say: Epic.

We're back at Crabtree Campground. Spiderman is low on food so he's going to do Forester tomorrow. Freebird, Hanne and I will take three days. It's cold! Hope I can sleep.

'Night.

Journal
May 16, 2018
Four Days Until Bishop

Mt. Whitney was spectacular. Left at 5 am. Good call. Freezing cold but climbing. Enough layers. Flash-frozen beard most of the way up. Rays of morning sun shooting through massive snow-capped spires. Yellow-pink lighting up the valley and other peaks to the west, trekking poles sufficient to maneuver the snow fields. Summited at 9 am with Hanne, Freebird and Spiderman and passed a few people coming down including Jumanji. Stayed on the summit for a good hour. Made tea before heading down. At the base we glissaded through ice and snow to the tents where we decided to nap for an hour before packing up and heading to Crabtree Campground to get a little warmer. Slept in to recover. Big warm sunlit field surrounded by the Sierras. Freebird took off earlier and we agreed to meet up down the trail to see about camping. Walked through so many different sceneries. Barren hills, streamlets pouring down from melted snow. Clouds looming over distant peaks. Incredible vistas of light and shadow dancing through the range. Hanne got a foot soaked at a creek-crossing, then the other foot a few miles down. The humidity and cold made it almost impossible to dry and she'll have to deal with wet socks for the next couple days. Made it to a little campground late in the afternoon. A couple other tents were...

(fell asleep)

Recalibrating the Clock
Letters Home #2

Sitting at Grumpy Bears at Kennedy Meadows and things are more or less in order...I think. Walk into the place and you've got a bar with motocross poster above the beer display and to the left a kitchen that serves some of the most satisfying food on the trail i.e. they know what hikers want. Protein, protein, fat, on a bun of some sort. Add bacon. Add avocado. Breakfast is called "Hiker Breakfast" and has two eggs, two bacon, a heap of home fried potatoes and a pancake a foot wide. Coffee is free as well as extra pancakes if you've got the appetite. To the left of the kitchen in the same room is a shower. You pay two or three bucks depending on who's running your card and get about five minutes. Turn the hot water on full blast and don't touch the cold water...just enjoy those five minutes. Complimentary Irish Spring and an array of shaving kits and painkillers behind the mirror if you look.

Down the street a few minutes is the General Store. This is where most of the packages come in for resupply and the store is stocked with all the things you'll be thinking of before heading into the Sierras. Across from Grumpy's there's another setup just for hikers run by the publisher of the Yogi Handbook and her friend. Jackets, ice axes, crampons and all the food essentials. You'd be surprised by how many hikers just crave Marunchan Ramen by name at the end of the day. I cannot exaggerate the satisfaction that comes with a mouthful of hot noodles, sodium and Cholula. Plus, it falls in the ultra-lite category.

Right now my pack is hanging from a tree branch outside and hopefully drying after a full disinfectant via Lysol and shower.

Seven hundred miles and daily sweat against the back of the pack have rendered some bizarre odors so today was the day. The rest of the contents have been gutted, spread across three tables, reconfigured, reassessed and repackaged. Ready for a streamlined system of instant access in whatever temperature as we climb to 10,000 feet tomorrow and summit Whitney within four days. From all reports, which are scant, everything above 9,000 feet is covered in snow. Mt Whitney is possibly a great block of ice as well but we are prepared. After some to-do I had my mountain boots, jacket, and stove mount. I picked up a set of micro-spikes from the General Store and an ice-axe from Triple Crown Outfitters. Some have said the axe isn't necessary. Probably true. To me it's like bear spray. Chances are I won't have a bad encounter with a black bear. They're skittish and avoid humans as best as they can...but turn a corner and encounter a mom with her kids and you've got a situation. There's plenty of snow coverage and we've already heard one report of a fellow having to self-arrest so these are just things you do. Also, a bear canister is legally required for a good portion of the Sierras so I had to pick one of those up too. You stuff as much food as is humanly possible in this canister and put it in the bottom of your bag. I have about fifty miles until it's legally required so I'll try to eat through as much food as possible in order to fit the extra jerky and freeze-dried dinners sent from my mom and Randy.

    We are at mile 704. Forty-nine days in. It's almost impossible to describe the level of things. All those expectations vs. reality. The songs that get stuck in your head. The memories that pop up. The pace of time. The type of exhaustion that goes so far beyond anything you've called exhaustion before. Feeling so physically spent that you're dead-sure you can't go another half mile, only to look at the maps and realize you miscalculated earlier that morning and you've got three more miles to go. The brain switches off. Emotions go on the back-burner. All physical exertion becomes mechanical and it's an interesting process to watch yourself go through, especially when you know you're going to feel that way at some point almost every day. At the same time there's zero sense of boredom at any point. All decisions are grouped into a few categories which revolve around food, hiking, and sleep. It makes things so easy when you're on the trail. The mind and body know what's in the mail. The moment you get to a town the inverse occurs and it's suddenly a mess of money and deadlines and social media blah blah blah. That is, I'm excited to get into town and find whatever nutrients and sleep my body has been craving and I'm equally excited to get back to the trail after a couple days.

A guy who goes by "Butterscotch" had given us a ride back to the trail outside Tehachapi and the only fee was posing with his stuffed animal for Instagram. He was all smiles and good vibes and had actually told the mechanics and engineers at the wind-farms to pick up hikers and had said the same to his local church congregation.

When people are asked why they help us out so much we often hear "because it's the right thing to do." It's simple kindness and as Butterscotch explained: "The PCT isn't an organization as much as an organism."

Everything works because you've got the hikers and then the whole system of Trail Angels and innumerable live updates from everyone that are always being sent in. The PCT water reports, the apps, the notes scrawled in the sand or left under rocks on faded pieces of paper and in trail logs. The entire organism becomes part of your life for these months. The idea of going alone sounds good on paper and there are certainly hikers that prefer a little more space, but it's impossible to be isolated from the basic paradigms of the trail for very long. Information is passed around every time you walk into a campground or come across another group.

   Last night at Grumpy's a group we hadn't seen for over a month came through the door around 7:00 pm. One of them walked straight over to us and asked about snow conditions in the Sierras. We told him everything we had heard from people who had heard from others. Some of it amounted to little more than rumors but we knew it was passable. It'd be rough and people who swore they wouldn't take an ice axe now had them strapped to the side their bags. All we knew is that one group and a few solo hikers had made it through. Sometimes you just want to know if the post office is close to the campground. Generally when someone else walks into camp or town you give them the rundown of everything you know or have discovered up to that point-then everyone's on their own if they want. When we headed out of Tehachapi we climbed up to a little bench put in place by the local Boy Scouts and decided to have a water break there. We only had eleven miles to do that day and there was no rush. An older man slowly came up from the north valley below and we talked for awhile. He'd just had knee surgery and was getting back into shape. He showed us his special shoe inserts for the metatarsal tendon that helps alleviate soreness up front (which we get a lot of) and said: "Just down a ways is where the girl from that Wild movie started".

   We said goodbye and good luck and ambled down the switchbacks over some train tracks and over the busy highway. A car honked at us from below and I raised my trekking poles in a wave. Trail Angels had left snacks and water at different locations by the off-ramp and I showed Hanne what Rice Crispy treats were all about. A few more miles and we were set up on a hill overlooking the highway, Mojave, hundreds of windmills, and a pink sunset that sent shadows dozens of miles across the desert below.

By 9:00 pm it was becoming obvious that the wind was only going to get worse. Huge gusts bore down on us and slammed tentpoles and guy lines every which way. It was so loud that it was becoming impossible to sleep...so I didn't. Hanne didn't either and when the sun rose we were both bleary and somber, shaking our heads while the wind continued to howl. It was a slow day up and down the mountain. Every break was a new temptation to take a good long nap and by lunch we were convinced to do just that on a bed of pine needles in the sun just off the trail. My head laid crooked against my pack and the needles kept jabbing my back but I barely noticed. Thirty minutes later we were back on the trail and stopped at two different cisterns for water.

Throughout the day we passed various hikers; old faces and a few new ones. Freebird and his buddy Red Flower have become fixtures in our periphery since Agua Dulce and I started to realize I was usually in the company of more Germans, Austrians, Israelis, Slovakians and Swiss folk than Americans. It's funny who you end up with at the end of the day. I began to wonder why I gravitated toward foreigners while the younger Americans tended to stick in little groups of the same age and preferences. Either way there's barely enough energy to analyze these occurrences.

If people speak German, they usually dive into a fast clip of data-sharing with Hanne that I can pick pieces out of and we continue down the trail. Sometimes people suddenly turn to me and say "How you say?" Or "What means?" But it's never difficult to put the meaning together. There are only a few subjects worth mentioning on the trail and we go over them a dozen times every day.

The wind was still hitting us relentlessly until we got below some hills and bushwhacked to the lowest point under some trees to camp. Since we were so exhausted from lack of sleep the day after Tehachapi we made dinner, said goodnight and were both sound asleep within minutes.

The next day was another study in contrasts as we were instantly enveloped in thick mists, more or less in the middle of clouds on the high crests, climbing higher and higher throughout the morning. It went from windmills and desert shrubs to an almost northwest feeling of damp grass, mossy rocks and tall pines with branches hanging silently in a subdued midday grey that followed us for hours. We walked quietly, took pictures and appreciated the stillness after the gales we'd endured.

We came upon a hiker called Yoga Bae sitting on the side of the trail reeling from shin splints.

"Look at this ankle. Does this look different than the other one?"

I put his ankles together to look and poked around a little. It was the same problem I'd had back around Julian. Muscles above the ankle going haywire trying to compensate for the extra stress. I dug into my pack and gave him the ankle brace my parents had sent to Big Bear a few weeks before. You could walk off shin splints if you were careful, but some hikers didn't know how to slow down. We told him to just take it easy and shorten his mileage until it healed and walked on. An hour later he passed us, charging up another hill. A couple hours later we caught up to him and Young Buck at a public campground by a spring with two outhouses that were probably the most offensive things I'd encountered so far. We made a tiny fire and looked at the stars and poked the embers and talked for awhile and fell asleep.

The next day we started out fast. Each day the new Asics were allowing my joints and muscles to heal and I was getting back to my original pace.

Fifteen of the twenty can feel like a frustrating mess until the mind literally gives up trying to control the various outcomes and "what-ifs". Other days it's the opposite. The first miles are a breeze and everything crashes in the last two or three. The body shuts down. Everything goes into autopilot. Words come out in mono-syllabic mumbles. You stare down the trail hoping your destination is around the next corner. You stop looking at your GPS because around mile two hundred you realized it makes those last two miles drag on and on while you count tenths of miles for the last half-hour.

That particular day started out rough, but we took an hour-long break early in the morning and talked about everything. All the things that build up over the miles. Things you thought you left behind. Things you didn't deal with before you left. Things that might never get resolved...but things you can talk about. Sometimes over the miles, with the extremes and nothing but the sound of the birds, wind and footsteps, the mind starts looping. The same songs start the same melodies in your head. Rhythms happen arbitrarily: 1-2-3-4-1-2-3-1-2-3. I even had a tough time with the trekking poles from Hiker Heaven because I couldn't get the meter of their tap, tap, tap next to my footsteps right. I kept feeling like I had to subconsciously keep time with everything. This is probably just a musician's problem, but it took a good two weeks until I stopped looking at the poles like long strange instruments that I had to learn. The good thing about the tough times is that the trail gives and takes. This is a great truth we've come to trust. An hour later we came over a hill and a couple guys with a pickup truck full of trail magic were parked at a crossroad with cold drinks and snacks. Another

German named Tim and Red Flower were there along with three Israelis: Sam, SloMo, and DoDo. DoDo was down from Lyme disease and recovering in Lake Isabella down the road with SloMo but they'd been driving a rental car for the past couple days for Sam who was a retired computer scientist. We all met briefly, enjoyed the snacks, thanked the Trail Angels and moved through hundreds of Joshua trees, leap-frogging Sam here and there. He'd hiked over 8,000 kilometers all over the world since retiring.

So, the trail gives and takes and soon we were trying to stand upright through vertical sandy stretches with more gusts coming at around seventy miles per hour, literally knocking me off the trail while I tried to brace myself and lean into the wind at the same time. I was worried about getting blown sideways into a Joshua tree and getting impaled by one of the spines. Our movements were slowed to such a degree that all we could do was laugh through the worst of it. At one downhill where the wind was coming directly at me, I put my arms out like wings, leaned forward and let myself fall into the wind. The sustained gusts were so strong I felt like I was almost floating as I careened down into the valley. For two more hours the wind didn't stop for one second and got most intense at the passes until we got to the other side of the mountain and ran into dozens of startled cows that stared and darted down the hills in front of us across the trail.

We were beyond spent but just by luck came across a campsite guarded by a tree and some rocks. The wind was low enough to get tents set up and get some sleep. The next morning started with another massive climb and we passed them less than a mile in and spoke excitedly about the approach to Kennedy Meadows.

The entire trail was beginning to subtly change. The spaces between passes seemed farther. The light was different. The air smelled different. In the far distance we could see massive snow-capped peaks and wondered aloud if these were The Sierras or another range before them. We began talking about snow, ice axes, micro-spikes and how far we could reasonably travel if we were post-holing the entire day. It wasn't an ominous feeling. I was thrilled to be so close to such a major stretch of the trail...but we knew the Sierras would require a different kind of hiking than what we'd become accustomed to in the past month or so. I would say rather, that the idea of the Sierras *loomed*...so, we hiked on through a fairly fast day, passing Freebird, Redflower, and a new girl called Snow White that we'd only seen in the trail logs. I knew she was Snow White right away just by the way her hair was cut and further down during a lunch break we ran into Israeli Sam again.

    He had great news: SloMo and DoDo were at the bottom of the section around Walker Pass at a day-use area in his rental van and we could all get a ride in to Lake Isabella with them. No $20 Uber or sticking our thumbs out for an hour. We made it down in an hour and a few minutes later Freebird and Red Flower came leaping down the trail as well. We all talked for awhile. Sam told us how artificial intelligence will eventually make us slaves if we don't get hip to coding (at least Javascript) and SloMo asked me all about the southwest and told us which places he planned on visiting after the PCT. I basically keep telling people the same idea: think of each state like its own little country and ignore what the TV says about America. It's all hype. People are people and most Americans will bend over backward to show you kindness. We've already seen it over and over again. Not only kindness but curiosity and willingness to share strategic info and their own stories and experiences.

An hour later we were in Lake Isabella at an RV Park on the edge of town, thinking we'd walk down to a nice Mexican Restaurant and dig into some salsa and chile, but from the first hour until we left Lake Isabella a day later the vibe was consistently off. We both kept wondering what happened here.

We got different information from everyone and after an hour and staring into amother gutted floor plan of an ex-Mexican restaurant, we shuffled over to a Burger King - dejected and starving at the same time. I won't tell you exactly how much fast food we ordered that night but it was so much that we confused the staff and put ourselves into light comas. The walk back to the RV Park was a two-mile snail crawl and I couldn't muster the legs for much more than a shower and sleep.

The next day we kept trying to figure out what went down in Lake Isabella. It felt like something stopped in the mid-nineties. I thought maybe due to the dam up the valley. Maybe it had been difficult to insure properties and done something to their value. Needle receptacles with great biohazard stickers sat in front of grocery stores where kids walked by and storefront after storefront was shuttered all the way through town. Still, people were great to talk to and we actually ended up having the best Mexican food of the trip so far. I've been trying to explain to Hanne what constitutes a good taco, where to find them, what's on them, what's not on them etc.

Back at the RV Park the tents were lining up. Freebird and Red Flower, Young Buck and Yoga Bae and Cherry and Leo - everyone sat in the community room talking about the Sierras. Even with a snowpack of less than fifty percent average it was a big unknown and people were grouping up and taking stock of gear. We headed out the next morning on a bus that drove us back to Walker Pass where we'd driven out with Sam and started climbing. We passed the Czech couple after about a mile and stopped to see how they'd been doing. They stayed out of towns for the most part and had taken their first zero day since Campo in Ridgecrest with some friends a few miles down the highway.

We climbed and descended. Climbed some more. Wound up at a campground with a couple tents scattered by a stream. Cherry and Leo were down below our site and we all knew we'd be getting into Kennedy Meadows soon.

When we finally did, it was right after mile seven hundred. We could see some of the Sierras clearly now and the whole landscape was becoming more and more epic by the mile. We happened to catch some fishermen coming in from the Kern River and they let us hop in their pickup truck and dropped us off at Grumpy Bear's restaurant in Kennedy Meadows which would be our hub for the next three days.

All day Scott drove hikers back and forth to the General Store to get their boxes for no charge. The only problem was that the guys at the General Store couldn't find my Sierra package so I was in limbo. I got the tracking number from Tad back in Albuquerque and it said it had been delivered but no one at the General Store could find it.

Thicker hiking boots, stove, extra jacket etc. I couldn't enter the Sierras without it so I waited and double-checked while the Sierras looked down at us just a few miles away...

I finished writing this in Bishop on the 18th of May. There's a portion including Mt Whitney and Forester Pass that needs its own blog.

Tomorrow a Trail Angel takes us to Lee Vining where we enter a closed access road to Tuolumne Meadows. We head into the wilderness for thirteen days and end up at South Lake Tahoe.

Thank you to all the supporters. I wish I could update the blog more but I do journal every night and compile mass excerpts /

notes on the phone. Service has been so spotty in the Sierras with weeks without signal sometimes. In Tahoe I'll have a coherent narrative of Whitney.

Journal
May 21, 2018

    A phone call home. The news that she isn't recovering from the marrow transplant; that it's a matter of months.
I was at The California Hostel when we spoke. I broke down sobbing. I don't know why any of this is happening and go from feeling numb to gutted. Strange moments of hindsight. Scores of regrets over lost time. Over wasted time. Wasted anger over nothing. Nothing at all. And I didn't get to fully appreciate or even know my mother as a grownup for fear I'd lose something. And those fears, at the end of the day, turn out to be ridiculous, childish patterns of thought. And now…I fly back to Arizona, essentially to say goodbye and I can barely process the idea. Can't imagine being unable to talk to her. The shock of all this…October until now. And the fact that I'm cut off…deep in the Sierras. God knows where; by Benson Pass I think. The only way I can communicate is via Spot GPS to let them know I'm ok at the end of the day. At the hostel I assumed the PCT was over and planned to just pack it up and go home, but she wouldn't hear of it. Sharing this with me is her wish. It was my wish. It was the idea behind the whole thing. Honestly, I didn't want her to go thinking I'd let her down or that she'd failed as a mother. On the contrary, she'd inspired me to be an individual. To be myself. It just took many different forms over the years, some of which were more accessible than others. I don't know how I'm going to process this or make sense of it. So much utter bullshit with the whole cancer industry. Makes me sick. Nothing but extortionist murderers to me right now…I still have to get to S. Lake Tahoe after N. Kennedy Meadows and get into Sacramento to fly back to Flagstaff on the 3rd. I'm terrified that I'll be too late. This all feels like the purest injustice I've ever known.

I love you mom.
Please wait for me,

May 17, 2018
Lauren

L: Mom said in an email she'd talked to you…how you doing?
W: Processing…pretty hard to take. I'm just taking care of things on the trail so I can get off in Mammoth Lakes in about a week and fly out of Sacramento. How are you?
L: Yea…processing. I'm fine, then I'm not. I'm headed there May 28-31. I'm sorry you have to come off the trail for this reason. Guess I'll be seeing you soon. Definitely not something I saw coming; feels really surreal.
W: Surreal…I can always go back to the trail whenever. Curious as to why they're not just going after whatever alternative ideas are out there at this point but I suppose that's their call. I'll see you pretty soon.

Kristin Says

W: Here's a video update - no service out here still but I made a message on the trail for mom if you get a chance to share - thanks for the kind words - love Will
K: She loved this…thank you Will! Made her so happy! Glad you are making progress! Love you so much! Your mom wants to know why you don't have your hat to protect you from that snow reflection!

Hitching to Lee Vining

W: Hello hello
L: Hey bro! So mom got REALLY weak last week and within just a few days she really went downhill. You could hear it in her voice, etc. She had an infection in her lymph node and they gave her a little morphine that really knocked her out for a

couple of days. They also have her a steroid shot that really helped heal the infection. When I got here yesterday, she was awake and really had a good day - tired but good. Today she was good this morning but had a hard afternoon...she's gotten very emotional and sad a few times and frustrated at how she is feeling so weak again.
L: I moved my visit up a week just because she seemed to be going downhill so fast. She is just so tired and weak. She eats with her eyes closed sitting at the table. I don't want to freak you out but I also want you to know how things are.
W: Ok - we just got out of the mountains and to a motel ten minutes ago. I have no phone service but can text as much as needed. We're going to try to find a way to Tahoe to get into Sacramento tomorrow. I'll just get the next possible flight into Flagstaff or change my flight if I can.
L: Ok. Kristin is staying here right now so they don't have a place for you to stay here until I leave unless the floor is ok.
W: It's ok - thanks for the info. Honestly it was one factor in turning around. Didn't know if conditions would get worse on the mountains and snow us in so I'm just getting a night's rest and then figuring out how soon I can get to Arizona.
L: Mom's been pretty emotional the past couple days. Heads up. She's good for about an hour in the mornings and an hour in the evening then she gets really tired and emotional. We've been sitting next to her, rubbing her head, arms, hands etc. Talking when she's up for it. Just being close. Helping any way we can.
W: Ok thanks for the info. We're almost to Reno and then headed straight down.

"We are now exposed to more images in a day than anyone in the 14th century would have known in a lifetime. Most of it is garbage. Most of it needs excising. Even if we're fearful that we might be missing something. We are probably not. We have to discard. We have to throw things away, cleanse the doors of our perception and work out what is worth looking at, what is worth remembering, what are the images that matter, what will we retain."

-Robert Hughes

Between Two Great Creeks

"In Bishop while we took a zero after Whitney and Forester Pass, I spoke with my mom at The California Hostel. The transfusion didn't take and the damaged cells are replicating again. The hospital basically said there's nothing more they can do. I arranged to get off the trail after the Tuolumne to S. Lake Tahoe stretch which seemed manageable at the time. I basically assumed the trip was over and I could come back in the future and finish it if I wanted.

Mom wouldn't hear of it of course and wanted me to stay on...in this way we can share our time in the best way possible. I honestly can't imagine getting back on the trail right now or what that would look like, but I'll just do what's best for everyone right now.

Yesterday was probably the lowest day on the trail although nothing's been easy since Bishop. It's too soon to write about or process and there are what feels like years of wasted time and regrets over petty miscommunications that occurred over the years. I only wish she knew how much I loved her all those years when it looked like I was choosing one strange path after another. God knows it wouldn't make sense to any mother but here I am in so many ways because of her. I'm just glad we've got the PCT to truly share. As it looks now, I'll fly out of Sacramento on the 3rd of June to Flagstaff, spend a few days in Sedona and get back on the trail around Tahoe.

Yesterday after three days of slogging through snow, mud and raging creeks Hanne and I decided over lunch at Smedberg Lake to turn around and return to Lee Vining via Tuolumne Meadows. Originally, we'd thought we could make enough miles to hit Northern Kennedy Meadows within six days but the Sierras aren't ready for us yet. We've basically spent the majority of every day post-holing for miles well below one mile per hour, dependent on Guthook GPS most of the time and backtracking as we've become the ones laying fresh tracks in the snow. Sometimes tracks have been visible here and there, but the weather has warmed and the mountains are in a state of massive change. Creeks passable in the morning are raging rivers by late afternoon. Shoes and socks are perpetually wet and we're just not making enough tracks to get there with current food supplies. Other factors are that we're both a little sad that we're not really seeing the Sierras. The lakes are all frozen, the trails are non-existent and everything's so wet that the places where you can actually see the trail have all become little streams...and I couldn't take the chance on the weather or possibly miss my flight not knowing what the passes were like up ahead, especially after seeing the slightly traumatized faces of hikers that had just done Bishop to Mammoth.

    One guy had run out of food and done a twenty-four-hour, forty-seven-mile, adrenaline-fueled push just to get through. We'd seen him last on San Jacinto over a month ago. Another older man we met just before leaving Tuolumne had fallen in the frozen creeks three times and waited four days in his tent until deciding to head out for his final push at 2 am just to avoid post-holing. The British fellow we met with a younger girl at Cajon Pass was now hiking alone a day ahead of her and missing a tooth. These are the ultra-hikers who passed us ages ago and we'd only chanced upon them because we'd had to either do Bishop to Mammoth or Tuolumne to Tahoe. Tahoe was the closest to Sacramento so we opted to jump ahead knowing we could return to Bishop after hitting Canada...but this is where everything stands.

    We turned around. Right now, we're back at McCabe Creek; fourteen miles from Tuolumne. We'll get in tomorrow, hitch down the mountain to Lee Vining, get a meal, upload, and get back in contact and update everyone and catch a bus to S Tahoe. When and if I return to Tahoe we'll head for Canada and then get back to Bishop to do Kearsage Pass (where we exited after Forester Pass) and do the entire length of the Sierras again when we can actually see and experience more than snow.

Right now, all I care about is getting to Sedona in one piece. There's only so much I'm going to offer over a blog; suffice it to say I couldn't have asked for a better mother. I don't say that to sound trite. I say it because this woman wasn't just a mom. She's always been a force of nature, instilling in me the courage to be myself, to answer the call to adventure, to go after my own version of greatness. She's why I'm here between two great creeks looking out a great white cliffs in the distance...grateful.

Journal
June 1, 2018
Back on the Trail

Pack is heavy. Feels like fifty pounds. Seventeen miles today. Mixed terrain. Snow. Hard-packed. No post-holing. Two passes. Incredible. Three sixty of Reservoir Lakes and another alpine lake in the distance. Suffering, but ok with it. Glad to be back on the trail with a pack and my legs and the sun and whatever it entails. They're probably right. This is the best thing for everyone. Took a few pics. Talked about Sierra City. About logistics of returning to the Sierras after the Canadian border. Burt Bacharach in my head for most of the day from Lost Horizon soundtrack. "Of the things that I will not miss" On a loop. "If you really want the things I have, just ask. I give it all to…" Repeat. Moments punctuated by pain for what my mother endured. Hits my stomach. A surreal shock that the mind can't really grasp. Felt better to be too exhausted to be devastated. Feeling like we're finally getting out of the snow…heading north-west toward the border of Oregon; feeling like there's no chance I can return to Albuquerque even under the best of circumstances. But where? What happens after all this? The trail has more answers. I will trust.

Journal
June 3rd 2018
Sierra Buttes - Mile 1202

A small doe curiously circles our camp atop Sierra Buttes. A panoramic view unmatched yet on the PCT. Late afternoon sun shoots through the valley. Layers of distant mountains are blue and grey, then lighter shades a hundred miles away. The sky is crystal blue and the pines and manzanitas so dense and so green I can't believe my eyes are seeing this particular hue. The air is still. Sixty-eight degrees. The occasional song of a bird in the distance. I try to take photos again and again, feeling that I can't possibly capture this level of grandeur, but I try, nonetheless. A few hundred miles north in Port Townsend, my uncle Kim took his last breath today through an assisted suicide. Cancer on his skin had spread to his lungs, all this at the exact same time my mother is going through what appears to be her final days. I pass a stream coming down the mountain through layers of dark grey slate. I'm reminded of a dream from years ago; standing next to water surrounded by dark slate rock...I pray for my mom's recovery and drink the water. I see time ebb and flow. See truths revealed. Cycles of perception unfold, meaning behind all things no matter how contrary to our desires. A great process united in perpetual movement...and I know it's miraculous. Tomorrow morning we're getting up early to climb up a lookout tower and see the sunrise. Then northeast toward Buck's Lake. An afternoon spent in Sierra City resupplying - meeting a few hikers - a true character from Ireland named "Peer Pressure", walking for Wounded Warriors...stories of Afghan combat. A life spent in the military. First Gulf War Vet. Loved his weed. Missing teeth. A recent widower and loss of a son soon before. A hard man who'd survived, and who made us laugh out loud with his jokes while we tried to pare down the weight of our packs this morning.

What do all these stories mean? How are they all related? We meet so many kind souls on this journey. It's like riding a river, a long story. Two men buy us a glass of wine. Another gives us his personal WiFi password so we can contact and upload. A barista gives us a free coffee. Locals ask 101 questions. Some people have done sections themselves. A man and his daughter follow us two miles out of town because they think we might have left one of our phones back at the campground. He takes her out to do trail maintenance with him "to do something positive." He's part native; done many of the stretches and here. Lauds the value of a Bud Lite and steak after a hike. Everything makes sense. Nothing makes sense. I feel like a passenger on some train of tragedy and hope; watching and doing what I can, but mostly as a hopeless bystander. The Fool on the Hill rings true. I know. I understand. I empathize. But there are forces bigger than me everywhere.

Understand / Innerstand

Our pace is cut in half. Two days out here and it's nothing but post-holing to the waist, thirty-minute creek fords also waist-high, wandering up and down until we find suitable crossing points, just looking for calmer waters. When the banks narrow the creeks shoot through with unstoppable force, flying over cliffs, smashing into rock walls, carrying debris...broken logs and pinecones. Most of the creek beds are covered in algae and it's easier to leave the shoes on. There's no way to stay dry out here anyway. The snow has melted through the gators within an hour and shoes are still wet from the day before. It's just going to be wet and cold. We jam our poles into the side of whatever trail we can distinguish, following the melting prints of a solitary hiker that seemed just as lost themselves, wandering around trees and sloping piles of snow that give the impression of passages until they don't. Then it's back to Guthook, backtracking, rejoining the trail. Five to ten minutes lost each time. We move forward but each slog is a miserable stretch from pass to pass. The mountains look free of snow from a distance but it's all perspective. Once we approach and begin climbing it's back to post-holing. The forests look desolate. Silent. Blankets of white with melting streams running below and out of sight. We fall through occasionally and keep moving. There's nothing else we can do. Frozen lakes are clogged with scores of black rotting trunks that go down untold depths. We stop after the big climbs, overheating and covered in sweat. Everything is already soggy. Five minutes later its too cold and we zip the jackets back up. Hanne lost her sunglasses at the Tuolumne River crossing and can't see with the afternoon sun coming off the long snow fields. I give her mine, which I stepped on earlier in the day and hang lopsided with one arm. We trade off throughout the rest of the day until we're out of direct exposure.

On the flats the snow sits in great heaps and we fall through over and over. I get stuck numerous times and Hanne drags me out with my own poles. A minute later I'm wrenching her out the same way. On the descents we glissade, skate, and fall our way directly over what would be switchbacks just to get to the bottom of the canyons. Then it's typically another crossing. The water is ice-cold. So cold it hurts; like being scalded. Blood vessels contract upon contact and the skin turns blue while the body calls everything back to its core. At this point I don't know how much further the snow goes. It looks endless. It looks like it's getting worse and there's more grey clouds in the distance. We're three days into what should be a six day stretch and at this pace it'll take at least ten. We don't have enough food. We're soaked to the bone and it's been nothing but snow since Tuolumne Meadows. We came in a day before it opened, hunkering down in a random site next to an overturned picnic table. All the cabins had been damaged from last year's storms and sat in gloomy disrepair.

The only ranger keeping tabs on the area had been an over-zealous rookie who tried to harass us until it donned on him that the park he'd sworn to protect wasn't open and it didn't technically matter that we weren't in the "designated backpacker area". We'd just nodded and gave him quizzical tired looks until he relented, but not before warning us about "The Plague".

Now we'd walked in three days and weren't sure how we were going to make it out. When we got to Smedberg Lake for lunch a strange feeling came through the air and clouds covered the sky. I looked into the distance and a chill went through my body.

"What the hell are we doing?" I exclaimed.

"I don't know!" Said Hanne. "I asked you this back at Miller Lake two days ago and you said quitting is out of the question."

"Yeah but…look at this. Five more days at least?" I didn't know it was going to be nothing but snow for a hundred miles. I mean, we don't even know what it's like up there. There's no trail. We don't know if the weather's going to hold…"
"What are you saying?"
I stared at the ground for over a minute trying to appraised the situation, raised my eyes once more and surveyed the terrain. I shook my head.
"We've just gotta get out of here…"
"I think this is a good idea." She said. "We can find where the snow ends, hitch up there and get to Canada…then come back when we can actually see the Sierras."
"I can't even see the most amazing part of the PCT right now. I already know what snow looks like!"

I was officially demoralized and kept shaking my head. Now it meant three days back…another hitch back into Lee Vining…and I didn't want to know what the news would be when I called home. It felt like an impasse. A stalemate. Maybe it got better just over the next pass. Maybe it meant walking into a white-out. We'd left Campo so early that we were now among the very first to approach the Sierras and there hadn't been any news one way or another.

June 8, 2018
Letters Home #3

Sitting on an old couch at the Belden Town lodge. Campsite is broken down; laundry clean. First clean clothes since getting back on the trail around Donner Pass over a week ago. We'd hitched out of Lee Vining after turning around - three days into Yosemite. The snow was nonstop. The creeks were raging. The lakes were covered by sheets of broken ice and snow. We didn't belong there.

At lunch along Smedberg Lake we looked into the distance, storm clouds looming, and made the call. We'd return when we could actually see the Sierras. So we turned around and hitched out of Lee Vining to Reno with a series of characters in van-living situations who are used to picking up hikers.

Picked up the rental car. Drove. Three days in Arizona. Another rental car. Through the night to North Kennedy Meadows at about 5:00 am trying to sleep sitting up in the car until a diner opened and I could retrieve my resupply package from Albuquerque. A good hot breakfast. Coffee. Back on the road to South Lake Tahoe to drop the rental. Hanne's bounce box was at the post office here and we walked to the bus station and all over town for a few more resupplies.

That night we looked at the best places to get back on the trail i.e. less snow. A few patches or slopes here and there are ok, but we didn't want to spend entire days making half-time with our GPS in one hand and two trekking poles in the other. It looked like somewhere around Donner Pass by Truckee would be the best option. Something below 8,500 feet where we'd seen the snow line before. So, one more night at a Budget Inn for $38 split between two of us was a good deal.

We rested and I tried to get my head and heart around everything I'd been through in the past week. Things were happening too fast, out of my control, and I didn't understand most of it, but we had to keep moving. The trail had been good for that so far and I wanted to get back into woods. Two more hitches from locals got us to a rest stop by Donner Pass. I felt like I'd forgotten how to hike that day. Awkward steps and trekking poles sliding around rocks and mud, but I was glad to have my Asics trail shoes back. We hit snow for two consecutive days after reentry, but on the third day we wound out of the high mountains to Sierra City, crossed a great footbridge over the Yuba River, hitched into town and slept in the yard of the local Methodist Church. This is where we also met the fake Irishman we'd heard about a month before at South Kennedy Meadows. Unfortunately, neither of us remembered the warning or description for our whole tenure in Sierra City and we endured his fantastic tales while we tried to repack and lighten our loads at the picnic table.

He claimed to be walking for Wounded Warriors. He claimed to be a combat veteran of virtually every conflict that occurred in the Middle East in the past thirty years. He claimed to be a widower and he claimed to have already gone southbound last year and done the Sierras in February. We were too busy to put two and two together until the morning after we left, hiking up the trail to the lookout tower at Sierra Buttes to catch the sunrise.

"Ohhh. That makes sense...that's why he didn't know what a Spot was. That's why we never saw him on the trail. That's why his pack weighed sixty pounds!" The news in South Kennedy was that he was a homeless guy who got rides to different towns on the PCT, used a rotating series of sob-stories, took his fill out of the hiker boxes, and lost his accent when he had a few drinks. The old bamboozler.

We climbed one and a half miles to the lookout tower while the sun rose and hit the cliffs all around us, turning the morning into a glowing cathedral of amber light. We circled the tiny steps running fifty feet above the summit and walked around the catwalk with railing that surrounding a tiny hut at the top of Sierra Buttes. We'd seen the very peak we descended days before in the distance; a hazy black spire that looked like the Matterhorn.

Thousands of feet below on all sides were dozens of lakes shining like little mirrors. Over the next couple days we crossed between some of them, and now that we were officially out of the heavy snow I began loving the trail in a way I hadn't before. The Northern California section was becoming dense and humid and it was easy to hit twenty-three miles per day until Buck's Lake.

We walked in along a quiet, impeccably paved road past giant resorts and family cabins for two and half miles until reaching Bucks Lake Lodge around 6:00 pm. The kitchen was officially closed but a man appeared through the two-way doors and said he could do burgers and fries if we wanted...and we wanted. So we ate and ate and managed to get some free chips and salsa out of the deal before signing the guestbook and heading back toward the campground.

It was dark and we just sort of snuck in and snuck out in the morning because we couldn't find anyone to give money to. Across the street we did a small resupply and I used my first pay phone in fifteen years to call the RV Park in Belden and ask about their shower and laundry situation. At this point everything was dirty. We thought we'd have facilities at Buck's Lake based on the guides we'd read but no such luck. I'd been wearing the same socks for three days and we were feeling pretty desperate to just clean up a bit.

A couple days later we made it to Belden. Through deep manzanitas covering the trail, down about seven miles of switchbacks and across some train tracks we came in on a small paved back-road that stopped at Belden Town with twenty-three official permanent residents and host to a number of seasonal festivals.

A few other hikers ambled about. Some took relief in the shade of the hotel porch. Others sat inside sipping cold beers, looking dazed but relieved to be off the feet. It's the "hiker stare". It's not a frown or any indication of discontent or malaise...more of a vacant, expressionless gaze; just glad to be done with the day's journey but too tired to say anything relevant about it with another round of Q and A with tourists.

All we wanted was a shower. One token for three bucks equaled three minutes and I was lucky to find some broken pieces of hotel soap someone had left on the counter. One buck to get the dirt off. One buck to actually clean under nails and behind ears. One buck to turn the water on full hot and wash out my hair over and over until the water stopped.

The laundry machine stopped on rinse and ran indefinitely, which took us two cycles to figure out. We put up the tent and finally had two bags of warm dry clothes. We sat by the window of the hotel restaurant and I tried to take stock of where we were at. There had barely been a moment to think since Campo and it felt like I'd been on the trail much longer than three months. We had so far to go and as soon as we hit Canada we'd turn around and head back to the Sierras for the last three weeks. As we came within a few hundred miles of Oregon I began writing:

"Minus the Sierra, we've walked just over 1,000 miles. 50 or so campsites, one hostel, a Budget Inn and dozens of improvised situations (wherever it's flat after 20 miles). We've relied on hitches at least 20 times; to post offices, back to the trail, to airports, into towns, etc. We've also done around 100 miles of unofficial side-trail to either get into town, find water and campsites, or walk from one side of a town to the other. At Belden we'd taken roughly around 3.5 million steps through sand, rock fields, mud, creeks, rivers, snow, hurricane-force winds, miles of non-stop post-holing through snow, from around 85°F to well below 0°F on Mt Whitney where we stood at the highest point in the lower forty-eight and looked down at its lowest in Death Valley.

    Most of the people I've been around have been from Germany, Austria, Switzerland, New Zealand, South Korea, Taiwan, or eastern Europe. The train of hikers moves all the time. Just today we ran into Vlado who we hadn't seen since the L.A. Aqueduct stretch beneath the windmills...it seemed like ages ago (I suppose it was) and when you run into someone who's gone through the same trails and storms as you there's an instant smile and exchange. "What did you do there? How's the leg? Where are you headed next?" I somehow remember most hiker's names after one meeting when I'm generally terrible at this back home.

    We've seen rattlesnakes, deer, lynx, marmots, picas, coyote, squirrels, chipmunks, lizards, hundreds of birds and listened to owls and bears in the night not to mention all the grazing animals that roam the land. The mountain chickadee has been present the whole time since the first week and I was only able to positively identify it outside Tuolumne Meadows when it finally fluttered up to a pine branch and said "dee-doo-doo".

    We've had sun sickness, sun burns, infected blisters, shin splints, sprained ankles, splinters, ant / mosquito / spider / bee bites and stings, metatarsal and toe nerve damage, and pretty much constant scabs and scrapes up to the knees from bushes and bad dismounts from blowdowns.

Our water comes almost completely from rivers, lakes, streams, and springs and I haven't filtered anything since we went into the Sierra.

We walk an average of about 17-23 miles per day with our longest day being 26 miles. Right now we're debating whether to go for a "30 day" since Northern California is probably the place to do it. We've been passed by other hikers who actually average 30 miles per day! Unbelievable, considering that on the PCT you are almost never walking any flat distances. Rather, you walk through passes, up and down all day one to the next. Sometimes if we're lucky we get to walk across the side of a mountain and wind around slowly.

And I'd written: "Most of the time, when I walk, I've got nothing but songs on repeat in my head. Songs and old memories and lately, what feels like some long-lost childhood spirit I'd long forgot or forsaken; feelings I'd stored away in safe corners, making sense of the mad rush of life. Stepping back. Way, way back...and I'm happy to be on the trail having brief encounters with exceptional people. Fathers and daughters. Retired world-travelers. Teenagers; inspired and brave enough to head into the wild. Sunsets and views so exceptional I lack words for most of it, capturing small moments with the camera. Strange sounds in the night that make us feel vulnerable and exposed and the next-day-summits and landscapes where I feel part of something so vast that I just have to shake my head in wonder and keep walking."

"The very shaping of history now outpaces the ability of men to orient themselves in accordance with cherished values. Even when they do not panic men often sense that older ways of feeling and thinking have collapsed and that newer beginnings are ambiguous to the point of stasis."

-C. Wright Mills

Remember

There at Mica Lake…high in the Northern Cascades. Looking down into it…the little trail meandering here and there through boulders until it reached its shores. When we came over the last pass the sun lit up the clouds like I'd never seen before. A different shade of pink, purple, orange, dark red, yellows, even green…all dancing into each other as we went through the rock fields. Stones of all colors and shapes. A conglomerate splayed out in various sizes…rounded with time, motionless as nature tends to appear at dusk. To the left and to the right, processes that remained untouched for millions of years. On the mountain tops, snow clinging to the rock faces still melting in late summer with dozens of tiny streams appearing between gardens of the heartiest-looking plants. The same process we witnessed in the early Sierras was happening up north. It happened all year long despite our privileged moments; a brief encounter with the magic side of the crest. Over any point would be miles of pure nothing. Animals creeping about, foresting, nesting, calling, prowling. Trees and snow and rocks and sun and moon and small ponds that were large ponds a month before. Dirt becoming mud. Mud becoming clay. Clay becoming stone. The world in its utter timelessness. The world, humming to a different tune altogether…cycles within cycles within cycles that we might appreciate from the precipice of our safe and well-groomed path. No, this isn't a mere planet. This isn't some lucky outpost in a galaxy we've named for convenience. This is a realm; interlocked in perpetual conversation, coaxing itself into replication in numbers so vast that no appraisal can amount to anything but hubris. This is where you live. This is what you were born into. This is your planet. Your home. Don't waste a single moment of this miracle.

The water in Mica lake is so clear that we can shine our headlamps through twenty feet of water to the pebbles on its floor. Snowmelt feeds the lake until it reaches the height of a tiny channel through a series of boulders, allowing the water to course down into the valley. At times I can't do anything but shake my head.
    I've said the word "Unreal" so many times it's unreal. I don't have the right words. The photos capture next to nothing but a two-dimensional rectangle devoid of any scale, context, meaning...or the way I feel chancing upon something like this after twenty miles. I don't have the capacity as a human to appreciate the scale of certain things. I just say "Unreal" under my breath and traipse on down, glad that there's a little flat spot next to a small cliff overlooking everything.
    The sun grows lower and shoots a kaleidoscope of different-colored rays through a long row of distant cumulous. This feeling is hard to come by. This is a sensation that approaches but rarely allows one to touch...not until it's down to the One Thing and all the endless chatter is gone. Only after I'm next to nothing, wanting of nothing, unable to coerce my rational side. When I've finally stopped identifying as a "human on the Pacific Crest Trail", it's there-as ever. As it's always been. As it will ever be.
    The word "Fresh" isn't what I thought it was; or I didn't know could be. I came close once in the Rockies. The High Rockies are plenty fresh. So fresh you can hear rocks dropping off the cliffs all throughout the night in parts. So fresh that the air is exploding with the smell of healthy organic life in bloom. It's a sort of intoxicating fresh that draws you up endless trails in Springtime...just to take in as much as you can before sundown.
    But here at Mica Lake, something stirs my heart to its very center. I didn't perceive survival as necessarily brutal, or even

overtly competitive. I simply saw the world asking the same of everyone: "Be strong, be vital, be alive, be here, listen, pay attention, and take care."

Back home, conflict would dominate our textbooks as if conflict was the only thing that had ever dictated the course of history. But I was thinking about everyone else. Long, long before the printing press. I was thinking of all the people who'd wandered and explored and hunted and lived and loved and prayed in the wild. The people without plaques and bronzes and chapters and regalia. People without streets named after them who felt the same wonder as I did right then. I thought of the average explorer. The average child. The average human creature finding their way through the world amongst the leaves and grass and mountains and animals...people who looked into the stars the same way I did and shook their heads and whispered in some long-gone language:

"Unreal".

"That which today calls itself science gives us more and more information, and indigestible glut of information, and less and less understanding."

-Edward Abbey

Your Place in The World

Over time the trail changes...what is this whole thing about? To walk five months from Mexico to Canada on a trail through mountains, little towns and ski villages...to sleep in tents, wake with the sun. To plod on through snow and mud. To ford creeks and swim in glacial lakes. To know what the animals are saying...or at least inferring. To find oneself at the mercy of the elements yet totally comfortable in nature. I've tried to add some romanticism to it; to say something that will convey the philosophy of my experience, but I have nothing. I can't quite describe what it's all about in plain English. Words are almost laughable at this point. I know. The others know...words simply aren't appropriate. Ansel Adams sold the idea of conservation through pictures. Shadowy walls of solid rock under halos of impending weather and for me, pictures were always enough. Even as I researched the trail, I found very little relevant information in blogs and books. Of course, everyone has a different way of absorbing information. The moments that meant most came and overtook my spirit instantaneously. I was rarely aware of actively "looking forward" to any particular moments outside those in the Sierra, which signified something personal and great in my mind, with each day holding enough grandeur to fill my heart, exhaust my body and leave me in a satisfied heap in a sleeping bag.

Some of the very most difficult days also brought the greatest rewards. In these instances the objective mind is completely bypassed and one enters a state of direct communion with the world. I had to acknowledge that I too, was being experienced by my surroundings. To feel this...to see myself as an animal moving through forests on padded protected feet, holding my home and food in a bag on my own back...to see myself

approach a level of instinct previously unimagined in terms of understanding my *place* again...how do you put that into words?
    When I returned so many things were clear. The level at which we are conditioned and herded about. The way our energy is controlled and directed and siphoned from cradle to grave...and whether or not we're willing participants, whether or not it's got a legitimate place in history rather than being the result of a strange schism...it might sound cliche. "The system". We imagine ourselves in it, sizing up our own level of engagement to defer responsibility, quick to point out how many *other people* are living just fine by it.
    The idea that you'll go on a trail and see the contradictions behind the curtain, that you'll come closer to an unfettered Self than you imagined existing, that the smallest things that you took for granted your entire life will hold almost religious significance and that the most basic motivations and paradigms that govern human behavior will be simplified and distilled through osmosis...the longer you walk. Well, yes. This happens. This is why you're on the trail, right?
    And yet so many of your daily occurrences fall outside the bounds of normal experience. There's a no announcement or degree to which you ought to expect any of this. It's a matter of living in natural systems for extended periods. What happens out there is more or less what you might imagine...only there's no way for me to describe it.
    The authenticity is utterly unfeigned. Maybe I can say that with certainty. The human body and mind, at its very limits, is a thing to behold. To those who have been at the very edge of existence and seen the way reality arranges itself just so, how synchronicity rises to the level of the commonplace and how so very much we have pretended and identified with is just that - it's a series of exposures. It's the silence; once awkward and unlikely, with some level of noise ingrained in the fabric of our

days, disappearing for weeks at a time. Natural sounds and sensations returning. And what is the overall effect of exposure to natural things as opposed to digital copies and odd shapes and colors? How can you write about that? The silence has a voice and nature has a language. It's only a matter of when and where it decides to speak.

This Wind

"So, *I have just crested the apex of a long and sandy hill. The footprint trails are being filled in by the wind. We stagger and fall sideways and lean forward and use the poles just to stay facing forward. All around are Joshua Trees, strong and resilient, dug in with their sharp fortifications reaching toward the sky…and we pass them one by one, eyeing our proximity to what a Joshua Tree is: A hearty plant that most people wouldn't want to be blown into. And then we're up on top where the wind continues to howl mercilessly and the valley extends below in a great amber undulation of sand and rock and plant life while ravens soar higher still, pivoting against arrows of wind like transient passengers, spreading and twirling and ducking.*

Now the trail drops straight down, turning directly into the wind for 300 meters and I lean in to see how much weight it takes to counter the blasts. The wind gives for a moment and my body pitches forward and I'm running at a forty-degree angle, arms outstretched, held upright by the air itself. The wind is so so loud I can't hear a thing and I fall toward the sun while tears glance off the corners of my cheeks. I'm so tired that I don't care what happens next. I just want to see what happens between me and the world this afternoon.

This is one moment in one day out of six months. Maybe it wouldn't have been so poignant had it happened down the trail. Maybe it was an accumulated series of poignant moments, but the conditions never acclimated to us (as they're prone toward in societies) Nature does not bend to your immediate needs, but it resonates with meaning at every turn. When I say "communion", this is what I mean. Slowly, the separation between you and your world disappears. The question I return with; the one that haunts me still, is how much separation there ever was, and how much is conditioned, imagined, re-imagined, and agreed upon."

Diatribe From a Motel 6

You see the pictures, the trail, the beauty of it all, which is good. These transitions are always beautiful in their own way. My mother is gone much sooner than any of us expected. You don't see me confused, frustrated, openly hating people and institutions under my breath, full of contempt for the slings and arrows; the self-pity or dull haze of watching one foot step in front of the other while an obnoxious musical phrase or unanswered existential petition repeats five thousand times in my head over a twelve hour period. I learned years ago not to profess anything truly authentic in public. I learned how to communicate on stage through music and symbols, not authentic confessionals that expose anything human, fragile, or vulnerable.

You're born. You make a series of choices in the midst of a given milieu, you adopt a workable identity, you might cry over a prolonged series of psychosomatic and largely imagined grievances, you act on behalf of a subjective idea of justice and value despite your permanently myopic condition, and you take a bow if you're lucky...or you're snuffed out and ground into history like sawdust, but I thank the stars each night that I'm here. Suggesting less than the miraculous would be foolish.

"So, go to the Sierra in May while the snow is still melting. While brittle lakes thaw and storm clouds roll in each afternoon. Go there when the streams turn into raging rivers in a matter of hours and subside deep in the night. Walk through the snow and mud until you know the different character of each. 'Till you're soaked to the bone and desperate for simple things. This is where you become part of nature and this is when you understand that here, not a single drop of water is a mistake."

January 5, 2019
Hyder Park, Albuquerque, NM

"When will my heart leave the trail? It comes in small aches. Acclimating to consensus. Resigned to...nothing. The branch sends forth a twig and on this twig: a flower, a cluster of seeds and yet another tree. The trail continues. All we know is what we know. Someday the "why" might approach, as if a timid fawn were to wander through our camp and meet our eyes by firelight. The world itself: beyond marvel, beyond comprehension. Still I walk. Still the path. I can feel a great force, as if drawn toward a new mystery. Another purpose. Past, present, and future...form a signature. Write a new chapter..."

"He remembered believing there had been a time when monsters roamed the earth. The brave-hearted fought flesh-and-blood dragons instead of shadowboxing their inner demons, the sport of modern man."

-Katherine Starbird

Journal
June 4, 2018

Climbed Sierra Buttes fire lookout station at sunrise. Epic. Perched over hundreds of vertical feet and staircases that hung above rocks far below. A semi-abandoned-looking ranger hut w/ stove, fridge, maybe room for a bed. Dated back to 1960s. We had a good pace. Passed six or so SOBOS over an hour. Strange. My head and chest felt light with aromas of the forest in contrast to the heaviness of the past three weeks. I can only pray. The thought of her suffering tears me apart and I feel as though one of these northern California stretches will be the last time I speak with her. Somehow, walking all day gives me perspective. At least enough.

Felt like I could feel something for the first time in months today. Since the beginning of all this. I don't know why. Old memories. Random dreams but totally benign or neutral content in contrast to the Freudian purgatory I'm used to. Feels like pieces of the past are falling into place or making sense. Things I felt for so long; elucidated or flat-wrong. Either way, energy flows where intention goes.

Passed dozens of little lakes today. Forest more and more dense. Tiny patches of snow. Cool breezes. Lunch by Grass Lake. Water from springs. We're at A-Tree Spring deciding on two or three days to Buck's Lake. Wanting to camp at a lake maybe...or a zero there. At least wash my socks. Scenery is out of a story book. No words. No words for anything.

Journal
June 5, 2018
Mile 1243

Calculating mileage needed to make this work. Too many zeros already. Ten-day setback with AZ trip...not that this is a problem...we just looked at the numbers. Need to be doing plenty of 20-mile days at *least* to get back on track. Oregon is 400. Washington is 500 plus a good 250-mile stretch of the Sierras still to do. We move forward. To Bucks Lake tomorrow. 21 more miles. Resupply. Sleep. Move on. Still 400+ miles in California. Although the 23 today felt perfectly fine. I'm ready to try a 30-day but Hanne is hesitant. She wants to enjoy the trail but I think we can accomplish both. We need to make tracks either way. Hiked 12 hrs today. Felt fine. Lost in my head. Old memories. Old songs. The energy is changing in a subtle way. The smells are so intense. Ambrosia to the senses. The wind has died down. Silent nights at 5,000 ft. No freezing. No extra layers. First time on the trail that it's just been comfortable to hike. Maybe we're just tougher. Three more hikers are just behind, camped at the lake junction. One girl from Ukraine. Didn't know the others. Hanne's pretty great to walk with. We get too intense for each other sometimes but we make a good team either way. Deep in the forest. Praying for mom.

Goodnight.

Journal
June 7, 2018l

Three 20-plus mile days ending up at Buck's Lake. Tiny resort village with picturesque family cabins and a clear blue lake. We walked the 2.5 mi detour from the trail and found the lodge. One free beer and the only thing on the menu was burgers. (kitchen wasn't officially open) Tried to update some pictures, but more enamored with food. Friendly local gave us some tips for crossing into Belden. We just nodded and thanked and ate.

Snuck into the campground down the street and snuck out in the morning over to the convenience store for breakfast burritos and coffee. Asked about showers and laundry but no such luck unless you pay for a room. We are dirty. My legs have dirt tans. My clothes are all covered in mud, blood and crud. Tomorrow, into Belden. Only 10 miles and we'll take care of all this at the local RV park.

We left Buck's Lake around noon and climbed up (which is usually the case after any town) above Silver Lake. Strange feelings and old bitter insecurities revealed themselves. The reasons I became over-defensive in my youth. Feeling constantly persecuted for being curious or different. Not knowing how to express my differences constructively. Getting bullied and having friends turn on me. The constant threat of violence and retaliation. The norm for rural Arizona in those days. How I shut off, always feeling like some severe form of retribution was just around the corner…for what? Yet, this chip on my shoulder ultimately led to everything interesting and essentially good about my life. It's as if being put through the wringer at such a young age helped me grow thick skin. But what's the cost? I may never know what things I've done merely to prove that I can do them and what things came from deep within. Sometimes it's a combination of both. I didn't choose the PCT to prove anything. I already knew I could do it. I did it because my mom and I needed it. I instinctively knew somehow. This whole year…one strange synchronicity after another. One great karmic cycle on display…but I don't know why cancer has to be part of that story. Why she has to go through this. Logically, it's the result of something. Chemical spray in the orange groves outside Hollywood…something. But my rage is spent. What fight is left I hold for the future. My future family. Myself. "Live and learn" was never so poignant. My mother lived an extraordinary life and she did it with a sense of grace and I'm not sure what else we can ask for. Tragedy of this scale hits in waves. When I stop on the trail for lunch. When I'm about to fall asleep. When I see an older couple enjoying their golden years together in one of these little towns on the trail. My heart just asks: "Why".

Journal
June 9, 2018
Goodbye. Somehow.

Finishing up a lengthy blog at the lodge restaurant in Belden Town and the text from my sister comes in saying mom is going downhill fast; maybe three days left. Stopped eating. Just lying in bed. I only responded "Ok, I'll have service in three days in Chester". Loaded up and walked six miles through bursts of tears, trailing quietly behind Hanne through the ascent and switchback. I can't believe this is happening. To have your life taken from you…

Yes, it happens to all of us. I'm glad beyond words we made our peace with each other…but to go through this. From being perfectly healthy to this outcome. The false hope. The chemotherapy. The loss of everything, even your home to cover the expenses when for what you know, you were about to retire and travel twenty more years with your husband. The shock to your value system and the way you lived and taught others. There's some level of cruelty to it that I can't fathom, and here we are, with the cold reality of it all.

Your mother gets cancer.

The combination of treatments and chemotherapy take their toll over the course of nine months. You watch it all. You even watch yourself change along with everyone around you. We all tried to do something. Anything. Research. Raise money. Pray. Beg and bargain with the universe. And there's nothing we can do. Nothing. We're fractured as a family and yet closer than ever. We never expected this…it came like some cruel joke and we scrambled to understand the diagnosis and move forward with the best information possible.

Everything has changed since this. My assumptions and easy beliefs. My petty qualms with everything, even myself. This thing we call life is too short. Say it 'till you're blue in the face, cliche as it sounds. So few people are mature enough to understand or take heed. Life is too short to waste. Period. No amendments. No liner notes. No small print.

And now. In the forest again. Hanne saw our first bear down by the creek a few minutes ago. Here we are: humans in the dark with whistles and bear spray.

I wish I could hold you now mom...through this night, through this hour of your life; that you would have no fear. None at all; that you rest proud of the life you had and showed to countless others. I hope you know that you were loved and respected by many. We count ourselves lucky. I hope you know that your life, for all measures and angles, was a grand success; a triumph. I hope you know I'm here with you...in the woods...until the end.

Journal
June 10, 2018
Bears and Cows

Slightly late start. In my head all day, quietly walking. Almost meditative. It's hard not to know my mom's status but we'll be in Chester tomorrow. 21.8 miles today with two detours for water adding another 0.9 but we generally take the packs off if we have to walk more than a quarter mile or so to get to a spring. 8 miles uphill starting off. Steady climbing. Almost 22 miles and no fatigue or soreness. The usual bit of numbness in the toes but I suppose it means we're finally getting in shape. Briefly considered doing a 30 but it would have been after dark. Physically I could have done it which is good to know.

Second bear today. They like to hang out around water sources. We were at Robber's Spring Creek Junction and I decided to take the bear spray with me simply because it was 0.3 to a remote water source. When Hanne saw the spray in my hand she laughed:
"Come on, really?"
"You'll thank me someday!" I said.

Two minutes later we rounded a corner and spotted a grown-up brown bear. When it saw us it took off in a dash toward the trees but I had my moment of smug. Without the spray I would have turned around and waited for the next water source. Hanne wasn't having it.
"I thought bears were afraid of people?" She said.
"Bears aren't afraid, they're skittish! Different bears have different personalities and I don't want to be assuming anything about how humans think they're *supposed* to act!"

Ok. I have a slight bear phobia. I'm working on it, but I sleep well with the spray where I can reach it when the branches start cracking in the middle of the night.

We ran into three cows and three calves earlier as well. They were using the PCT as their trail too. Statistically I'm sure cows are far more deadly than bears and if bears were really that interested they could take down these fat, grazing mountain cows in two seconds, but they like blueberries.

Volcanic rock. Deformed and broken. Mt Shasta in the distance. It has some kind of mystique for me still. Sun didn't set 'till almost 9 pm. We made camp on a butte looking down into the distant valleys. 16 miles (?) to highway access to Chester tomorrow. I will find out what needs to be done. Do I stay on the trail? Head back?

I'll do whatever they want me to do. I only pray, pray, pray she is comfortable and unafraid. Damn all this. I was so suddenly infuriated today I wrote in my phone: "Cancer isn't a disease. It's an industry run by profiteering scum." Fifty years "research" and ZERO headway. What a circus. What a scam. What a slap in the face to people that put their trust in these morons who do more damage each year than illicit drugs and car wrecks combined. Anyway. I'm angry, but the choice was ultimately hers. Nothing I could do. I only wish things were different.

Journal
June 11, 2018
Farewell for Now

Made it into Chester and got the final news. Mom passed away in her sleep around noon today. She's been asleep for three days-since I left Sierra City. It was peaceful and she was surrounded by loved ones till the very end.

They say these are the things you hope for when it's your turn. Yes. But the shock won't soon go away. There was nothing to prepare me for this…at least nothing outright. We were all blind-sided…to the degree that I'm not sure what the grieving process is going to be like. For months my mind has been asking "What else can I do? What can we try? What are the options?" And I keep watching myself compulsively doing this. What happens now…how will Randy cope? How will the family stick together? What am I supposed to do? How do I honor her memory? I just don't have the power to quantify this. I'm friends with the process of change. I understand it intellectually, but this…like this…happening to her. It's like the pages of the story book got mixed up. Thrown about. Massive printing error. Like the sun came up in the west one day for nor reason whatsoever. How do I honor?

Words are so small. Your life was so great. You cared. That has made all the difference. Are you here? Are you watching? Did you know you were loved?

Journal
June 13, 2018
The Grips

    I wrote ten reasons I'm thankful to have had her as a mother on a page from this notebook. Bought tea candles and searched around for a good piece of flat driftwood. Put ten of the candles on top of the paper - folded flat on the board. Gently pushed it out over the lake under a billion stars. Watched it slowly make it out past the shore. Twinkling softer, then brighter with each little breeze. Cried my eyes out. Wasn't thinking catharsis. Was thinking of something for her. There wasn't much catharsis today either: a raging hangover from too much sentimental red wine. Grips of paranoia and nausea back on the trail. Where's my family now? Will they still be my family? How will this affect everyone? How will I handle this? How *should* I handle this?
    The same old fellow who brought us into town originally, ended up passing by again and gave us another ride out. Retired teacher. Used to live in my niche of the woods in northern Arizona in the sixties. I felt he was a little lonely…and despite how ragged I felt I tried to pay close attention and make as much conversation as I could. We talked more at the trailhead before finally saying goodbye. Kind-hearted man. His friend married Chuck Norris and he's got a home in Chester. The stories you hear…
    Back on the trail I continued to feel like garbage; head full of suspicion, wanting to blame someone for something…anything to take attention away from my own heart. It kept hitting me over and over, taking my breath away. Feeling so surreal yet so final. So hopelessly final. And yet, I don't believe in death per se. I know the soul continues. It's the shock. The turn of events. All these things we never considered. I watched her eating at

the table in Sedona. Exhausted. Looking through the room. Through the walls. Trying to understand, prepare, but so genuinely...I don't know. Maybe shocked like the rest of us. Wondering "how did this happen to someone of her health and constitution?" What's the lesson? Is there one? I hope tomorrow is better. The rest will take time, but then again, there is no time is there? We've got to live. We've got to live, live, live.

January 1, 2019

"The Northern Arizona Audubon Society is proud to announce that it is embarking upon a youth birding and conservation educational program in memory of Dena Greenwood. Many chapter members knew Dena personally and were in awe of her enthusiasm for birding and the natural world. However, it is not as well - known that Dena had a passion for educating young people about nature and spent many years directly involved in this activity.

This new program will be called Greenwood Naturalists - Youth Birding and Conservation. The objective of this program is to provide nature oriented educational programs to youth residents in our area. While a curriculum has yet to be developed, it is hoped that Greenwood Naturalists will not only educate but also encourage youth to take action in conserving our natural world.

The generosity of Dena's friends has created a fund in excess of $6,000 to be used to turn this idea into a reality. There is much work to do but, it is hoped, that Greenwood Naturalists will be up and running by next spring.
You may make a donation by going to northernrarizonaaudubon.org, and then click Donate and you will see the Greenwood Naturalists link."

Journal
June 14, 2018
Twin Lake Sunset

Walked 20 miles in an absolute haze today. Barely the awareness of what I was doing. Where I was going...water break. Bathroom break. Lunch break. Walk. Swat mosquitos. Head down. Hills don't make a difference anymore. Uphill, downhill, flat, over logs, over snow. It's all one trail. You move forward. We crossed creeks on great fallen sugar pines. Made sandwiches next to a sulphur geyser (Terminal Geyser). Walked around a boiling blue lake. Warning signs everywhere. Some made sense. Others we ignored. You'd think after you lose your mother that you're in a perpetual state of mourning but it's more of a given. It's always there. Behind everything else. Behind "what the hell am I suppose to do about this situation when I get back home?" Walk. Through swarms of bugs lining up to suck your blood. Try to be semi-pleasant to others. To Hanne. She understands...but for how long? She's having her own experience. Wants us to be a team. I just don't feel much of anything right now. My primary motivation for the PCT has essentially left. Now it's a tribute, which is fine. That was part of the purpose to begin with: To share. Pangs of guilt. Second-guessing. Wondering if we'll ever be able to make contact. Somehow...when it's time. There are, at the end of the day, two Williams. Maybe only one the day I grow up. After this...then what? Another adventure. Another journey. I don't care. AT. CDT. Great Wall of China. Motorcycle tours of southeast Asia. I refuse to return to Albuquerque...except to produce the doc for Hanne. How soon can I get out? Sell the music gear? Again? Get another car? Save? Return to Flagstaff? I need a plan before this trip is over. I only feel drawn to finding more and more things to take pictures of. Travel photographer...Nature photographer... I could hunt for the rest of my life. Some kind of nomadic hunter, documenting as I go. What else is new?

Journal
June 17, 2018
A Bit of Hallelujah

Down to Old Station. Little stores and parks providing enough distraction. Subway cave and up to a lookout between the two mountains with Shasta in the distance still covered in snow. Every time we stop in, the biggest question on people's mind's is: "Did you see any bears or mountain lions?" Then it's advice we've heard a million times. "Oh, bear spray? Pshhh. Doesn't work." Or: "Oh yeah, you could shoot a bear at point-blank range with a .45 and he'll still tear ya to pieces." The oddest one yet had to be the position that cougars smell blood and to keep an eye out when anyone's menstruating. Hanne thanked him politely and we made our exit. We've seen two bears so far and they were both scared to death of us. Not to suppose every encounter will be so uneventful (knock on wood). Cougars however, prefer fast-moving objects with exposed necks and we don't fit the menu.

 The next morning we made a bid for our first "30 day". It went through a relatively dry and rocky section full of foxtails and plenty of mosquitos all the way to Baum Lake, and then a few more into Burney Guest Ranch around 8 pm. Famished, we nearly despaired when came upon a series of dark houses at the end of a long driveway but a small blonde woman appeared and showed us around, then treated us to burritos, salad, and lemon custard cake for dessert. Hanne literally cried tears of gratitude. $25 for shower, laundry, breakfast, and tent site. The owners were Christian and didn't mind letting anyone know, but I wasn't put off one bit. It wasn't preachy. Just plenty of crosses, quotes, etc. Kindest of the kind. True Christians if I had to imagine what they're like. We took long hot showers and fell into a dead sleep. Woke at 7 am for the breakfast, coffee, resupply (at their hand-selected-hiker-friendly store) and uploaded pictures.

    I shared some of what I'd written in Sedona with Aubrey, Kristin, and Randy as far as what I imagine might be a useable reading at mom's memorial. Their response touched my heart…the tears are still falling. They fall for her. They fall for Randy. They fall out of utter disbelief and inability to understand. I've been so angry this past week since Chester. Just hating the whole maze of existence, but honestly, it was Burney Guest Ranch that brought me serenity for the first time since I got the news. It was simple kindness. Unexpected rainbows overhead and communicating with everyone back home if briefly. Also, a Siamese kitten crawled up my back and sat on my head for a good ten minutes. We hugged the owner goodbye and headed down the trail, passed a younger Swiss girl with an older Australian man and stopped for the longest random chat. It was fine. We only had eight miles to Burney Falls State Park where we set up the tent. Planned the trail to Shasta and watched the sun go down. If there can be anything from this trip, just let it inspire. Let it show what love can do.

Journal
June 18, 2018
Understanding a Little

We camped in a wide-open campground at Burney Falls State Park and slept in until 9 am. Hit the snooze over and over. Both of us were in deep sleeps and couldn't be bothered. Ambled over to the Burney Falls area and walked down to see majestic water mists spilling a hundred feet into pristine blue waters. Walked back up to the general store for coffee and sat on a stone ledge outside and talked for half an hour about everything. How did I feel? What's the impact of all this? Why did she choose the route she did in the end? Should I have tried harder to convince her? At what cost? Did I do everything I could? Kristin was amazing as always. It's a great mystery to me. Why? Did she feel like she didn't deserve her golden years with Randy? Was there a hidden psychological component to her condition? What would have happened if she never went in for that blood test? Why, over and over in her life, did she so blindly subscribe to authority and hierarchy? What was the importance of a piece of paper from a college? What were the true dynamics with her brothers? What did she *really* feel? Did she feel loved? Respected? There's so many other angles to one's life story and as we hiked it all sifted through my head and heart. We crossed over a great dam and had lunch on the edge of it. Then just a few more miles to a campsite where a few other hikers were set up. We all sat around a great fire and talked and shared stories and laughed at all the crazy adventures we'd had so far. What a time. Three months in. So much has happened. It's a completely different world out here. Sometimes I don't want to leave and it's becoming more and more vague which world is the real one. We get into civilization and sometimes it's more like Disneyland than society. All this useless artifice. Plugged in.

Proxy living. Staring at TVs. What is the *real world*? Digging burrs out of your socks? Slapping mosquitoes? Feeling water from dense shrubbery make its way down into your shoes? Looking up at billions of stars? Drinking from streams? Walking thirty miles with your life on your back? It is whatever you choose if you're aware enough to even realize you have a choice. And in the midst of all this…a strange hope. Though my life is also short, a hope that understands, puts context to our relationship. The whys and hows. What we were actually trying to communicate to each other all those years. Where did we fail? Where did we succeed? I lived in her shadow as a child, terrified of failing. Years later in Flagstaff I had this moment where I realized I'd *never* live up to her expectations because we were playing totally different board games. Less than a year later: this diagnosis. Reconciliation. Love. What was important in the end was that we both cared.

"The hillsides are wild
Your hair is covered in dirt
I understand what the wind is saying
Every muscle aches with joy"

One Day Was Day One

The sheer blur of the movement. Of thoughts. The hyper-vigilance of the sights, smells, sounds and sensations coming from the environment. It was difficult to feel as though I were wandering far off into the woods on some epic journey. Hanne and I walked down the trail asking each other little questions, trying to sustain basic communication in the middle of the heat and our own determination to define these first moments, both foreign and surreal in every sense of the word. In the beginning you don't know what you don't know. You have no idea. The reality of your endeavor accumulates and seeps deep into your soul through a series of situations; broken tent poles, swarms of mosquitos, choking down instant coffee, waking with tremors and shooting pain in your calves, and deciding what to do when a plume of smoke suddenly appears in the middle of a Cascade forest. The first day contained very little of the final sentiments that overtake you after months on the trail. There's very little to evaluate because all those initial evaluations are false. The excitement is real…the anticipation is unbelievable. A glint of perspective emerges slowly, but you can see it on the horizon from day one.

"This is what I'm doing now. Take mental notes as best as possible, realize there's going to be huge missteps and awkward trials, and keep moving. Just keep moving."

As much as I tried to rationalize what I was doing and philosophize my way out of the initial anxiety, the more something *else* began taking form; something I didn't have a name for; a language I didn't know how to speak just yet. I put my head down and kept walking: "March 19th, 2018. This is the only day that exists."

Hannelore

"So, why'd you want to fly all the way over here to do this?".
"Well, I traveled here for sports a few years ago and saw the Sierra Nevadas with some friends and loved it so much..."
"I can't wait for the Sierras."
"Yeah, so I read this book and I thought I want to do this, but I don't want to do something so competitive anymore..."
"Competitive?"
"I wanted to do this for the right reasons..."
"Ok."
"And I take some time to think about this and I almost decided *not* to..."
"Really?"
"Yeah, but then I decided it is time and I'm ready and I just do this for me to enjoy the trail..."
"What sport did you do?"
"I was a bobsledder."
"Oh, wow! I used to race road bikes!"
"Ah, so you know what it is like trying to integrate after competitive sports..."
"Yeah, (I suddenly realized) I do. I became a musician after that. There's no medals for writing songs."
"Yeah exactly...it's like 'Who am I now? Everything was easy because you had a clear goal."
"Yeah. Maybe the trail is like that..."
"What about you?"
"Well...so my mom found out she was pretty sick in October and I wanted to do something that I could share with her because she's a naturalist, always in this field of study and work and it's her life...and I just wanted to do something we could completely

connect on while she goes through this. I think I needed a reset as well."
"A reset?"
"A reset button…sitting in a studio all day. I'm not sure why. I thought music was the answer for a long time, but I don't know if it makes sense anymore. I guess I have to figure it out."
"I see…but you bring music on your phone?"
"No, I cleared everything out to save the battery. Only resupply lists and The Halfmile app."
"What about Guthook?"
"A band?"
"No. It's the best app for the PCT!"
"Oh…no, I printed out paper maps."
"Really? Why?"
"In case my phone breaks or something. I have maps for each resupply point so I don't have to carry them all at once."
"So how do you do your resupply?"
"I bought everything in Albuquerque and my friend is shipping it to me…"
"Really? Why?"
"I don't know. It was fun to plan out. It felt like the safer route."
"I send only gear from my friend in Sacramento to the Sierras."
"Kennedy Meadows?"
"Yes."
"I can't wait to get there. I think if I make it there, I'll feel like I did something pretty amazing either way."
"Only six hundred or so miles to go!"
"I'm going to try to take it one day at a time…"
"Yeah…it's only a mind-game."
"Totally."

Some nerve running down my neck into my back was starting to sting terribly. I lowered my head to stretch the tendon…

"Man…"
"What?"
"This nerve is acting up already." I pointed at my neck, looking for sympathy. "
   It was bad when I was backpacking Europe ages ago but I didn't feel it when I was training."
"We probably get used to this pain." She shrugged.
"I hope. I hope it's not something that I have to deal with for five months."
"You'll find out!"

   The afternoon wore on and we stopped for some lunch and surveyed each other's rations.

"I'm sorry…your food is crap."
"What?!'
"I'm just saying."
"Uh-huh. And what do *you* have for lunch?"

   She brought out a perfectly arranged bag of various organic grains and proteins in different configurations and dropped an electrolyte tablet in one of her water bottles. I watched it float to the bottom and start fizzing.

"Is all that from Switzerland?"
"Some of it but also from San Diego."
"Are you doing a gas stove?"
"Jet-Boil."
"I'm trying the cold method."
"Bad idea."
"Why?"
"You will want something warm at night."

"I'll be fine. I have everything I need."
"I will be drinking water every thirty minutes. I think this is the best idea." She said
"Yeah. That's not going to happen."
Why not?"
"Your water intake is going to change every day."
"I carry eight liters."
"What! Why?"
"All this desert! In Switzerland we have water everywhere. It is not a thing to think of. I see no water in this place." She said, waving over the hills.
"Yeah...I have four liters, but it's supposed to get better in the Sierras."
"Yeah...do you bring the...how is it...purification tablets?"
"No, just the Sawyer filters."
"The Squeeze?"
"Just two of the Mini. I'm not going to try and filter water that looks gross though."
"Gross?"
"Oh. No, it means like "Bleh!"
"Ah, ok. Yeah, I don't do this either. They say not to rely on the water caches either."
"Yeah...definitely going to make sure I have my own. Where is the next water by the way?"

   She brought out her iPhone and scrolled...

"In this canyon here." She leaned over and nodded at the screen."
"Seven more miles. No problem."
"Yeah, I maybe camp here tonight. Where do you camp?"
"I'm not sure...I thought Lake Morena but maybe it's too much for the first day."

"Yeah, this pack is heavy."
"Mine too...way heavier than how I trained."
"I didn't train too much. I train out here on the trail."
"None at all?"
"Just a few day hikes..."
"Wow...well, I guess it's possible to get in shape out here. As long as you have good shoes."
"I'm sorry...but you have the wrong shoes..."
"What do you mean?"
"I worked for a bio-mechanics company after bobsledding. They make custom insoles for athletes."
"So, what's wrong with these?"
"Too soft and your soles are too thin. You will feel all the rocks."
"But I trained in these and I thought they were super-light...and I didn't get any blisters in all the training so I guess that's my main concern...avoiding blisters."
"You will see."
"What kind of shoes do you have?"
"I wear Lowa with custom insoles. Shoes and insoles are seven-hundred Swiss Franks."
"What? How many dollars is that?"
"About the same."
"What? I got mine at a discount shoe store!"
"I know. They are last year's model. I know all about this. I can tell when people walk what their problems will be with back and hips and knees."
"What about me?"
"I don't know yet. You will know in the next two weeks."
"Hmmm. Shall we go?"
"Yeah. Time to go."

We trudged on as I fidgeted with the straps and whatever other parts I had access to. Shoulders cramping, neck straining, but nothing overwhelming. We'd hike for a couple miles, set the packs down and grab some water...take a deep breath and hoist them back up.

The only animals so far were the occasional birds chirping lazy midday songs in the branches of various bushes and trees, and little lizards who liked to cock their heads and size us up before scrambling beneath the nearest pile of stones. I'd read all about the different animal species on the trail, how to behave, what *not* to do when you turn a corner and come face to face with a cougar. Oddly, the protocols tended to change from one experience to the next or sounded something like "I knew a guy who knew a guy who heard that this happened to a guy..." As far as I knew there hadn't been a fatal cougar attack on the actual trail system since the late 1970s but that didn't stop me from turning my head at every sound. It tended to be little rustles in the bushes or leaves and by the end of the day I surmised that the vast majority of all these little snaps and crackles were either lizards or squirrels merely reacting to our presence.

It was around 3 pm and we had been walking...exchanging small talk...and I'd been trying my best to remember the different plants of the desert. Sage and creosote; each with their own distinct aroma as we walked down to Hauser Creek. It was hot but I barely noticed. There was still little else going on inside my head other than: "Wow...this is happening."

We pushed through the brush and over some rocks at the bottom of the canyon to find the creek but after a few cursory glances it was evident.

"Huh..."
"Yeah."

"What are you going to do?" She asked.

I honestly hadn't thought about it although I wasn't disheartened. I'd given much more thought to food than water and knew I could last until Lake Morena in the morning, but the thought of camping by a wash in the dirt instead of being lakeside on my first night didn't sound amazing either.

"I can go further...I think I want to be by a lake anyway." I said.
"Yeah, I think so too."
"How do you feel?"
"Fine...yeah I feel fine."
"So, we go for it?"
"Yeah, you think so?"
"We can do it...only a few more miles."
"It's uphill from here...over all *this*." She motioned to the other side of the canyon we had to climb out of; a long series of switchbacks...
"Alright...let's do this."

    I was pretty good at climbing mountains; all these three-hour jaunts up Mt Wheeler and the San Francisco Peaks, but I slowly started to fatigue after we got out of the canyon. I'd never in my training done more than fourteen official miles and never with the full weight attached to me.
    At the top we came upon a long sloping bluff with patches of small green shrubs in what looked like typical beach sand that felt completely different from what we'd been on for most of the day.

"I think it's hitting me" I said, wiping the sweat from my forehead.
"Yeah, I feel it in my feet." Hanne said.

We both started slowing down...

"Almost there. Should we take another break?"
"Yeah. Let's take one more break."

I struggled this time to remove the pack and swayed as it tried to drag me down by my right arm.

"Man...this is nuts. I felt so good earlier but I'll get used to it...just have to build those muscles up."

I leaned my chin down, wincing until the nerve in my neck relaxed a little.

"We're close...it says in Guthook that there's a bathroom with a coin-op shower."
"What's a coinop?"
"You know; coins to turn them on for a few minutes."
"Oh yeah I know what those are. That sounds amazing."
"We'll get used to it."
"Ready?"

The sun began to slowly arch down into the west and a chill came over the high desert. Through tufts of high grass and gnarled crags I finally saw the far edge of the lake and a wave of quiet relief swept over me. I was going to make it down there to the human stuff with the water and the showers. An hour later with sunset rapidly approaching, we stumbled down into the campground through a maze of RVs and small families. I felt wrecked, but not as wrecked as the training hike I'd done back in October. Food poisoning caught me in the middle of an ascent up the Sandias. Back then I'd been too stubborn to turn around, figuring pain was something I needed to get used to. I'd spent the next week drenched in cold sweats under my blankets, but this. What was this? It felt like my joints were coming apart, but I'd made it through day one and I'd met someone from another country. That was good enough. Now all I had to do was put up my tent and do it all again tomorrow.

There were already a few hikers spread out across a designated patch of grass with a small shelter and some benches to the side. A group of older Chinese men were having a few beers and laughing hysterically about something. We made small talk and eyed each other's gear with innocent curiosity or pretended to be preoccupied with something vaguely more important than socializing.

Hanne and I dismounted our packs and let out great sighs of relief. We'd done most of our first day together and it had been pleasant enough as first days go but it suddenly dawned on me that I knew of no particular etiquette that should inform us what to do now. We're we automatically trail-friends? Does someone walk with a person one day and another person the next day? I was confused and tried to push it out of my mind. I'd trained to walk alone as had she. We'd seemed to have a few basic things in common but in the middle of the desert on the first day of the PCT? I glanced around, surveying the ground for a spot to pitch my tent.

"I guess...I'll go over here." I nodded.
"I go here." She pointed twenty feet away across the grass.
"Cool...well. I'm going to set up the tent and hit the shower."
"Me too. You have to get coins from the people we passed at the entrance. I think they have food too."
"Ok, well...nice to meet you. Good to talk with someone the first day." I said
"Yeah. I think I start early tomorrow."

"Yeah, me too."
"Ok. See you sometime maybe."
"Sounds good."

The Day Before

On the way to Campo Alana and I had made a visit to the Mayo Clinic's outpatient facility. My mom and Randy had been in virtual confinement at a place called "The Hope House" since the marrow transplant and we were going to stop by on our way west. A long stretch of fresh asphalt led around a series of massive buildings painted in southwest adobe colors and we wound through until we came to her building, which looked like an upscale urban apartment complex.

Randy appeared at the top of the stairs which led into a common room where caretakers and family could cook and mingle. Things had gone as planned. She was in excellent health for her age; having avoided every vice, junk food and a host of other potential toxins her entire life. Before we'd left, I'd already received the pictures of her without hair. She hadn't wanted me to be shocked when I saw her but I wasn't worried about the condition of her hair as much as losing her altogether.

The truth was that I couldn't bear to see her going through any of it; the thought of how a simple diagnosis had upended everything she believed and taught and caught her completely unaware after a series of bruises showed up on her arm one week and a bloody nose a few days later. Randy had urged her to go in for her regular checkup and mention these anomalies. There could have been a million reasons from dry air to bumping into something in the middle of the night and simply forgetting about it.

He led us up the stairs and we entered their little room. Mom was sitting on the bed and gave me a big hug with a huge smile.

"You remembered to wash your clothes first, right?"

Her immune system was at zero, having been taken down by the chemo to "restart from scratch" after receiving completely

new blood from a match in Germany. The match had been 100 percent; obviously, the best you can hope for.
"Yeah, everything's clean. How do you feel?"
"Just tired...they said everything went as well as it could have gone though so now we just wait for my levels to start returning to normal. They'll do tests every couple of days until I'm strong enough to go home, but this is just the first phase of recovery. We ordered some pizza for you guys on your way out there...are you ready?"
"I'm ready. I mean, a little terrified but that's expected. I'll just get out there and keep walking as far as I can walk!"
"I can't believe your actually going to do it. I'm so proud of you!"
"Thanks. It just felt like the right thing to do. I have a blog set up so I'll be sending you my updates and pictures and calling as much as I can."
"You might have a hard time getting reception in some of those mountains."
"I know. Verizon is supposed to be the best but there's some stretches where it'll be a zero signal for a few days."

She smiled with the same glimmer she always had when her curiosity was piqued.

"Can you imagine how people used to navigate those trails? John Muir and Ansel Adams out there by themselves..."
"I know. It's insane! I have these topo maps, but I've got this other app on the phone that can measure my location down to 10 square feet."
"Well, we got you something else, but you have to help Randy set it up before you leave."

Randy pulled out a Spot GPS from REI that would basically broadcast my location in time-increments of my choice as I made my way up the trail. I got online and went through the registration process until a little indicator popped up on the screen.

"Wow...so you can print this out at the end of the trail and it'll show everywhere I went?"
"I think so. Basically, yes."
"Thanks guys. This is awesome."
"You just stay safe out there and keep us updated as best as you can" said Randy.

We spent a few more minutes together in the room. I answered questions as best as I could, but I was often in the dark as much as anyone else as to how the whole journey would play out.

"I'll text when I get there and send some pictures in the morning...just concentrate on staying balanced and taking it easy right now. Don't try and push yourself too hard even if there's lots of birds to look at out there."
"I will. It looks like we're both on long journeys from here huh?"
"Yeah I know...we'll go on this one together."
"Ok love...you two better get going."

We got back on I-10 and drove toward the sun, stopping a couple times to refuel and grab water until night came upon us. We listened quietly to music and talked about our futures. I'd dated her for two years.

We'd half-tried for awhile but couldn't get on the same page and called it off for good in 2013. Now, she'd been accepted to a

nursing program in San Francisco and would be driving north for her orientation after dropping me at the border.
"Do you think we'll forget about each other?" She asked. "I mean, this whole thing...it just seems so big. We're both doing these huge things right now. What if we're just different people after you finish the trail?"
"Yeah well, we were always different people. I'll always be here though. You know that."
"And you'll call as much as you can?"
"Of course. You're taking a huge step here and that's pretty awesome. I really think you'll be a good nurse."
"I can't believe the amount of debt I'm going into right now..."
"I know, but give it a few years and decide where you want to take it. There's so many directions you can go in this field."
"We'll always be friends though, right?"
"I think so...thanks for taking me out here."

Day One Continued

I found the showers and put my coins in one by one. They came shooting out onto the concrete floor. I reached down and picked them up, tried again and caught them this time and took them to the next stall.

This time it worked and cold water immediately came out of the showerhead. I waited for it to get hot. I turned the knob clockwise, then counterclockwise. After half a minute it warmed about three degrees and stayed put so I got in and immediately began washing as fast as I could. My toes were the dirtiest but my head and hair were full of sweat as well. I had no soap and my towel was an eight-by-eight inch ultra-absorbent square from REI.

I hadn't even thought of how to dry myself on the trail…but it was a special material designed to absorb large amounts of water fast and it worked. I marveled at this rag for a moment and put my clothes back on, walking barefoot across the cement and nearly running into a blonde lanky kid grinning ear to ear. He was probably in his early twenties, but he had an easy confidence about himself.

"Hey man what's your name?" He smiled.
"Oh…uh, Will. My name is Will. How's it going?" I asked.
"Oh, good man. How about that first stretch?"
"Yeah man, brutal. But this campground is pretty nice. Where are you from?"
"Oh, I just came from L.A. I was living in my van but I got the opportunity to do this so I was like, cool - guess I'm doing the PCT this summer!"
"Right on."
"What about you?"
"Oh well…yeah, pretty much the same. I'm from New Mexico."

"I hear ya. It's gonna be insane! Well, take it easy man. I'll probably see you out there.
"Cool man. Sounds good. Have a good night."

    Something was taking hold in the pit of my stomach. My mind was beginning to race back to the film Never Cry Wolf by Carrol Ballard that we'd seen as kids. It was one of my mom's favorites. I even occasionally joked it was her fault I became a musician. She'd bought the soundtrack by Mark Isham and I'd sit in front of the stereo zoning out to these hypnotic arpeggiated sounds for hours. There's a scene at the very beginning when "Tyler" (Farley Mowat, the author) is standing in a train headed for a small Alaska town to do research on grey wolves in the middle of nowhere and he's slowly realizing the madness of the whole scheme.
"But I can't return now...I'd be a laughing stock. Still, I wouldn't last one minute out there."

    I felt sick for a moment, but I couldn't tell if it was from the exposure, exhaustion, or the realization that I'd committed to walk 2,650 miles.

    "And for what? Maybe she needs you there right now...and who is all this for? You or her? What exactly are you trying to prove here?"

    A lady and her family were the official campground hosts for a few weeks, collecting fees and dolling out shower tokens but they also had a massive spread of free snacks for hikers on a foldable table and gallons of water beneath that. When I'd received the tokens, she invited me back for a fire they were going to get started. I could see its glow in the distance and began wandering over, stumbling in pain. I crossed through a portion of someone else's campsite. An elderly man chuckled:
"Got the hiker-hobble eh?"
"Haha...yeah, I think so..."

"Don't worry, it gets better."
"Oh good." I said. I didn't know what else to say. I just wanted to be by the warm fire and kept moving in its direction.
"Have a good night."
When I arrived a small contingent of hikers were gathering around, picking through snacks, cracking beers and joking about the first day...Our host appeared smiling.

"Oh, there you are! Did you get some water?"
"Yeah, I think I'll get it on the way out in the morning...do you think there'll still be some left?"
"Oh yeah. Don't you worry about that. We restock it as soon as it starts getting low."
"Thanks. This is really amazing, what you guys are doing. Is this your first time doing this?"
"Oh no. We do this every year for you guys. We like seeing all the hikers and making sure they've got enough food. The first day can be pretty insane huh?"

...I must have looked dazed in the fire light.
"Yeah...I'm just...I think it'll be good."

I was starting to lose the capacity for rational conversation and stared blankly into the fire.
Hanne appeared in a few minutes and stood above us. She was six feet tall and the men in the group suddenly went silent.
We'd spent the whole day together, but now we were around new people. New attitudes and energies. Everything felt nebulous and distant and I didn't know which way the vibe would move next. I didn't want to follow other people around but maybe it was a good idea to hang out with others for a week or two just until we all got our feet under us. Maybe there was safety in numbers.

"Hey! How was the shower?"
"Good! I feel so much better!"
"Yeah that was good. I feel like I'm crashing hard though…did you get some water?"
"Yeah I'm good to go."
   We all attempted small talk for about half an hour. Nervous energy around new faces…six or so of us, sunburned and teetering on collapse with a million unknowns in front of us. One by one we broke off and wandered back to the hiker area. Light chatter drifted through the trees until it was nothing but stars and a dozen or so tents silhouetted in the grass. I crawled in the tent and zipped up the vestibule and tried to write something legible about the first day but my mind faltered and sleep overtook me in a matter of minutes.
  I woke with the sun and poked my head out to survey conditions. I'd slept ok but it was cold. Super cold. I'd tried to curl up and get the bag zipped all the way, but I woke up every couple hours or so. I felt ok but the knees were still aching. The grass was frosted over and my tent was covered in a thin layer of ice and I went into auto-pilot, pulling things out, shoving things in, trying to swallow granola bars. Then I headed for the water. No one was around yet but I heard muffled voices from inside the host's RV. I hastily poured the water into my bottles before realizing I didn't know where the trail was…
"Wanna know where the trail is?" A voice came from behind me.
"That'd be great!"
"Just walk right back through and stay to the right. You'll see it when you're almost back to your camp spot."
"Ok awesome. Thanks…"
"Yep. You stay safe out there."
"I will, thanks…"

I picked up the pack and felt the weight of the new water.
"Alright...just take it slow. Looks like a solo day."
   I walked back toward the site along a gravel access road and noticed that everyone else was gone except Hanne. Her black two-person tent stood covered in frost, conspicuously silent.
   "Well...I guess that's the PCT. Maybe I'll see her later."
I felt as though I should have waited to see if she wanted to join up again but I didn't know if she was a late riser...or anything else about her strategy for that matter. I felt like I needed to get going.
"Today" I said...
"Today the whole thing really begins. It's you and the trail. Stop when you want. Take pictures when you want. Heck, you can hike into the night if you feel like it."

Journal
June 17, 2018

    What's authentic; I mean, the authentic reality of a situation? This word we use so casually. The feeling some people crave. This idea we skirt around hoping to avoid ourselves indefinitely...even though it's happening every waking minute of every day. Your life. This precious thing. This miracle. This extended moment. Breathing, eating, sleeping, laughing, loving, hurting, learning, getting knocked down and getting back up. The music. The moments. The wind in the pines far above. The rush of a cold creek and the crackle of a fire, staring listlessly at the flames, offering a word or two...looking back up at the stars.

    This whole thing was nothing more than an idea that got stuck in my head; that suddenly propelled one foot in front of the other. A reclamation as much as a tribute, a five-month "thank you" to a mother who had shown me the value of authenticity at a young age.

    Living on a hill overlooking the Verde Valley in northern Arizona. The endless distractions of the outside world versus our quiet home on half an acre. A wood stove burning through winter. Books on adventures great and small. The men and women who explored and loved this land and lands beyond - that I dreamt of in the back room we built, lying on the forest green carpet of my room just reading and dreaming. I owe that capacity to her.

    The bicycles. The drum kits. The books. The detritus of teenage experiments everywhere. The old stereo in the living room. Fifth Dimension. Beatles. Roberta Flack. Vivaldi. Bread. John Denver.

The whole time you're waiting for something more. Compulsively longing for something you're too young to understand under the soft gaze and gentle hand of a mother.
 Years later...sitting next to her at the table, watching her too exhausted to open her eyes while she tries to eat...finishing her salad for her, helping her to the couch just to lay down...to watch this occur within a period of months. Holding back tears the entire time. From a routine checkup to chemotherapy to failed marrow transplants...from the healthiest woman you knew to the weight loss, the hair loss, the loss of everything just months before retirement.
 And yet there I was, a week off the trail in Sedona surrounded by friends and relatives, surrounded by love and endless cards and gifts from people who she inspired through a very innocent sort of authenticity.
 I go through old pictures; boxes of history dating as far back as the marriage photos of grandparents and faded snapshots of great aunts and second cousins gone long before I knew them...and there's this young woman, this kid, with long blonde hair and a chipped front tooth and eyes like you've never seen. There's something different about this human and I can't stop looking because I can't believe this is my mom. I see the toughness yes. The conviction, the beauty, but something else. A magnetism. A quality. It's because I suddenly recognize this quality that I understand something. A puzzle piece lies down in my mind and years of missing narrative appear like missing chapters in a long book.
 I hold her hand while she lies on the couch after beating me in scrabble one last time. She whispers 'Did we miss anything important? Did we talk about everything? I pause and say "I just want you to know how grateful I am."

This feeling of gratitude overwhelms me on the trail daily. Sometimes I wonder how I actually got such an authentic, loving human for a mother...

Did I deserve her? How do I begin to honor her life? The last words we said to each other were:

"I just want to tell you how grateful I am."

She sighed and said, "Why were you grateful?"

"Because you cared."

"*One good test of whether an economy is humanistic or not is the plausibility of earning the ability to drop out of it for a while without incident or insult.*"

-Jaron Lanier

Journal
June 19, 2018
Three Months on the Trail

Passed flip-floppers all day heading south. The woman who gave us pizza at Silverwood Lake. The guy who saved my Cheezits from ravens at Whitewater Preserve. Old Faces like old friends. Exciting info on north and south situations. A lot of people just didn't want to do the Sierra in those conditions, but most are skipping up to Ashland and just heading south, hoping the snow has melted enough. We're going to Canada, then back to the N. Tahoe / Truckee area and heading south to Kearsarge where we got off at Independence. Time has flown by. Barely a moment to look up with everything that's happened on the trail and off. I went through old pictures from the beginning of the trail and I barely recognize myself. Kind of an angry too-cool-for-school look in my face. We found out Cherry and Leo got off at Bishop after Leo slid down the last ice ridge at Forester Pass. Unbelievable. They wouldn't have made it through in those conditions anyway, but there's a chance they skipped way up ahead like us. The Aussie at camp had a video of it. It was a day before we'd gone through. He was fairly convinced they got off the trail. 23 miles today. Abnormally sluggish. Needed more sleep. Hot. Mosquitos. Bear poop everywhere. In fact, we think just heard one poking around outside in the bushes. Trying to hide or string up food. Mt Shasta looks like a monster of a mountain in the distance. Getting closer and closer. Two or three days away. Oregon is nine days away. Unbelievable. Hope you are at peace mom.
  I love you.

Journal
June 20, 2018
Very Beary

Not sure if it was charging us or running away but today's bear encounter left us both a little spooked. Thrashing of the bushes. Silence. Not concerned with our whistles and clacking poles. We retreated, then moved through as fast as possible.

Good energy day. Mind and body pretty sync'd up. Good solid strides. Making sense of the past. Imagining the future. In the present. Forgiveness.

Short on food but we'll make it into Shasta tomorrow. Something about that mountain has captured my mind for ages. I've even drawn pictures of it for album art before. Place of mystery. Sasquatch stickers and fridge magnets at the local gas stations and minimarts.

Journal
June 22, 2018
Mt Shasta

Today was mom's memorial service. I hadn't been online in four to five days and didn't even know until I went to the Black Bear Diner in Shasta this morning. When I got ahold of Randy he said the place had been overflowing with people standing in the back, and that there were many tearful tributes, that my words had been read, etc.

When I spoke with Aubrey and Lauren later, I learned that Tom had shown up as well and spoken, stood by Randy and that it had been a moving ceremony. In my mind none of this makes sense still but logically I can accept it. Like the other day; logically accepting that a bear might be charging me, feeling the blood drain from my face, thumb poised on the lever of the bear spray...but unable to believe it's actually happening. No matter what's empirically happing in front of your eyes, in your life...the brain or the heart still says: "But, no...this wasn't supposed to happen."

Good to talk to them both. Wish I could have been there and I need to make an effort to keep communication open with Randy. God knows what he's going through. I can still send pictures, updates, etc. I suppose he's the closest thing to a parent I've got. No communication at all from my real dad in Louisiana as of yet.

Shasta is a bit like Sedona, with a great 14k mountain looming above it. I like the place, but it's time to get to Etna. Money is precariously low. I'll have to get more by the time we reach Oregon and hoping the options are still there but we'll just have to see. Randy and mom did so much to help already.

Last night blood-curdling shrieks from the woods behind the KOA for hours. Almost sure it was someone with severe

Tourette's but damn. Unnerving. Train flying by with horn every hour. Awful anxious dreams.

Stomach in knots. That's life sometimes. Yesterday was 24 miles in less than nine hours and I didn't bat an eyelash. Fastest pace on the trail so far. Tomorrow will be climbing with full pack again. Not even sure I bought enough food to make five days. New to this type of resupply strategy.

Camping with the Aussie and his Swiss pal again. He's the talker of the two. Ex vice-president of mid-east operations for…something; doesn't mind skipping parts here and there on the trail. Hike your own hike. Nice people.

Hanne's third pair of shoes bought today. Hope they work. Her heel problem is reaching chronic status. Need a permanent solution to arch support and constant cracking of callouses.

…and a special goodnight to you mom. I hope you know you're living through me on the trail. Through the beauty and the pain. I move forward.

Love, Will

Journal
June 23, 2018
Leaving Shasta

    Resupplied last night at grocery market in Shasta City. Must be at least ten crystals per resident…but a great town with great people. Black Bear Diner was fantastic. We camped at the KOA again with Aussie and Swiss girl. (Did I write this already?) Woke and walked back into town for coffee and hitched out.
    Friendly guy picked us up and drove us to the trail. Talked about bears. I keep hearing the grizzly and brown bear are from the same family. I know grizzlies are only in Alaska and Canada, upper US and Montana now and they're huge compared to black bears, but the brown bear is a bit larger too and I'm pretty sure this is what we saw at Robber's Creek. Anyway. Climbed all day. 18 miles. Still worried about Hanne's feet. Hope these shoes work. A fire in the distance southeast of us sending a plume of smoke into the air.
    When it got dark at our campsite, we could see hills glowing orange and red. Surreal. We are perched on a large mountainside with a massive view of Mt Shasta and everything toward Mt Essen. Four 20-plus days to reach Etna. I'll be out of money here. Hope I can keep going but I'll accept whatever happens. Every day since the beginning has been indescribable. Challenging. Beautiful. There's no words for a good 99.9 percent of this.

Journal
June 26, 2018
Ugh...and Full Moon

A climb. Seven or so miles. Stomach churning. Messing with me all day. Stomach and brain intimately connected unfortunately. Slow. Sluggish. Moody. All in the stomach. Always some bug or something my body doesn't like. We climb through the heat. Sun burns on arms. Wasn't expecting after three months of this. Not bad just a light red. Beautiful scenery. Moments of feeling lost. What do I do after all this? Even though we were profoundly different...there's still the connection...on many things we were the same. Our particular sensitivities etc. "Who am I?" Should be the proper question. Ideas percolating. How to spend my future. How to even *have* a future. It struck me when Hanne said last night that we're only halfway in Etna. 90 days out. I feel like I've been living out in the woods for ages. A shift in perception. The idea of having something to go home to. All the mindlessness of the past ten years in Albuquerque. The relationships. The jobs. The bands. All lifted like pieces on a chess board and flung over a mountain cliff. Irrelevant. That's the scary part. That's what happened from Europe in 2004 to New Mexico; being completely lifted out of one's self, one's previous comfort zone and knowledge base. Who am I now? No more phone calls. No more "stop worrying, leave me alone." Feels like a double-edged sword right now.

June 28, 2018
Letters Home #4

10 pm in Etna, California, local RV. Hot showers and a small site in the grass for 19 bucks. Laundry is just a stone's throw away and the breakfast diner is a quarter mile up HWY 3. It's a full moon tonight. The third full moon since we started. I remember the first, just as we were coming out of the San Jacintos. The night I probably earned my trail name. There'd been a light breeze and I'd still worn base layers to bed. I still wore a pair of faded black jeans, still wore a pair of Nike gym shoes and still carried ten pounds of food between every town. Tonight, all I hear are crickets and the faint drone of cars passing to the north. We've been out here one hundred days now and every day still presents a series of unique challenges and perspectives. The best way to get over blowdowns, what the terrain looks like when there's water nearby, what foods work best in the morning, how to consolidate gear even more, how to walk when your toes go numb, how to repackage food in Ziploc bags, how to score free amenities, how to hitch a ride and on and on...and each day it changes. Each day asks for something you've acquired through some level of improvisation. Duct tape. Super glue. Needle and thread. Walking, eating, sleeping. We've gone entire days with less than fifty words between us and we've gone days where we've both watched the other person cry out of exhaustion, frustration, or the realities back home and we've sat at the fire contemplating how incredible the whole thing is. How grateful we are just to be here; to wake up and spend the majority of every day wandering through forests and granite and sun and wind and dirt and the far-off sound of streams.

    Same night in Etna: Waking up at 3 am to the sound of four sprinklers pelting the tent with buckets of water. Our backpacks

and shoes lie outside and get immediately soaked. We jolt up and unzip the rain fly trying to get out only to be hit ourselves, grab the gear, tripping over guy lines in a frenzy.
"Do we move the tent?"
"Where to? We'll get soaked!"
"I'm already soaked!"
"There's no time!"

    Jets of cold water are coming at us from every direction. Hanne retreats to the other side of the road with some of our gear and waits. I dive head-first back into the tent, taking off my shirt and using the dry parts of it to sop up water from myself, sleeping bags, and the tent floor. Otherwise, everything's dry. I wait for twenty minutes until the cycle finally ends and poke my head out. "Hanne! Where are you?" She appears in the darkness shivering with her rain jacket on and gets in the tent.

"We are *so* getting a free night."

    We try to sleep and get a few hours before breakfast at The Ranch House is down the street. Bacon, sausage, three eggs, hash browns, and two pancakes for twelve bucks. Another day. Another adventure. I'm still processing everything. Day by day. Walking 20-30 miles every day is probably the best way but sometimes I feel distant. Unable to talk to the people closest to me. I watch my legs move. I hear my breath quickening uphill and slowing downhill. I answer questions from day hikers and small families on sections that cross and integrate into the PCT. I swim in lakes and stand quietly on cliffs looking back toward Shasta and a plume of billowing white smoke coming up from a fire by Mt Essen. The days are quiet. We walk, break for water, break for lunch, find a spot by evening, cover ourselves in mosquito repellent, ration the food, trade a few items, write in our journals, and fall asleep.

A week before we came from Old Station into Burney Falls, providing dense foliage and mild days and plenty of bears. The first two took one look at us and dashed away. The third didn't care so much. In the middle of the wilderness the trail is used as much by animals as humans. Every morning fresh deer tracks follow shoe prints for miles and water sources especially seem to attract bears. In fact, all four times we saw them were next to creeks and springs. While most bears are just as startled as humans when we encounter them, I don't agree that they are basically "large raccoons" and I've learned that locals tend to exaggerate every story they've ever heard for the fun of it. The truth is that bears are highly complex and vary by individual just like humans. Some have learned that they can walk into a camp of backpackers and force them to flee in every direction. Some have never seen a human before. Some are spooked by high-pitched whistles. Others are aggravated by them. As for me? I've carried grizzly spray for 1,500 miles. I've had other hikers and locals tell me 1.) It doesn't work 2.) It works better than a gun. Now, grizzly spray was developed by a guy who'd endured multiple attacks up in Alaska (this came from another hunter in Chester). Either way, I bring it in the tent each night. Why not? When we passed our third bear we banged our trekking poles and blew our whistles from about 40 feet away just off the trail. The result? A raging bluff charge through the bushes. Then silence. I'd had my thumb on the spray ready to deploy thinking "Ok here we go, aim low and..." that's all the time I had. We retreated 100 yards back, listened, decided to quickly and quietly move past and pick another spot for lunch away from water about a mile up the trail. Of course, it's a strange sensation realizing you might suddenly be in a critical situation when moments before you were simply daydreaming about gear design, but it was a lesson: Don't listen to "stories".

    Listen to your own experience and intuition. Humans love the idea that they can somehow predict and control nature. They love imagining all the solutions and options readily available; that the right tactical gear choices will save them, but it amounts to little more than a buffer between you and the wilderness. All the accidents I've heard of so far on the PCT this year resulted from a lack of situational awareness or plain bad luck. That being said, I've not heard of one critical injury so far. The vast majority of hikers have a deep respect for the reality of the trail and services like Guthook and message boards constantly update everyone on everything from animal sightings to the best coffee in trail towns.

    We made it down the trail and passed our Swiss friend; an older man going solo that we'd met at Burney Guest House a few days before.

    I asked, "Have you seen any bears yet?"

    "Bears? No. There's no bears. The whole thing is a myth. There are only what you call...the deers out here."

    We made our way down to Castle Crags State Park, passing one last juvenile bear near the main road.

"Just keep walking. He's far away."

    We hitched to Dunsmuir then hitched to Shasta nestled below the imposing mountain. At 14,180 ft it looms even from miles away, trapping circular clouds around its summit and sending half of its would-be ascenders back before reaching the top.

    We just needed to do laundry and resupply before hitting the local KOA and after showers we were close to sleep before a combination of train horns and someone with the worst case of Tourette's Syndrome I'd ever hear started shrieking in the woods by the tracks, unleashing the most profane string of psychotic howls for hours. Eventually he fell asleep but I only sussed it was Tourette's because at 7 am it began again!

We packed up and went to the grab breakfast at the Black Bear Diner. Huge plates for 12 bucks. Some of these diners knew what hikers were after. Afterward we ran into Ah-solo and Thriftshop again. They'd met early on the trail and we'd camped together a few times. They were staying at the KOA as well and offered their site if we wanted to stay another night (you only pay per site).

Hanne's feet had been in poor shape for over a month and she needed to heal and try another pair at the gear shop, so we opted to hang around. We thanked them and headed to Fifth Season where she finally settled on a pair of super-soft Altras. Since then, she's been ditching me on the trail like Southern California when I was trying to walk in gym shoes.

We passed people we hadn't seen for over two months in the next few days; mostly pairs who'd flip-flopped because of the lingering snow in the Sierras and gone up to Ashland Oregon near the border to head south back toward Bishop or S Kennedy Meadows. Hopefully there'd been enough snowmelt to let everyone through by the time they reached the North Tahoe area.

We saw Mt Shasta in the distance for days after leaving. The heat went soaring to 90 degrees and our first day back on the trail had an 18 mile climb back to around 7,000 ft. This is where we saw the plume of smoke in the distance. Four days later we came out of the mountains and stopped at a paved road leading eight miles down the crest to Etna. No less than a minute after setting our packs down a woman in a pickup with her son asked if we needed a ride into town. We hadn't even put out our thumbs yet. We crawled in the back.

"I'm gonna drop you right at the city limits because the cops have given me problems for letting hikers sit in the back if that's ok."
"Absolutely no problem at all. Thank you!"

And here we are, catching up in Etna at the Wildwood Crossing coffee shop. Three days from Seiad Valley and three more to the Oregon border. I can't believe we're only halfway done (technically mile-wise) but we're now averaging 20+ miles per day without major aches and pains…and my phone is about to die.

Take care / love from the trail.

July 16, 2018
Losing Track
Letters Home #5

    The weeks have flown by recently. From Etna to the Oregon border to Shelter Cover where I finally got enough WiFi and free time to write. Sitting in a great red plastic chair by the lakeshore listening to a retiree chastise her husband who's trying his best to dock their little outrigger. Country music blends with banter from tourists, hikers, and birds. A perfect cloud cover and calm waters but most noticeably: no mosquitos. We've been at it since Ashland with a nearo (near zero) in Crater Lake pushing 25 to 27-mile days since the border, measuring food and water, stopping at small resorts along the various Oregon lakes to pick up food and take advantage of the free camping provided by most of them.
    As we near the 2,000 mile marker it feels like I've finally got enough distance and perspective to enjoy some hindsight and organize my own energy a bit. For four months it's been go! go! go! Feeling the body adjust to the initial strain wondering "how on earth do people walk 20 miles every day" to the time spent trudging through endless snow in wet socks for weeks, changing trajectory and moving up through the Northern California section dotted with tiny towns, big American breakfasts, and the friendliest people imaginable in the great "State of Jefferson". There's finally moments where I feel like I've got some serious miles under my belt and that the trail has knocked any remaining hubris or unrealistic expectations I've had out of the picture. When I began hiking, I'd say ridiculous things like "this is just how I hike. This is what I'll do every day. This is what I need to maintain a comfort zone". I think most of that was gone by the time we exited the Sierras but the longer I spend time on the trail the more the comfort zone moves and becomes irrelevant.

There's no reason to assume any day will be similar to the last outside of the fact that I'll walk twenty or so miles down the trail. Any number of things happen in any order from squirrels stealing my food to amber dusk light illuminating the last two miles of a stretch in a way that I've never experienced before.

Twenty miles in any direction will usually lead you through a different climate, geological strata, elevation, ecosystem and temperature. Each destination affords separate challenges and benefits to the body of the experience.

Immediate comforts are the first to go. Backpacks tug on shoulders, sun burns, joints and muscles don't understand what you're doing to them and you become intimately aware of how your body prioritizes healing. On the other hand, you're easily in the best shape of your life and suddenly, after four months of adapting these to the reality of the trail, you can finally sit in a big plastic chair at Shelter Cove somewhere in the middle of Oregon and take a deep breath.

Hanne and I spoke while I wrote this blog...what have we actually learned out here? Maybe how life gets distilled down to the basic elements day after day. You become intimately acquainted with the core elements of your own personality. When we started the PCT we both wanted to control every aspect of the experience but as the months wore on, it became more important to understand the actual limits of this idea. Instead of "I need to control this experience" it became "how much can I actually control?" Then, "how much of the little that I *can* control do I actually need or want to control?" Food. Walking. Small tactical decisions from town to town. A good place in the forest for lunch, the cheapest options, or when we ought to hit the trail, but these are more like day to day guidelines that can't be interpreted too strictly. It just doesn't work. At each town, village, and resort we sit down for half an hour and decide the best general approach for the next stretch.

How far is it? How much food do we need? How many days will it take? What info do we currently have on weather, fire, and mosquitos? Outside of that, the best strategy is to get up early enough to walk twenty or so miles and walk twenty or so miles. Of course, every day things happen well outside of our control and comfort zone. What Hanne and I discussed was basically the psychology of pushing through when you realize your comfort zone is probably compromised indefinitely; when you don't have any choice but to keep moving. What do you do when there's no immediate solution and plans A, B, and C are equally punishing? You just walk. You adapt. You might suffer but you stay on the trail.

Just after Etna we made our way over a few more passes and came along the Klamath River in the early morning, walking along a barren half-paved road that passed farms and fields; rusting Ford F-2s and the old XX symbol of The State of Jefferson, over a great steel bridge built in 1967, along a busier road that lead into town, to the heart of Seiad Valley and footsteps of the Seiad Cafe.

We sat down and ordered the breakfast we'd been waiting for. Eggs. Hash browns. Bacon. Toast. Large milk. Coffee. Short stack of pancakes to split between us. In the corner were an assortment of books about the PCT: A hard copy National Geographic publication from the 1970s when people hiked in street shoes and cut-off jeans. Old analog photos before the trail gained any real popularity. The book followed a couple as they made their way slowly through the same conditions as us. They'd often sidetrack to explore different summits in the area. Where were these people now? They were kids in their mid-twenties who did the whole trek before the northern and southern trails were officially met and established. Before cell phones, GPS, and the tools that most hikers now consider indispensable.

We finished what must have been a good 1,200 calories and went next door to buy more food; just enough to get us over the border and into Oregon. We sat under a big shade tree at a bench and sorted items for breakfast, lunch, and dinner. After another massive milkshake, we headed back to the road and met the trail; spending the rest of the day moving through eight miles of blazing vertical switchbacks and back over to the cool side of the pass toward a grassy field that held a couple tiny ponds.

We filtered our water there, pitched the tent and tried to sleep until high winds began howling all around us just like outside Tehachapi, shoving the tent to and fro and keeping us up all night. No sleep. At this point it wasn't a huge deal.

We slept in just a little and took off toward the border through fields of flowers and sloping plains that let us observe Mt Shasta from the north side now, still rising high above the horizon and a week behind us. In the morning we took a side road that met a dense trail through the forest and over some train tracks leading to Callahan's Lodge on the far north side of Ashland.

Oregon. Finally. The land changed immediately. Greener. Passes were less pronounced and sloping along one another into the blue-green distance. We were famished as usual after three days of trail food and went straight for the breakfast lounge. Callahan's was family-owned and operated and had a special hiker-package that included a space for camping, free breakfast, free bottomless spaghetti dinner, laundry, and shower.

We checked in and inquired about transportation into Ashland for resupply. We'd been going for over a week now and supplies were dwindling. A woman who'd been hiking in the area and stayed at the lodge overheard us and offered to take us to the Safeway down the highway. So, we left our packs in the event room just right of the lobby and climbed into her minivan with her two kids. We answered a lot of questions about thru-hiking on the way. She wanted to take her family on the PCT someday.

We always tell people "You can do it. Anyone can. Just get out there and start walking."

We spent a good hour picking out food for the next stretch and took a bus to the local Fedex to send a couple packages up the trail where resupply was more challenging. We called a cab because Uber and Lyft were officially banned in Ashland and hitching on the highway wasn't allowed. A fellow showed up a bit later and drove toward the exit only to find that it'd been cordoned off by police cars. A fire on the California / Oregon border had jumped the I-5 and forced that section to close due to visibility issues. We backtracked and ran up parallel to the highway on 66 trying to take a side road into Callahan's but just as we got there it was being blocked as well. It was a brush fire; growing by the minute. This was all the info we could get. As for us, there was no way back to the lodge. All roads were closed and our driver offered to take us back to the cheapest hotel back at the exit.

I assumed there was still a way to sneak back in but as we read the news it became apparent: we were stuck for the night with all of our gear 10 miles south in a building that could be evacuated at any moment. We stood in the parking lot between the motel and a gas station while a family of ranchers spoke quietly to each other. Their horse trailers lined up, side by side. Some were on the phone. Another girl was crying. A little while later we learned that their ranch had been one of the first casualties of the fire, killing 17 of their horses as well. Everyone that had to exit the I-5 was standing around, looking stunned, and waiting for updates, but it was apparently that things would get worse before they got better. We checked into the motel with nothing but our grocery bags and phones and got some Mexican food across the street. Everyone at the restaurant had been sidelined by the fire as well and we craned our necks toward the windows to see how bad the smoke was getting.

In the morning, I woke early to check the news. The highway was back open for the moment and we had a brief window to get back to Callahan's. I called the same cab company and we got out within 30 minutes. As we approached, the sky darkened and the smell of burning forest surrounded the exit. We got back inside and checked the status of the fire. Still only five percent contained and double in size from the previous day but no immediate order to evacuate the lodge.

The owner overheard our story and offered us an upgrade to an indoor room at no extra charge with an extra free hiker breakfast. We took everything down the hall to sort into laundry and later, it was long showers, beard trims, and all the little things we'd forgotten or put on hold since Tahoe. Little patches applied to bags and sleeping pads, packs turned inside out and cleaned, items carefully rearranged for optimal space.

More data coming in: Now the fire had crossed the Oregon border just a few miles south and an eleven-mile section of the PCT was officially closed. Our only option was to walk the paved parallel road we'd tried to use the night before and hope for a hitch to the 66 were we could get back on the trail around Green Springs. Unfortunately, the stretch was remote with only private residences scattered here and there and we got within two miles of the 66 before we caught a ride to the junction.

This road was a bit busier and soon enough an official Trail Angel with another hiker in the front seat picked us up. She'd heard about the fire and drove us up and over a pass until taking a left toward Hyatt Lake and Green Springs.

Her three-year-old son was confused as to what a musician actually does. I told him I make pretty sounds. This satisfied him and he changed the subject to fish.

That evening we camped by a lake and got showers again (just for the dirty feet) and watched the smoke change the colors of the sunset. I had something going on in my sinuses but it wasn't that bad. By the end of the day, it looked like the winds had shifted a little and the sky was getting clearer.

The next stretch would lead us 100 miles to Crater Lake. Although the terrain had broadened out a bit, much of the trail was littered with burned pines and charred ash mixed with dirt on the forest floor. While it wasn't exactly scenic, we made good time averaging about 25 miles each day until we came upon the park and headed into a small free campground set aside for hikers.

Summer season was in full swing and like most of the campgrounds and state / national parks, it was overflowing with RVs: gigantic houses on wheels that provide every comfort imaginable with satellite TVs, extendable awnings and rooms, ensuring a safe distance from nature no matter how close you actually get to it. Granted, these are by and large retirees and there's no real judgements. We talk to plenty of them and many are familiar with the trail. I've yet to have a negative experience with the glampers. Some have posted up at parks for entire months complete with tartans and regalia on full display. Many are here for the fish. Some tow outriggers behind them and some couples have little more than a shell attached to the back of their pickups but wherever we go from park to park and lake to lake they're part of the summer scenery. I remember camping as a child only meant we loaded a tent, sleeping bags, and food into the back of our Chevy pickup and headed somewhere north. We'd wind up through Utah and camp at Zion and Arches, then further north into Yellowstone and the Grand Tetons. At night my mom would read books to us and we never imagined anything was lacking from the experience.

Give a young boy a stick to roast something on and he won't complain much. I still feel this way, but the season has gotten too dry and all the fires have me spooked. Now, I don't even zip up my sleeping bag. It's too hot and the risk is too great. Pine needles are nothing but tinder when it gets too dry and I'm happy with the Jet Boil and my noodles.

In the morning we grabbed the resupply from Ashland, took showers, and did a small load of laundry before hitching up to the Rim Trail which had to be used because of another fire closing a portion of the PCT a few miles out around the crater. I don't know why the Rim Trail isn't the official PCT because the view over Crater Lake is unreal. Is it? A massive collapsed caldera six miles across with a cinder cone sticking out of the water...and water so blue and pure I was doing double takes the whole time, trying to get as many pictures as I could. Of course, pictures never capture most of what we see and experience out here. Sometimes written descriptions are even better than photos because you can let your imagination fill in the blanks.

We were able to walk around the rim for half of the day, taking it slow and stopping for snacks while we leap-frogged with our Czech friends that had suddenly reappeared after nearly three months. The last time we'd seen them was Bishop after Kearsage Pass. They'd had some adventures of their own in the Sierras and we were happy they were still on the trail and doing well.

The trail that day was the longest stretch of flat easy hiking I could remember in ages. The only problem was the growing number of mosquitoes. We were entering a section of the PCT so notorious that it had forced people off the trail for good. We'd carried Deet and other Deet-free sprays since Sierra City but what we began to encounter over the next two days was more like something out of a horror film than a thru hike. Clouds of hundreds of these high-pitched vampires flew behind us at all times, taking advantage of any exposed skin, and swarming when we stopped for the briefest moment. After a day of this I decided to forget the Deet and attach the legs to my hiking shorts and wear my thin windbreaker at all times. I was missing my mosquito head-net and resorted to closing my eyes, curling my lips back, and giving my face a good spray of the Deet-free stuff. Everything but my mouth, nose, eyes, and hands was covered with some kind of synthetic fabric they couldn't get their little straws through. It was hot. Ninety degrees plus. When Hanne and I stopped we just gave each other hopeless looks of resignation. The only option was to keep moving. 25 miles per day for three days. When we passed other hikers going south the conversation was only about mosquitoes.

'What's it like on your end?' 'Bad. What about you?' 'Really bad.' 'Ok hang in there. Have a good hike.' 'Ok you too, bye.'

We could barely stop for conversation before the swarms took over. During lunch we pitched the tent and dove inside with our food bags, then killed the fifteen or so mosquitoes that came in with us and took off our extra layers for some temporary relief.
"I had no idea it was this bad."
"Me neither...unbelievable."
    Late in the afternoon of the third day we found our way down to Shelter Cove on the shores of Lake Odell. It felt like some mythical realm of mercy. The moment we stepped onto the resort grounds the mosquitoes stopped. Completely. Not one. We checked into their cheap hiker campsite to the side of the RV grounds and immediately ordered burgers and "the biggest coke you have." Half of what I eat and drink out here I wouldn't touch back home but after 25 miles I couldn't care less. It's all getting burned off in a few hours. When I approach towns, I do exactly what my body tells me it wants. If it's black licorice, cold milk, Fritos, or ten of those little clementines, I just assume my body knows what it's missing.
    We took a zero day at Shelter Cove. Hanne's feet needed a rest. After three pairs of shoes we're still trouble-shooting the

pain. I needed a break as well. The pads of my feet to the tips of my toes start going numb after a few days and the distances we covered weren't giving them any relief. The shoes I bought in Tehachapi (that had literally saved my saunter) were now a few months and over 1,000 miles broken in. The tread had begun to fall off and come unglued. It's about time for another pair but I will swear by these Asics Kahanas until the end.

It's 11:30 am at Shelter Cove and we're waiting for our friend John who we haven't seen since South Kennedy Meadows. He's headed back down to finish a portion of the Sierras and will drive us back to the trail before he heads south.

I finally bought another mosquito net and Hanne bought full mosquito pants. We're heading back out for a four day stretch to Bend. Now we know what to expect and we walk with a little more confidence. The comfort zone will change again in the Cascades and again when we re-approach the Sierras for the final stretches. What can you do? Adapt. And keep walking.

"After you have exhausted what there is in business, politics, conviviality, and so on - have found that none of these finally satisfy, or permanently wear - what remains? Nature remains."

-Walt Whitman

One Fine Moment

Sometimes the finest moments come from the finest summits with the widest views. Sometimes they come because you're at the very beginning of a great adventure and you don't have the level of control you're used to. Your instincts kick in and the body and mind become one extended moment. Some moments are fine because you've gone without for a length of time and the small things you took for granted become luxuries. Other times a fine moment can be found walking silently through the woods when the afternoon sun hangs low and golden through the trees, casting blue shadows, knowing it's less than an hour to camp. Sometimes it's your first creek crossing and sometimes it's your last. Sometimes the finest moments belong to you and no one else at all. It's a smile and a whisper or a shared moment when you suddenly realize you care a lot about someone else. Your little trials and missteps and all the laughter in between. Keeping each other safe and warm. Sharing your last piece of pepper-jack. Taking care of things when the other person has had a rough day. Sometimes it's letting all the details slide and getting from A to B. Sometimes the finest moments come from what you *don't* do. The words and opinions you *don't* share. The silence you keep until you have something that actually helps. Of course, on a thru, a great many of your finest moments will come just after you've crawled inside your bag, closed your eyes, and fallen asleep so fast that you can observe it happening. Those last five seconds stretch into one fine, fine moment.

Zurich, CH
All Cities Are the Same Now

    I didn't induct though a boundless etheric field of space-time and miraculously conglomerate on earth via quadrillions of cogent genetic impulses that operate on an unquantifiable causal principle and exit from another human being into physical existence with a limited lifespan so I could talk to you about television, Goddamnit.

February 9, 2019 - ABQ
The Walls Are Closing In

You ask yourself to write about the trail…you ask yourself to make some pithy observations about 2,650 miles of dirt, snow, forest, summits, passes, creeks, rivers, lakes, waterfalls, ice, springs, suns, moons, stars, campfires, lizards, deer, bears, snakes, and mosquitos. On and on and on. Words. More words. Maybe somebody gets on the trail and sees for themselves…the accumulated magic. Maybe someone gets into camp after dark and realizes their hands are so cold they don't work, unable to put together a tent or undo the straps on their pack. Maybe the next morning they wake to the smell of another wildfire with ashes falling all around like snowflakes, unable to trace its origin through the thick clouds of smoke. Man, how do I really write about something like this? All I wish is that I was back on the trail. At least five to ten times per day I catch myself lost in a moment. I had no idea how much the aftermath would affect me. Life feels different. Some days I can still identify old patterns. I see old friends here and there, but I've lost whatever waning interest I had there to begin with. It's not isolating. It's not liberating. It's me…away from where I want to be. I shouldn't say I miss "The Trail." I've learned what a thru-hike is all about. It's just "Trail" wherever Trail is. I miss Trail. I feel like I belong on a trail that's all. And being back in society…I don't know how many people go through it, but all thru-hikers can empathize to a degree. Society seems almost deliberately ridiculous, like it's set up to siphon your energy towards all manners of irrelevance. It doesn't feel real. It doesn't feel immediate. It doesn't feel normal. I sit on a computer so I can finish this book but I'm sick and tired of staring at screens. I hate the concrete. The noise. The cars. The trash. The crass, closed-off humans gathering and dispersing and talking about the inane rubbish everywhere I go. The posing. The posturing. For me, there was no real post-trail honeymoon. I felt trapped within 24 hours of being back…and I've been ready to get out; ready to move ever since.

February 10, 2019 - ABQ
This is What Post-Trail Depression Feels Like

There's something about the vagabond that a lot of city cats just don't cotton to. It's not on their radar and it's not their fault. When you spend lots of time in the same place you get familiar feedback which stimulates reliable patterns and modes of behavior. Ten years in the same place you feel like you've got the lay of the land and you don't have anything else to learn. To the vagabond this equals death. There's no difference between physical and spiritual death. No point in hanging on to a life that doesn't engage you. And we wonder why such levels of clinical depression and anxiety and malaise in the west. So much nonstop complaining. It couldn't be more obvious, but for me it required a gigantic step back to realize something we already know: This whole civilization thing has reached terminal levels. It's great when you've just invented the light-bulb or connected running water to a distant town. Make no mistake; these are magical moments, but it's clear that we're now more preoccupied with feeding the machine. Now it's only a matter of how much faster. How much more. How much *muchliness* can be crammed into it? If it's boring to a child, you can bet it's going to be boring to millions of grownups no matter what level of access they pay for.

    I found that what humans need has nothing to do with information, status, even freedom or social stimulus. These reductions are only valid within the calculus of post-modern existence and maybe 50 - 80 years of available records and research. Well, to me it's all bunk now. It's all information within the confines of a thing we call "civilization" isn't it? This situation that we've found ourselves in for less than 100 years; we're all clamoring to get front row seats to. We're so completely wowed by it. So entranced. Why are we all so obsessed with color of the bed sheets in the loony bin? Yes, Virginia. It feels like a loony bin because it's a loony bin. This is why people do thru-hikes. You want my reason? My real reason? Because I allowed this to become so damn boring that I didn't know how to participate anymore. People with nothing to say. No light in their eyes. Nothing interesting whatsoever. They're either drunk, self-obsessed parrots; desperate for the next Big Thing, chained to whatever keyword and trigger the news handed them yesterday; enchanted like children with loud screens and actors, pronouncing their moral aptitude through their "tastes and preferences", outraged by things they'd never actually *read* about or experienced. Phony academics. Phony artists. Phony intellectuals devoid of context and heart. I live in an age when they're all given public platforms and I wanted to be far, far away from all of it because I was *becoming* it. Culture has turned into a social engineering initiative gone either very right or very wrong, but do I blame anyone? Did I ever open my mouth and condemn anyone? No. We all have our own paths. I can do little more than be the best version of my own self; a self that evolves and climbs and descends and runs and falls and weeps and loves. I'm a human. It's not my place to condemn. It's my place to find my place. Where can one be most effective? In his own space. In his own confidence. In his own truth. It is my love that breaks my heart and my empathy that condemns *me*, not them.

    I went out there for the same reasons thousands of people, fed up and harassed by modernity, go there. People willing to live without the insanity that the 99 percent swear by. I didn't understand it. I didn't understand anyone and I had to watch it. Powerless. You know what it's like? It's like watching clowns setting fire to a circus tent in slow motion every day of your life. *That*, my friends, is why I decided to walk from Mexico to Canada. Not to follow in the footsteps of John Muir. Not to smash specimens of flora and fauna into a leather-bound book. Not to add content to a blog. Not to prove a single thing. Not even to do something "different." It was to get away from the whole thing for two minutes.

    Simple, measurable beauty in the face of an impending experience. An experience none of us chose…in a window of time. In little moments and consistent doses. It was about putting my body and spirit up against the side of the summits. It was about all the hardships. Each and every one. It was about the early May fords that tested my balance and resolve. It was about looking into the distance at Smedberg Lake, low on food, surrounded by unending snow and ice with a fear so immediate that I started shaking. It was about sending candles into the midst of Lake Almanor the night my mother left. It was about blessing my uncle Kim's transition on the edge of Sierra Buttes just a week before. It was about saying goodbye the only way I knew how.

    Now I sit in a big coffee house in Corrales, New Mexico. Alone at a table. Well-caffeinated. A controlled propane fire across the room. Now I've said the things I wanted to say. I've checked out. I have no faith in this. I only have faith in silence.

"Depression: the healthy suspicion that modern life has no meaning and that modern society is absurd and alienating."

-Neel Burton

Journal
July 2, 2018
The State of Jefferson XX

    The body adapts. The mind follows. It's a balance that takes time to occur. To look at uphills and downhills with the same resignation. To know you can make it either way. To approach tactical problems with a level head instead of throwing your trekking poles over Forester Pass, but there haven't been many of those all-encompassing feelings I used to get as a younger man. Not to suggest that I'm not literally agape at some of the sights. I regularly shake my head in wonder on the trail. I love the adventure and I love the satisfaction that comes after 25 miles. Falling onto the sleeping pad. Lying on my back. Asleep. Deep sleep in less than five minutes. You don't always feel what you expect to feel…but you feel something *else*.
    Walking into Seiad Valley next to the Klamath River, past old farmhouses, long grass, trees shrouding a six-mile paved section into town. I just felt that old feeling. Something so delicate. So easy to lose. The feeling I had from reading books like "A Walk Across America" or "Hey Mom, Can I Ride my Bike Across America" or "Kon-Tiki". This deep feeling. I don't know how to describe it. Pure romanticism. At the local cafe there was a book made by National Geographic from 1975 when the idea of a thru-hike wasn't on most people's minds. It was all about the PCT with great period photos from real film. No gadgets, no high technology or Guthook. Kids in Converse shoes! Anyway. Today was a romantic sort of day in that sense. Just the enormity of what we're doing finally donned on me. It seems so normal when you're surrounded by other hikers and trail and hiker towns and Trail Angels. It becomes your life. How you think and plan; so unfathomably different than the world we came from. Exhaustion becomes routine. The mind accepts it instead

of running from it. You no longer shun discomfort because you don't have an option. You may, of course, attempt to minimize the physical suffering. We do this daily…hourly even, but the legs keep moving. Tan lines develop. Calves grow. Beards grow. Freckles come out. Blisters come and go. Dirt invades every corner of your body. Clothes smell like a science project. We keep moving. You'd think the tendency would be to wring our hands and complain that there's still so much to go, but it just doesn't happen like that. After fifteen miles all you're thinking about is what you're eating for dinner. After twenty, you're not even thinking. For me, this surrealist sense of humor kicks in and I start doing comedy sketches with marmots and bears in my head. It's nearly uncontrollable. Then you're at camp. You have to set up the tent. Blow up sleeping pads. Roll out the bags…put things in different places for different levels of access, then make dinner. By the time that's all done, you're just thinking about what needs to be done to do it again the next day.

Journal
July 3, 2018

The wind last night picked up to the point where neither of us could sleep. Finally subsided around 5 or 6 am. Hadn't been that bad since outside Tehachapi and surprising, considering we were in a fairly protected valley. Either way, today was a long slog but some of the best views. Shasta through meadows of little pink flowers from the north. I wonder how long we'll keep seeing Shasta. It's just unbelievably big. Rising from the earth and towering over everything around it. Passed a few black cows with clanging cowbells. Springs and water sources were trickles, but solid flows. Met a hiker "Zig-Zag", a teacher who's finishing up portions he missed in 2016 due to the fires. From Etna to Seiad Valley and beyond: whole ranges burned to a crisp. Black and white trunks and some of the ones still standing actually bleed a dark red sap. These are the ones that got burned around the base but not enough to take them down. The first time we came across it we thought a cougar had a grisly lunch right at the tree! Tomorrow we'll say goodbye to California for close to two months. Wow. I can't believe it. Can't put everything in focus with enough perspective right now. I've come to love this state. It's forests, towns, people. We've had so many great experiences since Campo, which seems like a year ago. I knew *nothing*. Took desert sun and Sierra snow to straighten me out. The process is indescribable. So intense. So subtle. Can't believe how many people I owe this experience to. My heart swells for this state...

"In his own way the modernist becomes as irrelevant as the fundamentalist. The fundamentalist has something to say to his world, but he has lost the ability to say it. The modernist knows how to speak to his age, but he has nothing to say."

-William Hordern

Journal
July 4, 2018
Land That I Love

24 miles today. Five miles from Callahan's Lodge. We are officially in Oregon territory. It was almost sad to say goodbye to California. For three months we've been walking slowly north. I remember when just the *idea* of Kennedy Meadows seemed like some improbable dream. Just keep walking. Keep walking. Good days. Bad days. Happy days. Sad days. And now we're here and Oregon already feels different. I looked back on all the folks that went out of their way to help us complete each day and each section with nothing but gratitude. From the hot dogs in the Mojave to the free rides. Everything that's happened; racing to hitch to run to rent a car to return home to say goodbye to my mother. I don't know what time will make of all this. Slowly, some form of acceptance but it'll take a lifetime to understand. Your whole life is a process. I hope everyone is coping well enough back home. I'll call from the lodge. Not much to report otherwise. Green green evergreens / pines / grass. Clouds today are a welcome change. Cool soft breezes and forgiving terrain. Oregon promises to be beautiful even if it's the shortest duration of the three states. Ready for a shower and clean clothes.

July 7, 2018
As It Happened

Got to Callahan's Lodge.
Checked in.
Had a big breakfast.
Left packs in ballroom.
Got a ride into Ashland from lodge guest / fellow hiker.
Resupplied at Safeway.
Back up the street for coffee.
Hanne called The Howdies in Silverton to see if we can arrange a meeting up the road.
To the outdoor store for bug spray, gas, new spork.
Took a city bus up the street to UPS after USPS.
Walk across street to Goodwill on off-chance they have some cheap hiker shorts that fit better. No dice.
No Uber or Lyft allowed in Ashland.
Call cab. Wait. Wait. Wait. Cab arrives.
Get to I-5 exit toward Callahan's.
I-5 is closed due to fast-moving brush fire on Oregon / California border.
Look for detour-find parallel at 237 & 66.
Get there just as it's being closed off as well.
Stranded. No way back to lodge other than 20-mile walk sneaking through road blocks with grocery bags.
Cab driver takes us back to Chevron @ I-5 exit.
We debate. We think.
We open a bottle of wine.
We go to a Mexican restaurant across the street.
We give up. We fall asleep.
Wake up. Check I-5 status. It's open. Call same cab.
Cab takes longer than before. Wait. Wait. Wait.
Takes us back to Callahan's.

Callahan's is shrouded in smoke.
We enter lobby. We get an upgrade to a room because smoke is inundating designated hiker camp area.
Use our Free Hiker Breakfast cards and get 3 eggs, 3 bacon, 3 pancakes, with milk and OJ.
Wait in lobby until room opens.
Sort clothes and start a load of laundry. Wait. Wait. Wait.
I grow listless in towns. Nowhere to go. You sit. You "check things". Pointless newsfeed drivel. Take a shower. Trim hair and beard a little.
Sort food into bag for carrying in backpack. Clean out pack.
Throw away stray accumulated wrappers and broken tooth-care products and plastic bags.
Clothes are drying.
Sort everything in backpack. Fresh clothes.
Smells like smoke everywhere - permeates the building.
Go downstairs. Grab a couple IPAs.
Talk to a Canadian hiker named "Snowman".
Ask what his plans are per fire news. He's going through.
We order our included hiker dinner: plates of spaghetti.
Hanne gets a piece of pie for dessert.
I'm out. Fall into bed. Strange dreams.
Wake up. Last hiker breakfast. Check out the news.
Fire has spread to 20,000 acres and only 5 percent contained. PCTA website now has official closure from our location to Hyatt Lake.
We debate. Sky is less smoky but I can tell it's closer. Just different wind direction...
Helicopters overhead with bags of flame retardant thump through the sky.

And sleep...

We get out at the turnoff to Hyatt Lake Resort. We'll head seven more miles down the trail to make tomorrow (to Fisher Lake) easier.

Scandinavian from S Kennedy Meadows and Snowman pass a few miles in at the same time. We leapfrog a bit with a German named Mario. Down-to-earth guy.

Smoke thick and covering entire sky…plants covered in ash for miles. Get to campground full of cars with shower, bench, potable water (I hope)

Cook dinner. Exchange snacks. Hanne wants separate tents tonight. Can't argue. I need some space too. We try our best to help each other but it's a lot of proximity sometimes. Nothing personal at all. We're all about keeping the energy flowing. Live to hike another day…we eat and hike down to Howard Prairie Lake. Looks a little clearer in the distance…

Watch a deer come cautiously out of the forest toward us. We sit on a tree stump together and survey the lake. We're both tired. Combination of smoke and pavement and the stress of the last 3 days.

In nature you walk, eat, sleep, take pictures, experience the woods, talk, act like a human, align with the flow.

Towns are welcoming at first. Showers. Coffee. Maybe a soft bed or a glass of wine to take the aches away…but the glamour lasts no longer than a few hours for me. On the trail I feel like I know what I'm supposed to do.

The one interesting thing about all these recent towns is the nonstop ubiquity of John Denver. He's everywhere…wherever there's a radio. Brings me back to earth. Reminds me of why I'm out here. Other times I burst into short tearful moments out of the blue. I can't believe she's gone. The logical side of me doesn't understand either. It's a void that doesn't make sense at the moment. I can't believe Randy has to cope with this now. I can't believe how quickly it all happened. My other uncle in

New Mexico sent me a video of a paraplegic weight-lifter via Facebook. I have no idea what in God's name he thinks he's getting at. Case in point: no one's interested in his blather right now.

    A song drones in the distance. The trees sway. The sun goes down. Birds sing their final melodies. A young Portuguese couple talks quietly in the next campsite.

    I can't believe my actual luck as a human...on this trip. But the truth is, the luck seems to follow when I'm engaged in the upmost attempt to be my best true self. Not the self others might want, not when I'm engaged with any level of proving anything; but when I'm chasing that connection. That communion with a sort of energy out there...that blue glow of a crystal lake or pure snow or mountain ridge against the sky. That sweet ambrosia of the forest that you only smell once in awhile. That unfolding mystery that I still subscribe to. That I trust.

    Before we left Ashland, the girl in the coffee hut gave me a free coffee "Because I'd had a rough enough day already..." I went to the ATM and broke a $20 and gave her $5. "Thanks. That was awesome of you."

    Trail magic. I don't know. Counting one magical moment to the next. Carry the sadness. Memories of my whole life. The triumphs and failures. Just a human.

December 12, 2018
Three Journals

    A gift from Hanne who spent the last of her existing trail funds and took a plane from Zurich to come visit me in Albuquerque.
    So, I walked from Mexico to Canada along the Pacific Crest Trail. It took six months. My mom died the day I reached Chester; exactly halfway. By then we'd all known it was only a matter of days. The shock was profound, but I don't think it would have made any sense whatsoever if I hadn't walked through it. It connected us in a way I never imagined and through that, it reconnected my Self with my Soul. I said goodbye that night with ten candles set on an old weathered plank of wood with ten reasons I was grateful to have her as a mother and set it adrift on Lake Almanor. I had one and a half bottles of wine in my system and nearly surmised to become captain of a great canoe heist, but Hanne talked me out of it. I watched the piece of wood slowly float out into the dark, glittering water with tears streaming down my face…because I just didn't understand. I didn't understand in a universe that I'd only recently come to regard as intelligent and full of purpose, where everything held some sort of meaning. I felt like a victim then. I felt at the same time, a sort of awe and reverence and gratitude. I knew it had meaning and that nothing happens by chance, but it felt so final. So unfair. So fundamentally wrong.
    And I kept walking with Hanne…over mountains, through fields, around volcanos, by streams, past people, past other hikers, Trail Angels, nomads, vagabonds, explorers, seekers and searchers from all over the world.
    Hanne's favorite podcast said something like: "Give up your personal history." Yeah, but I like my personal history. Most of it anyway. I've had an amazing life for better or worse. Yet once

again, everything's changed. If there be life, let it be magical. Let it inspire. Let me let go of the person that needs *so much*. Let me give instead. Let me practice magic by giving.

Journal
July 10, 2018
(Mosquitos are From Hell)

We made it. Only three 25-mile days between stomach issues and swarms of Satan's Little Helpers trying extract blood from us at every turn. It was rough.

Every hiker we came across lamented the mosquitos of Oregon. Unheard of. Unprecedented levels of high-pitched annoyance and itching places you forgot about.

Well, we're here. Crater Lake is a great place even though we haven't seen the lake yet. We heard it's the deepest lake in the states.

We've decided to chill tomorrow. Sleep in. Get breakfast. So, five or so miles up on the rim. Get the resupply and call home. Blog. Coffee. Do what we need to do basically. There's always time constraints but they're guideposts, not laws.

Ran into Pavlina and Petr after two and a half months the other day! When was the last time we saw them? Whitney? Wow. They're doing well. Had the same experience in the Sierras as we did. Jumped up and have probably been ahead of us for a few weeks. Good to see them. (They've gotten *really* fast)

A bunch of us convened on Crater Lake. Snowman and a few more plus a kid from Michigan. Good little group. We're all in the hiker campground right now. All us crazy hikers with our crazy stories.

Journal
July 16, 2018
Shelter

Crater Lake: a sight to behold. Walked the alternate rim trail for hours. Officially entered into "Mosquito Alley". I would call it the stretch from Crater Lake to Elk Lake. Right now, we're twelve miles outside Odell Lake and Shelter Cove. Did a zero there…breakfast and dinner. Resupply box from Ashland and a few more items from store and hiker box. We're learning the routine. The walk was three days at 25 miles per day from Crater Lake. Ungodly swarms of mosquitos. I'd lost my head net. Used the DEET liberally. Couldn't care less what chemicals "may harm you in the state of California". Although, all studies I read turned up nothing particularly alarming. Still got nailed a dozen times. Mosquitos flying in my mouth. Kamikaze mosquitos into my ramen. Following us into the tent. Never experienced anything like it. Otherwise, a fine sloping series of stretches. Amazing that such a small creature can drive you nearly mad with frustration. Got to Shelter Cove at Lake Odella; a great fishing resort / RV park with hiker rates for camping. Not a single mosquito on resort property. I don't get it…but was beyond relieved to sit outside enjoying our dinners and walk by the lake instead of cowering in apprehension. Met John and planned a zero with Kris when we get to the youth camp three days away. He brought watermelon, Gatorade, home-made blueberry muffins and gave us so much great tactical advice as we go through his part of the PCT (They live in Silverton, OR). He dropped us off at the trail up the street and we braved more mosquitos for a few hours (this time with a head-net) and made our way up the hill. We'll get to the youth camp and the next morning we'll meet Kris and finally get some good internet to handle 101 things on hold, work on Hanne's Visa extension, make phone calls, patch the hole in my sleeping pad, and sleep in a bed for one or two nights. John and Kris have been a great resource through this, lending time and energy and advice.

Glad to have the mosquito net more than anything. A level of added security instead of having your day and energy hijacked by those little bastards. Got a care box from Aubrey too. Some Darn Tough socks. NICE. Really nice of her. I need to keep the postcards going. I'll be out of money again by Silverton. Will have to make that call and see if the trail continues. Should be fine...

Love you mom.

Timberline Lodge Lobby

    Finding favor through fine sand. The footprints of others shadowed under a full moon. Silver light shooting through pines. Mt Hood under the heavens in a silent wreath of snow. Beyond the brush to my right, a vertical drop hundreds of feet to a rushing stream below. I can hear it now…the only sound. Everything else is silent. I am silent. My mind is silent. There's no more pain. I understand my feet are swollen. I understand it's 1 am; that we've been walking for 17 hours.
    "Hey mom" I say.
    "I'm out here." Whispering as if to give coordinates.
    "Just look at that." and I motion to the mountain.
    In the distance Timberline Lodge is glowing yellow and orange. I feel like I'm in Russia. In Chile. High in the Swiss Alps. Somewhere without a name, a place that exists in the imagination-for the imagination.
    I don't know what day of the week it is. I don't know what happens when I return home…how I return home…where home is anymore. I wonder if I've ever wanted a home to begin with and what home really means.
    We cross a small creek with a flat piece of wood over it. At the top of a hill overlooking the lodge we find a clearing beneath a tree. 35 miles. This will be our longest day on the PCT.
    Immediate sleep punctuated by flashes of nerve pain until 8 in the morning.
    We wander down to the lodge. In the bathroom I find an old rag in an open janitor's closet and scrub the black dirt from my feet and legs. Hotel guests appear and disappear. I barely notice. We're here to grab our resupply box and sit down for the breakfast buffet.

An hour later we're charging phones and answering mail in the great lobby. Tourists wind through with kids in tow. Time to get back on the trail.

Journal
July 18, 2018

    Two fast 20-something-mile days. Terrain pretty flat with some more burnt forests, plenty of lakes and ponds, streams, grass, forest...MOSQUITOS. DARN THEM TO SHMECKENSTEIN!
    As if I'm the first hiker to have that sentiment. Little we can do, however. Just continue to move north. Some say Elk Lake is where it lightens up but we're at a pond ten miles north and it's still pretty brutal. Tried to patch my pad tonight after submerging it in the pond. Might work. If not, more patches at REI by Silverton.
    Crossing the lava fields tomorrow and a restricted area called Obsidian. I bet there's lots of obsidian around there. The fun thing about having no cell service is that you can't Google things ahead of time. Time and experience go back to their normal flow. Of course, Guthook takes 90 percent of the guesswork out of the PCT, but we can't be Luddites out here every day. Hanne likes the info. I just hike. Grab water here and there. Eat. Hike. Swear at mosquitos.
    Yesterday spoke to Randy for a moment when Hanne got service on a hill. He's going to send some more money my way...don't know how much. Feel irresponsible and under-prepared for this magnitude of a journey...but I learned. Being grateful...will do a thank you blog because honestly, it took lots of people to make this happen. Hitches, family, friends, ex-girlfriends, cousins and random strangers...here we are doing the legwork yes, but it begins to feel like you're part of a team, a network that wants you to keep moving. Other hikers, glampers, coffee shop owners, forest service workers. Back in the "real world" it wouldn't matter. Out here, we're part of something special and I don't dare take it for granted. As Randy said: "It's

a tribute hike now". It always was, but when I've got a level head and few minutes I say "Hi" to mom. Like other friends who have passed, I don't know if she's gone or what that means. I don't know where the spirit / soul goes when we die but I know it isn't the end. Hanne and I were talking about what happens after this. Two more months out here. Plenty of hiking still to do, but it's starting to occupy more space in our thoughts.

A moment into these somber reflections, two bare-tooth dobermans leading six horses and three riders bursts out onto the trail scaring Hanne's socks off *and*, just as I write that, the most insane sounds outside the tent. What the...

Hmmm. Sometimes a tree falls just as you're about to fall asleep and it's probably the worst jolt of the past few weeks, but that's the trail. At least it landed over there.

At this pond we've got got four other hikers. We came in around 9 pm. Ate dinner. Got into the tent. One more day and a half and it's showers and a ton of...(pen runs out of ink here)

Journal
July 24, 2018
New Things. Old Things.

The last page of this trail journal. Bought a new one in Silverton. Got off the trail for three days after Big Lake Youth Camp to stay with Kris at her and John's house. Go, go, go. Nothing but driving to stores. Blowing tons of money on new shoes, patch kits, total resupply for Washington all boxed. They'll ship from Silverton! It's a huge help and as far as Trail Angels go, John and Kris are more like Trail Magicians.

Hanne got her Visa application forms all printed out. I reprinted my thru-hike pass. We ate out. Grabbed coffee. Cooked Kris dinner and just talked about whatever. Still, something nagged me the whole time. Still can't put my finger on it…forced proximity to cities or something? Spent most of the side-trip deferring to Hanne…you know, we're both awesome on the trail and we both get moody in the towns. Like being thrust into The Rules again…and there's no real rest in towns. It's just getting ready for the next stretch and we don't like more than a day of it. There was just so much to do in Silverton. Sigh. Anyway…we're in the Cascades. One more week in Oregon. That went by pretty darn fast. I've mused what to do when I get back after this adventure…something's coming together. Slowly. But it's too early to tell. Just glad to be back in the woods. Need to recharge. Really love the campgrounds and resorts and state parks as far as places with any amenities but cities just don't do anything for me…still, thank goodness for John and Kris. We love those two.

Journal
July 30, 2018
Ore-gone

Woke late. Really late. Hanne still sore from the 35 miles. I didn't mind sleeping in either. Hit the trail around 11 am. All kinds of dynamic terrain within ten miles. Rock creek crossing. Tons of people on the Timberline Trail route. Up a long steep climb through forest. Past Ramona falls and out to a picnic bench by a trailhead / parking lot for lunch. Then further up-n-down. Mostly forest. Crossing boulder fields, riding crest lines and zig-zagging down small valleys. All in a day. Helped two lost hikers within 20 minutes. One was just going the wrong way on the PCT. The other was a day hiker who missed the junction to Bald Mountain. Good pace. Quiet mind. Just feeling solid again. Hanne says "Stop gassing me!!!" Haha. She's usually in front. Always after lunch. What can you do…

Beautiful sundown. Smoke from a fire below. Every day, at least once it seems, I feel sincerely lucky…then I get tired and think about food. Tomorrow waking early to do the 20 miles to Cascade Locks. Maybe a zero. We'll see. We don't really need zeros anymore, but some towns are just nice to hang out in for a day. Plenty to do. Four-day resupply. Laundry. Shower. Calling home. Met a couple SOBOS this evening. Young guy with his friend. Fresh-faced and happy. Hah. We are too…underneath all the grime and miles, just not as openly exuberant as we were the first month. Refreshing to see though.

Journal
August 1, 2018
Washington

We spent a day in Cascade Locks. Beautiful grassy tent site on the Columbia River in an RV / camping park. Decent food. Nice people. The SOBOS are really starting to appear. Talked to a few on the trail and in town. They're all smiles. Heard the snow was bad up north about two months ago but it's all gone. Bags really need a wash. Getting that hiker trash smell to them. Did the resupply in a little market for four days good. Dinner at the Alehouse and Thunder Island Brewery. I've opted out of beer this time. Taking care of my stomach, even taking activated charcoal supplements, which I feel are doing wonders right now. The grassy hiker area was full the first night we got in. Talked to a few people. I want to ask these SOBOS how Washington has been. Breakfast twice at the Bridgeside Diner. Tough getting through to everyone this time. Phone tag. Sent a chess computer to Lauren's oldest son Andrew. Also, three postcards to Aubrey, Lauren and Tad back in Albuquerque. Looking at Europe for one-foot-in living. Might be the way to go. The right choice will present itself. Felt really rested and peaceful in Cascade Locks. I think I'll return to there if I can someday. Kind of blue collar. Small. Just felt right. We crossed the Bridge of the Gods this afternoon around 2 pm. Windy. Trying to take pictures. "Welcome to Washington". Wow. Started walking up and up almost immediately through dense humid jungle. Kids everywhere headed to the lake a mile up to swim. We crossed a few little bridges and made about thirteen miles to a saddle overlooking Columbia Gorge and Mt Rainier. Everything is still smokey. Nice breeze going on tonight. We're scaling back to 20 miles per day now. Gonna take four zeros in Washington. Come in nice and slow (like 20 miles is slow) but yeah, compared to the pace in Oregon we need to chill just to enjoy the days a little more. At 25 per day, we got into camp late and slept in too much. 20 per day feels really solid now. One month 'till the Canadian border. Unreal. I don't feel like I've written enough or taken enough pictures, but it's all a big experience that'll take ages to put into context. For now, enjoying August, then head back to the Sierras for three final weeks. Feel like I'm already getting post-PCT blues before I'm even done. I could hike / live like this again and again. And some days I think "Man, when is this over?"

Goodnight, mom.
You're with me always.

January 21, 2019
Leave

I want to hide.
I want to go back to Campo on March 19th, 2018.
The cool morning air. The smell of the dirt. Everything leading up To this moment...
The unknowns.
When my mother was still on this side of the veil with us...
When it meant something.
The sheer proportions of an adventure...
Too large to measure.
Too unreal to evaluate in any sense.
Until months down the road.
Until it had sunk in and saturated our bones.
Until we were strong and made of nothing but lean muscle.
Waking with the birds and sniffing the air for the same information As the coyote.
It becomes so trying to add dimensions to this idea when you're Back home.
You had a hard enough time knowing what was what on the trail...
And by the end of the whole thing, all you cared about was the Right pass under the right dusk light.
Chasing view after majestic view deep into the day.
The sheer simplicity of that life matched with the silent Understanding of what each day entailed...
Nothing left untied yet able to improvise a hundred times without hesitation...
None of those bored whims to torture the weary hiker...
Three months later my knees still hurt when I try to run.
I still wake up thinking:
What is this?

What is this madness I capitulated to?
I'm speaking of the before *and* after.
All the time spent making music...
Like some kind of causal loop...
An experiment gone astray.
People like us...
We were meant for the mountains.
To feel more at home under clouds of stars.
Cities make such little sense.
They feel insane.
Like prison theme-parks.
We tell ourselves to readjust. To accept. To move on.
The city cats all tell you in unison to do the same.
People who've never been outside the city.
Who walk from room to room.
Climate-controlled sanctuary to climate-controlled sanctuary.
They drone on about that one time they "went on a hike".
Or suggest I watch *"that hiking movie if I like hiking so much."*
(True story)
And it dons on me:
The city has everything...
Except spirit.
The one thing that makes life worth living.

"Modernism had two great wishes. It wanted its audience to be led toward a recognition of the social reality of the sign (away from the comforts of narrative and illusionism, was the claim); but equally it dreamed of turning the sign back to a bedrock of World / Nature / Sensation / Subjectivity which the to and fro of capitalism had all but destroyed."

-T.J. Clark

Journal
August 2, 2018
Deep Forest

Energy changes again. Deep forest. Almost rain forest. Clouds for the first time in a month. Morning mists-walking over and down a crest picking berries. No rush. An 18-mile day. A sort of rear-view mirror presents itself asking me how much I'm truly attached to music. Where it all comes from, what it means. What I observed even in the midst of it…feeling like I was on the sidelines even when I was front and center. Always the watcher…but the music remains. Its a strange relationship. It's in my head all day since I was very young and I never cared to combat the condition or overthink it. I assumed it was always there, like an appendage and nothing could be more natural. Music to the rhythm of my steps in the forest. One note for each rock I step on while crossing a creek. Either way, I've been keen to ignore music from outside sources for the majority of this adventure. Nothing on the iPhone. No iPod. The most we listen to is Phil Collins or Roxette here and there. It's all Hanne's music. Roxette is actually way better than I remember, but it begs the question: What do I do when I return home? I feel an obligation to make sure Randy's doing ok. God knows what he's going through. As for me…I feel anger still but it's not rage. It's a feeling of quiet resignation at the indignity of it all. Watching your mother have to capitulate to the system she tried to change. There aren't words a son can have or write so I don't. The only thing left is to know I'm out here doing this for her, while she was still here and now, in her memory. How did I know the PCT was going to be "it"? I've fallen in love with this trail over the past four months. I've lived out here. Slept out here. Met each day and each challenge day in and day out. Small miracles and random acts of kindness have defined the trail. So many inspired well-wishers young and old. So much love for the land. The people. The country. With all the inane broken records back in society I find the America that I truly love; that I'm truly proud of every day. Looking back in the rear-view mirror I'm almost shocked by what I'd bought into. I realized I was far more entertained by this chipmunk eating berries than by any television back home. Everything is integrated. Everything means something out here and Washington is beautiful so far. Actually looking forward to the next day. 20 more miles. Night, night.

Journal
August 4, 2018
Take Me Home Country Roads

As we entered the camp area tonight the first sound we heard was the wild shrieking of a teenager in the adjacent woods. Either the longest temper tantrum I've ever heard, schizophrenia or drugs. Hard to know these things. When we sat down for dinner the shrieking was accompanied by the POP! POP! POP! of a couple shotguns about an acre away…God knows what's being shot at this far below visibility. Finally, entering the chorus two acres in the other direction were the harmonious subtleties of two chainsaws cutting…wood I presume. The other two girls across the campsite were audibly not amused; trying to laugh it off. Eventually all subsided. I finished my Ramen, two Cliff bars and some cheese. Basically, I understocked food for this stretch. Other than the very end it was a beautiful day. A few lakes. Clouds. Thunder. Even a brief 30-min rain shower that had us scrambling for gear we hadn't used since Belden. And oddly, just as the rain started, we bumped into Shiva who we also hadn't seen since Belden. Nice pace. Good trail. No crazy hills. They're coming, I know. A good day to just meander around my own mind thinking of ways to make an income back home. Hanne also likes the travel-van-camping situation. We could give it a try at least. Tomorrow we wake early and go ten miles to the Trout Lake junction. Lunch, resupply, a good Nero, then ten more the next day. Time to wash. the. bags. The funk is real. Can't wait to have a clean bag again. Easy to forget but the bag is covered in more sweat, bacteria, and grime than anything else and it doesn't have the luxury of getting washed every few weeks. Anyhow, Night mom. Hope your spirit is free as a bird.

Journal
August 6, 2018
NOBOS and SOBOS

Got off the trail to resupply in Trout Lake. Started walking with our thumbs out. Brent stops up the road in a little red Honda Civic and takes us into town, giving us a brief tour. We set up camp behind the general store on a grassy lawn with a few other hikers. (It's starting to get cramped in some spots) the SOBOS are in full effect now. Cleaned up the street in the worst-smelling camp shower I'd ever encountered. Almost aborted, but I came out smelling a little better, nonetheless. Burgers and huckleberry shakes down the other way and more coffee. We stayed the night and cooked in our little pots and pans; spiral pasta and sauce with garlic and onion. Sorted the resupply we'd sent from Silverton. Checked to see status of possible exit from Hart's Pass. Starting to strategize getting back down to the Sierras. It's all coming up. A sort of sadness taking hold. Watching Hanne the other day picking berries, realizing I'm going to miss her. Neither of us know exactly what comes after this. We've been romantically involved since SOCAL. We walk. Avoid the topic. Sometimes I dream of just leaving for Switzerland. Other times I feel compelled to write more music. And, when I've got my head on straight, I feel like having some kind of future. Some kind of something. How do I get there when I have the soul of an explorer?

Journal
August 7, 2018
Too Many Hikers

Beautiful views of Mt Adams. Through pines and grassy flower-laden meadows. Sometimes I wish I could remember all my insights into the natural world, of this experience, that percolate through me each day. Unfortunately, after dinner the brain turns off immediately, then the body. Either way, we're out here. Noticed that we're often so far outside civilization that we don't see airplanes all day. Pretty remarkable. No contrails that litter the skies of any city back home. Of course, we're not "outside" civilization. Civilization was we know it, is a blip. The earth is 70 percent water to begin with. When I was at Kris and John's in Silverton I glanced at a globe they had upstairs. Our entire six-month trip amounted to less than a couple inches of land along the side of a continent that amounted to a large island beset by thousands of miles of ocean. And here we are. No way to escape the myopia of each stretch. It consumes to the body and requires the mind to retire. Day in and day out. There isn't the slightest chance of real boredom occurring. It's daily destinations that require everything you've got. I don't believe the PCT is a place to become spiritual, although these moments happen. It's just too tough. What it does is clear you out. There's just no room for bullshit. Maybe what most people are calling spiritual in the post-modern world is just a glimpse of their unbullshitted selves. So many hikers today. Lots of SOBOS. Everyone's on the trail now. Seems like you can't walk a mile without passing someone. Of course, everyone's kind and generally friendly. Leapfrogging with a character called Tika who sleeps in a hammock. Gregarious. Another couple we met in Trout Lake, "Ghost Hiker" and her friend, are crossing our paths here and there along with a younger girl named Lana. What are we all doing out here? Tika asked if I was tired... "...now that we're getting closer to the border." I said "Sure, but I'd rather be out here than back there."

   Some people we've spoken with are actually aching to get back to their careers and normal lives. I just don't care. Doesn't interest me in least other than finding a way to fund the next adventure. No real attachment to anywhere anymore. I'll occasionally long for a warm bed and a movie but even things like media take on a different meaning out here. I realized I can run entire movies and ideas in my mind all day if I want. I replay songs, scenes, whatever at my whim. To imagine we stare at TVs when the mind has such profound capabilities. Makes me ponder plenty. And now it's time for sleep.

Love,
Will

Journal
August 11, 2018
Mystery

Morning shrouded in mists. Long conversations over spiritual matters. What it means to be out here. There's an element of needing physical grounding. To be rooted and aware of the physical world. I'm prone to fantasy. My imagination goes…places. I can spend four hours on the trail thinking about one particular topic. One idea, looking at all the angles. Other days I feel dumb as a doorbell. Today was lively though. Washington has yet to disappoint. We walked through fog and clouds. Lunched by a pristine lake. Took our time. A little too much time…since by the time we found camp it was well after dark and my hands were almost immobile. I have this syndrome. I forget the name, but basically my body over-reacts when it thinks my core temperature is being threatened. It can be a balmy 50 Fahrenheit and one of my toes will suddenly lose feeling and turn white. Kind like frost-bite without the frost. Anyway, it was epic on every level today. Passed quite a few day hikers as we came into Rainier National Forest. Some days completely re-invigorate my purpose for being out here. Also figured it would have been July 30th if my mom's soul had been reincarnated according to Buddhist tradition. Same amount of days it takes for the pineal gland to form after conception… Love. Goodnight.

It's Already Mid-August
Letters Home #6

We took our first zero in three weeks at Snoqualmie on the 15th of August, tripping down a rocky dirt road beneath the ski lifts and into a valley filled with smoke from three separate fires. We booked a room at the Summit Inn, washed off the most obvious layers of dirt and headed straight for Commonwealth; the only open restaurant in town. The last stretch to the middle of Washington had changed the way we experienced the trail with more milestones, old faces and the Canadian border now a little over two weeks away. We'd been out here on the trail for roughly five months and it wasn't until Snoqualmie that we realized how much everything had changed since March 19th when we showed up at Campo with heavy packs and too much water. There was this idea at the beginning that *some* change was imminent, that I'd walk a scenic trail dominated by alpine forest and bucolic sunsets and campgrounds, slowly finding the relevance of the whole thing...that it might appear one morning and I could nod to myself while I stuffed things into the bag for another day, but this isn't accurate either. The truth is I didn't know what to expect. I didn't know what I didn't know and for most of this journey I've simply tried to assess where I am, where I need to be and what needs to be done to get there. I did not anticipate the actual umbrella under which all this might occur. I can only say that yes, walking 20 to 30 miles per day for five months in the wilderness will undoubtedly change you. It would change anyone and to those day hikers that we pass full of questions and wistful "somedays" we still say, "Just start walking." We've met people from age 17 to 75 on the PCT. People who have taken years to complete all the sections. People who were terrified of being alone at the beginning passing us a thousand miles later with confidence and a completely new energy about them. People who got off the trail to nurse injuries then got back on and kept going. We all learned how to adapt in the end. It's been the only hard and fast rule. The trail doesn't automatically change anyone. We both agree it's not a cure, not a place to come for that all-encompassing moment of revelation. It's brutal. It's exhausting on a level I didn't understand before regardless of whatever competitive sports or journeys I'd done in the past. It also required us to do the one thing we weren't anticipating: let go of control. Put your thumb out and hope for the best. The trail doesn't get easier even with the relatively forgiving stretches in Oregon. What happens is that the body and mind begin to anticipate a sort of grind and you start pushing through with less and less complaints. You become acclimated to a certain level of pressure. You slowly understand the cycles of your own inner animal-that regardless of how well you eat, how much you paid for your gear, and how long you spent stretching in the morning, you're going to have days where you just feel off, nauseated, and moody.

    We sat eating bacon-wrapped stuffed jalapeños at Commonwealth with the same childish satisfaction we felt during our first burgers in Big Bear. Now we were actively working on our exit strategy for Hart's Pass. We'd have to set up camp, wake up, tag the border and return that evening. Then wake up and get a ride to Stehekin or Mazama where we hoped to shuttle into Seattle and find transportation back to Bishop to finish the Yosemite stretch before the end of September. We looked at all the old photos on our phones of the first few months, laughing at how inept we were at certain points and choices we "strategically" made, but what mattered was that we were here, that we'd kept moving...and for all the struggles, bites and bruises there hadn't been a single moment of regret.

    At the Washington border we'd come out of a fairly steep series of switchbacks into the tiny town of Cascade Locks along the great Columbia River. On the other side through the near-constant fire haze was the town of Stevenson. Connecting the two was The Bridge of the Gods, a great steel structure dating back to the active trading days along the northwest waterways. Of course, these passages are still much-used and great cargo ships churn through hourly.

We pitched our tents on a fine grassy embankment at the RV park where a dozen or so other hikers were set up just above the south side of the river and decided because of the timing and scenery and hiker-discounts everywhere that we'd take a zero here.

I'd never felt so calm on a zero before. Typically, there's so much to do that towns are far more stressful than the trail, but we took our time wandering here and there from grocers to coffee shops and showers. A different sense began to overtake us (and I think all the other NOBO hikers as well). Finally. Washington. While it felt like we'd been in California for a year, Oregon had seen us averaging 25 miles per day and I felt as though between the pace and rabid swarms of mosquitos we'd nearly breezed through to where we found ourselves now...perched on a picnic table watching flocks of geese and an old red and white vintage steamboat take tourists to and from the eastern docks.

More thoughts on what happens after this. It's on everyone's lips now. 'Where's home for ya? What's your plan? You guys got jobs to get back to?' Other hikers laugh it off. We joke that the good thing is that you've got six months to think about your angle of re-entry. Although I rarely think about it in a tactical, adult way. It's a lifelong balancing act between adventure, creativity, and basic survival. The older I get the more I appreciate things like plans and logic. On the other hand, this journey has uplifted a whole series of assumptions I had back in January when I was convinced I could take a four-season tent on a 2,652-mile hike. If I'm to become tactical with age I hope it's the same sort of tactical that allows me to appreciate these sorts of things. The people I've met on the trail alone have already upended what I thought about the hows and whys of life. The support I've received and words of encouragement have been enough to convince me to stay on that silent rarefied course. It doesn't need approval. It creates its own sort of weather like the High Sierras. So, when I think of "what to do" when this is finished, I think "Wait...I'm not on vacation. It's just the appropriate bridge to whatever comes next."

Four days after Cascade Locks we came out at Forest Rd 23 and stuck our thumbs out until Brent from Trout Lake stopped in his little red Honda Civic and turned the hazards on. He drove us the 13 miles into town and gave us a quick tour of the amenities including one cafe and one public shower at the one campground up the street from the one general store. We thanked him and waved goodbye and the ladies at the store said they'd let hikers camp on the lawn as long as we pitched our tents after the sun left the grass and had them up before it hit the grass again in the morning.

We sprayed the bags down with degreaser and hosed them off for the first time since Campo. We never took to the term "hiker trash" which was a sort of badge of honor the younger kids claimed. It meant going as long as you could without showering or changing clothes until you basically resembled a sort of homeless shade of brown and smelled so awful that it literally stung people's noses wherever you went. We felt this was a bit rude to families and day hikers or people whose services and charity we depended on. There were a few stories of 20-something characters abusing the selflessness of others and using the PCT as a free-for-all (probably because it was the first time mom and dad couldn't tell them what to do) but these were few and far between for the most part. We just didn't understand what was so wild and natural about smelling like garbage when hygiene was natural to every wild creature in the forests we walked through. Either way we had started to realize our bags needed attention...badly. So we did our best that evening.

We updated pics and wrote home and ate at the cafe and shared a huckleberry milkshake and bought onions and garlic and pasta at the general store and cooked it all in the Jet Boil and my camp stove. We've become pretty good at cheffing with what we've got, packing small amounts of olive oil and seasoning for each stretch.

When we wanted to head back out to the trail the next day we called Rick on the Trail Angel list at the store and he showed up in about 20 minutes and gave us some local history and talked about his volunteer work on the PCT, going out with crews and making sure the trail was 18" wide. As we were waving goodbye at the trailhead, I realized I didn't have my phone on me. Hanne rolled her eyes once but half-smiling because I lost things pretty much on a weekly basis. Sunglasses, knives, satchels, my spork, the sacred Cholula, and now my phone, but we didn't skip a beat and our thumbs went back up and ten minutes later old Brent came swerving into the trailhead with his Civic and twenty minutes later the lady at the store handed me my phone. Some hikers had just brought it in from the bench where we'd been waiting for Rick. Then, Brent said he'd take us back to the trail AGAIN and twenty minutes after that we were headed for White Pass. After a few minutes it was clear he didn't remember picking us up the day before, so we went through our story again.

This stretch took only a few days, but we got an incredibly close look at the Miriam fire and the crews that were trying to contain it. We also started passing more and more SOBOS heading the other direction. They seemed full of the fresh optimism we'd felt back around Big Bear; many dealing with the same early thru-hike foot problems we'd dealt with as well. It's also been good to get their perspectives and info from up the trail. The day before White Pass we were hiking up a barren stretch before Goat Rocks and we noticed a massive plume of vapor expanding above the horizon. It wasn't smoke but I'd never seen a storm grow so fast. We were mystified but we were hiking directly toward it over the Knife Edge by Goat Rocks and soon we saw smoke mingling with the cloud. The hotshots must have just dumped something on the Miriam Fire we thought. Only moments later though, a SOBO came careening down the side of the Knife Edge, seemingly in a panic, saying something to the effect that *this* fire wasn't the Miriam Fire at all, but a new one that had sprung up just hours ago on the west side of the detour we hoped to use. This meant we were essentially walking through a fire sandwich with Miriam burning to the east and this one on the other side…which gave us pause, because we assumed we were walking far to the west of the closure and now it looked like we were hiking directly toward a new fire that was burning so fast it'd taken over the whole side of the mountain. We thanked her for the info and debated what to do.

"If this is a new fire we might be out of luck. The wind is heading east up here but it looks like the smoke is moving west over there. How fast can fires move?"
"I don't know…very fast. We shouldn't mess with it."
"But then we lose the window if they close the detour."
"Not worth it."
"But then we have to backtrack three days."
"Hmmm."

   We spotted some tents far below by a stream and decided to see if they had better info. Half a mile later we spotted yet another fire burning down in the valley.

"Wait a minute, which fire was she talking about? This little one? Because this is pretty far west of the detour. The big one *has* to be Miriam. Was she confused?"

We made our way down to the tents and realized it was Ghost Hiker and her pal we'd just met in Trout Lake.

"No, no. The big one is Miriam."

Ok, that made sense. So we got as close as we could to the detour trail that night and hoped to push through before this smaller fire caused any problems.

In the morning we found the PCT closed off with long strips of yellow tape and official detour notes from the Forest Service. The air was incredibly smokey but we pushed on, crossing a few streams and hopping over logs to get to the highway that would take us into White Pass.

Around noon we caught a ride in and sat at the convenience store with some other hikers. News was that the detour we'd just taken was now officially closed as well but people kept walking in saying they'd just done it.

Across the street hundreds of tents lined up in rows. Hot shots were brought in from as far as New Zealand to fight the blaze and we set up above a lake behind the store in a dry patch with a lone picnic table. The best part about White Pass was that the coin-op shower kept running after your five minutes were up, which gave me enough time to get the deeper dirt out of my toenails. It's the little things...which brings us to Snoqualmie Pass. We're hoping to finally get past the smoke during this next stretch, but it seems like the whole northwest is smokey right now. The plan is a seven-mile climb today then two days to Steven's Pass. So close. And so many more miles ahead.

Love,
W

Journal
August 17, 2018
Exhausted

We are in the northern Cascades. And they are slow-going. Epic climbs and descents. Rocky footwork all day. Stomach still not 100 percent but took another round of charcoal. Didn't leave camp until 9:45 am so we didn't arrive until just after 10 pm. Headlamp batteries toast so I used my phone to see the last couple miles. The morning scenery was gorgeous. No two ways about it. Walking through clouds, lakes and creeks with wooden bridges all day. Some sort of fairy tale. It was that last 5-mile ascent that killed me. I knew it would. Oh well. Pray for recovery while I sleep. More of the same tomorrow but we'll get up earlier. Ate a full bag of freeze-dried something so I think I got enough calories. We're just shy of halfway in Washington as far as miles. The map has us well north of center and it's already the 17th. We should get to the border on the 1st or 2nd. Different moods / thoughts. Sometimes anticipating, sometimes dreading the end of all this, but we're far from the end. Very, very far.

Journal
August 18, 2018
Memory and Motion

Lost in my head most of the day. Seems to be cycles that plague me from time to time. I just let it flow; never try to condemn whatever I'm processing but sometimes the mind is too loud. Nine times out of ten it has more to do with digestion, but I think the system is clear. Wake up to the smell of burning wood with ashes falling around the tent. Whole side of the next ridge was a white-out of smoke. Passed a local on the way down and talked for a minute. He said it was the same three fires around Stehekin and east of Snoqualmie. Either way he seemed unfazed so we walked on. Agitated sinuses, eyes, etc. Passed whole families and plenty of other hikers. They all seemed perfectly in their element with the summer fires. It's a yearly thing. Today was tough but not like yesterday. Just plenty of up and down. A few stream crossings but not too many sights due to the smoke. Made it to a little spot next to three converging streams and set up camp next to a guy going by Sunshine, watching old episodes of The Office on his phone when we came up. Talked a bit about the trail etc. Tomorrow: Into Stevens Pass, shower, meals, laundry. Off to the final stretch!

Stevens Pass

"I've had a dream somewhere along the line...a dream about this place. A place like this. A place that means the same thing as this. It's the end of a long day and we've come over the mountains, under the ski lifts, along a grassy ridge and down into Stevens Pass. We've walked up through the trees toward the Mountaineer's Lodge that hosts hikers throughout the season.

"Don't step on that!"

The power lines leading up the dirt road to the lodge have been brought down by a fallen tree, splintered in the middle of the road, its great trunk recently cut up and pushed aside to allow access.

The line runs the length of the road all the way up to the lodge... Two people on the third story balcony wave down. A man and a woman.

"Hello! Welcome! Come on up! There's no power but we've got spaghetti and salad!"

"How do we get in?" We shouted.

"Come in through the bottom and take the stairs to the top!"

"Ok, thanks!"

We dragged our legs up the four flights and came out on the balcony where pots and plates and bowls of salad and bottles of wine were laid out along the top 2x6" rail 30 feet above the driveway.

"Heaven...we're here. Thank you so much."

I immediately dropped my bag and sat in a small plastic chair in the corner.

"Food?"

"Yeah definitely...in a sec. Just have to sit here...for a minute."

The great red lodge stands silent and dark save for a dozen or so tea candles and lanterns dropped in strategic locations from the balcony. Then, a great room with a long wooden table lead further in toward the kitchen. The oven is heated by gas, so they've got loads of noodles bubbling up top and a pan of homemade tomato sauce steaming to the side. The smell of garlic.

The smell of wood. Old wood.
Something was transporting me to a place and time I hadn't known for ages. It felt like home for some reason. Maybe it was the gentle candles alongside the dusk light, changing from amber to deep orange while we sat together and looked into the distance.

Then, it was blue and darker blue and then a pair of silhouettes appeared in the distance where the road curved back into the forest.

"Food and wine up here!" We called down.
"There's no power and it's awesome!"

Down in the very bottom floor of the lodge are the showers and laundry. There's no dryers just a room with fans blowing from every direction where you can hang your wet clothes. It smells like hiker. Bad.

On the very top level where the roof comes together, there's a smaller room with sleeping pads lying alongside each wall and a door that leads to a tiny balcony with stairs dropping all the way down to the driveway.

The level below that the third floor and it's also nothing but bunks and pads for hikers, mountaineers and skiers, all who rent the lodge in different numbers throughout the year.

I learn our host is a fellow from Seattle who had done a stretch of the trail a year before and fallen in love with the lodge when he came through and decided to become a volunteer. All that entailed was greeting guests, collecting fees, having them log in and cooking a breakfast and dinner for everyone which typically used all hands on deck to chop, boil and otherwise prep the massive meals that made their way out to the main room.

The kitchen, living room / lounge area and eating tables were all on the second floor and the kitchen itself came stocked with every imaginable tool, blender, spatula, and corkscrew one could imagine; all collected over the last century and stacked, hung, and hidden in corners from the ceiling and the walls. Cutting boards sat ready in rows next to towers of mixing bowls like stacked like Russian dolls…

We lugged our packs up a set of narrow vertical stairs to the third floor dorm and set them on the top bunks and headed back down for food.

The two silhouettes were Belay and Cheeky from the US and Ireland. The same glowing smiles and delight in the small things was written across their faces like most thru-hikers. It said "Ahhh, rest." Now we were all in Washington just days from the border and we'd seen enough trail to understand what a treat this great old lodge was.

For most of us it had been a combination of rugged sites (flat areas good enough to pitch a tent), a few designated campgrounds and KOAs…a few hostels here and there and PCT-oriented places like Hiker Heaven and Hiker Town in southern California. Once in awhile we'd grab a cheap motel and even did a couple Air BnBs those first couple of weeks while we got our legs under us. To set up in a mid-century ski lodge like this felt true to the spirit of the adventure I'd set out on and the old charm and ambience of the place took me somewhere deep inside myself; somewhere in the imagination that I'd set out to encounter one way or another.

We poured wine and dove into the food, sharing our best stories well into the night. When the rest of the group learned Hanne had competed in the Olympics for bob-sledding the questions came in twice as fast and it turned from a rustic mountain sanctuary to a magical night between total strangers.

The laughter reached fever pitch and echoed down the dim hallways until BOOM! The electricity came surging back all at once, triggering half a dozen appliances, machines, and pumps. It was a long night…and we fell asleep in the dorm with a tiny window propped open to smell the pines. It just felt right. No matter what had happened. No matter the past or the future. Ineffable was the word.

Journal
August 22, 2018

    As it grows nearer, a sort of calm descends. For now. I overheard Hanne crying in the afternoon and asked what the matter was.

"It's only 30 more trail days and I don't want to go home and I don't want to leave you."

    I've thought about having to say goodbye to someone you've come to love through 6 months of thru-hiking or something similarly intense. It's a bond that feels stronger than any bond I have back home, wherever that is. I imagine going to Switzerland, just taking everything back over the ocean and starting over…again, but we also understand: Nothing will compare to this in terms of sheer living, adventure, and love. There's no way to describe to people what this is like. My blogs are totally inadequate. Words mean nothing out here anyway unless its tactical information. How do we *return* home? Especially when neither of us really care to? I could keep walking and roaming indefinitely if money permitted. And what are we going back to? My mother will be gone. Most people barely noticed, but some old friends have cheered me on. Every sentiment on social media just seems absurd and useless. I sleep better in a tent on a punctured mat than a bed now. Just like when I did the bike trip at thirteen. Nature and nonstop camping seems normal. The trail truly *does* provide and the mystical synchronicities are known by nearly all of us. Now these sunsets and quiet moments are becoming a bit somber. A bit more visceral. The adrenaline is on the wane and we know it's two stretches and back for three weeks in the Sierra. And then what? One day at a time…still. Awareness.

Journal
August 23rd, 2018
Epic

Head finally feels like it's cleared a little from the discombobulating smoke we've been dealing with. Moderately clear skies exposed vistas, summits, glaciers that boggled the senses. Twice this week I've felt the overwhelming "magical something". At the lodge and then today. It's not one tree, one lake, or mountain. It's the moment. Standing atop the last pass before heading down to Mica Lake felt so otherworldly. And then, reaching the site while a distant pink and yellow sunset danced on the water. All these moments, coupled with the aroma that comes off the mountains. It's some sort of ambrosia to me and I feel dazed and bewildered; enchanted by such direct access to beauty.

Dozens of pictures today. Epic climbs. 20.6 miles. Blowdowns everywhere. Leapfrogging same Swedish, German, Latvian, Estonian, Aussie kids since Stevens Pass. Two more days 'till Stehekin. No SOBO news from fires / closures. Wish I could send these pictures to mom. Felt first moment of clarity about it in awhile. The crushing disappointment she must have felt when the transplant failed. The shock of the diagnosis alone. Every bit of news just took more and more of her will and it was so painful to watch. I don't know how long I'll be processing this. I just don't want denial, avoidance, or nihilism. I want to honor a life. To show that she made a difference.

Journal
August 27, 2018

    A few days between worlds…the Holden Lutheran mining co-op hydroelectric-volunteer-resort where that we opened our wallets again, getting laundry / room / breakfast & dinner plus a free shuttle ride to the ferry to Stehekin. It was all surreal as villages and towns and our general existence over the last five months goes. One interesting coincidence, bizarre encounter, friendly passerby to the next. The ferry ride was beautiful if too short. We bought a couple drinks, enjoyed them on the bottom deck, then went up top to feel the wind and spray coming off the boat. We've met so many people the past week; seems like everyone from Stevens Pass or before is now part of this larger movement toward the border. We cross paths, wave from campgrounds, share benches during resupply.

    Once again, I'm the only American which gives me a sort of easy detachment from having to be anything. Stayed a night in Stehekin. Cool little place. Not even a village or town - just a place where you can get in or out by boat or watercraft. Dinner, blah blah. Internet I couldn't care less about, but it's got to be done. A few postcards sent and resupply. Had to get separate permits for N. Cascades National Park. Every night had to have a specific campsite tracked and locked down so we opted for a 60-mile in-and-out to touch the border. Hanging food is mandatory and we've got no problem with that. We like it high and far away. We're at the first site tonight. Eleven miles from the High Bridge Ranger Station. We'll do only six more to the HW 20 and hitch to the East Bank Trail at Ross Lake for the final approach. Have I already written this? Anyway. The grade should be easy up the shore so we hope to make some miles, hit the border, and head down to Bishop. Maybe stay at the hostel again.

Feel like mom's passing is finally getting past my shock barrier and hitting my heart. Last two days just waves of sadness. Not for anything in particular. Just...can't believe my mom is gone. Can't believe it happened like that...that uncle Kim passed away a week before. It's so much...yet so little was said. What's the parallel narrative here? A brother and sister dying just weeks apart? Out here on the trail I see how nature works every day. It's so child-like. It never holds onto anything. It just does what it can. The rivers flow where they can. They stop when they can't. It's a revelation of pure humility, and I trudge through with my human baggage. Wondering, watching, waiting...just hoping to understand.

Journal
August 28, 2018
163 days

   Slept in. Way in. Sound of the creek at 6-Mile Camp had us dozing back until 10 am. We only had six and a half mile to reach HWY 20 so we took it easy. I think that's the general plan for the last four days up here.
   We had lunch at the pullout for the PCT just before Rainey Pass. Put our thumbs out and caught a ride from Matt, who actually works for the Forest Service and helped create the closures from Hart's Pass. No hard feelings. We talked for twenty miles, then he dropped us off at the Ross Lake Trailhead and gave us each an IPA. Probably the best beer I've had in 2,300 miles after sitting in a cold stream for 20 min. We made our way three and a half more miles up the East Bank Trail and found Sunshine up at the Hidden Hand Campsite watching his shows. He waved and smiled wide and we made our way up to the cook area. Had some chili and whatever else was floating around. Then we hung the food bags twenty feet in the air (after a few false starts). Tomorrow we make about nineteen to twenty miles alongside the lake to Nightmare Campground. Good wide trail. Can't believe the border is two days away. Can't believe any of this. Also, whole family of deer in the middle of camp tonight. Love you mom.
Will

Journal
August 29, 2018
Who am I?

The hike took some unexpected detours here and there. We're not used to operating without the PCT map I guess. Plus a BIG series of switchbacks as we made our way uphill away from Ross Lake and toward Nightmare Camp. I love it. Haha. Stomach so messed up from the chili last night and felt sluggish and heavy. Thoughts and memories from adolescence left me struck dumb. "Why on earth would I think about that in the first place? Why did I care? What bizarre creature lived within me as a child?" But…it's all a wash. It's the past. I can't make sense of it. Looking at my modus operandi from the past year alone leaves me shaking my head in disbelief. What kind of life was I expecting when I allowed so much habitual compromise? Something had to give. Something was rotten and needed a full surgical removal. Anyway. Just strange. Thoughts make up the fabric of the day and fit the spaces between steps. Some days it's nothing but music. Others, it's "The Past". Others, I wonder what the future holds. All I know is that tomorrow we hope to touch the Canadian Border.

Canada

Ditched camp at a 7:45 am and left the food hanging. Put all extra gear into the tent and made ourselves as light as possible before heading north for one final stretch toward Canada. It's hard to know what to say in those moments when you're on the verge of something like that…and in another way, we've been out here for five and a half months now. This has become life and second nature. Another day on the trail. It's easy to forget that there's a destination at all sometimes. The journey is truly what the PCT is all about. It was mostly downhill until we hit a smooth forest service road taking us the final mile up; walking around one gate, then the border monument up to our right. Four kids from last night's camp are waving down yelling "Congratulations!" We scale a sheer muddy slope and make it up to them. Fist bumps. Hugs. Laughter. Bewilderment. Inability to understand what we've done. "It will take some time." said the Italian. We take pictures. More pictures. We know the Sierras are next, but there's still a sense of finality to this. It's as far north as we go. This is Canada! For us: some 2,300 miles hiking since March 19th. I write a small "thank-you" in the trail-log, dedicating the journey to my mom…the one who made me adventurous to begin with. She had no idea how I'd interpret the word…but there I was today…with her.

Thank you.

Journal
August 31, 2018
And Out

We walked back south to the trailhead. Stopped at the same picnic lake. Almost autumn-like on this last day of August. A difference in the air. I felt detached, somber, reflective. Maybe for the first time in five and a half months. Maybe the first time I've felt like I could breathe. Let go for one moment. More memories flooded in. Light came softly from behind light clouds, illuminating the foliage and flora in a glowing green. Change was in the air. When we made it out to the trailhead Sunshine, Stiina and Kristians were already there with T-bone and a hiker from Portland. An exceptional moment. Everyone was headed to Vancouver or Seattle and flying home within the week. Unreal. Goodbyes were brief but heartfelt. We hitched into Concrete, WA with more Forest Service workers; two girls in their early twenties. Wound over the bright blue lakes and dams. Everything we spent the past five days trudging through was passed in ten minutes. Dinner at the only open restaurant. Another hitch with a Christian woman who wasn't sure if we were homeless or hikers at first. It happens. She had us bow our heads in her Rav4 and prayed that The Spirit of the Lord would find us. I'm ok with that. Amen. Sleeping at the KOA. Tomorrow: Seattle.

Coordinates: 39.1728, -120.2575

Just northwest of Lake Tahoe; having joined the Tahoe Rim Trail for two and one half days and parted just a few hours ago, splitting down to the left, by the top edge of a ski resort and into a valley far below where a campsite appeared next to an active and fresh stream. Good views of the lake earlier. "Biggest alpine lake in the world" said the gentleman who hitched us from town to Echo Lake Pass.

Space. Stars. Absence of wildfire smoke. We sit at lunch recalling how we felt and who we were before we'd even entered the Sierras; before we understood what post-holing for nine straight hours actually does to your morale.

We tried to piece it together. Tehachapi had been the last time we saw John and Kris on the trail. Where I bought my second pair of shoes.

"Remember the wind? So bad we couldn't sleep a couple times. So bad I thought I'd get blown off that mountain outside Lake Isabella."

I hadn't thought about any of these experiences at much length since Oregon. The pace changed. The wildfires sprang up and filled the sky with haze all the way to the Canadian border. And now we were suddenly back here, just thirty miles south of where we'd got back on in late May; after going home for three days essentially to say goodbye.

I'd called Aubrey from a Safeway parking lot in Tahoe and realized again how warped time had become out here. It hadn't even been three months since she'd been gone but I felt like I'd been out here at least a year. At least. I don't know what causes the time dilation to occur. I assume it's because of the sheer energy and movement taking place day after day; never seeing the same thing twice. I haven't known the day of the week offhand for at least three months. It only mattered as far as post office hours go.

When we were here last, everything was covered in snow. The lakes were frozen. The creeks were raging with the first rays of summer sun but there had been a late storm and we'd turned back. Outside of Tuolumne Meadows we'd had lunch at Miller Lake. It was there that I suddenly knew at a gut level...and could feel and imagine what life would be like without her. I shuddered next to a broken crag and walked down to the water to try and scoop something clean for my ramen.

We'd gotten out four days later and moved up to Donner Pass to beat the snow and come back when the weather was in our favor.

Oregon blew by in a cloud of smoke and mosquitos. Washington was a beautiful, wooded and mysterious place. Thick mist hung in the morning air. Streams crossed the path everywhere and moss hung beneath ancient grey slabs of metamorphic Cascade stone.

The further we got, the more aggressive the climbs until switchbacks lasted five miles and took most of the day's expendable energy to get through, but it was stunning; unlike anything I'd come across before. The thru-hikers around us looked somber. The end was coming. They kept to themselves as did we. Small calculations inching us closer by the day.

We'd learned after Snoqualmie from an exuberant day-hiker on a corporate retreat that the PCT had been closed all the way from Hart's Pass to the border. He casually told us as we ate our lunch leaving us both stunned for a moment.

"Ok. I guess we'll find out more in Holden."

Holden was a Lutheran-run sort of volunteer-based village tucked away in a valley a few days ahead. We trudged on. We passed a few more hikers. News was spreading fast. There were feelings of betrayal, talk of mutiny, threats to walk through the thirty-mile closure come hell or high water or legal repercussions. To some hikers the monument was everything. It was proof that they'd stayed true to the trail for five-plus months. There would be champagne and high fives and midair jumps of joy caught on phones here. It didn't seem fair, but as the day wore on we realized we'd already done a few reroutes due to fire. The idea was to go from Mexico to Canada on foot right? The trail overall was a well-groomed foot and equestrian path and every detour we'd had to take reminded us how good we had it on the official PCT. So what if we hit Canada at a different spot? There had to be options.

"We'll make our own monument if we have to!"

We walked through more mist and more smoke. Epic switchbacks with quarter-mile turns steeper than anything since Seiad Valley; camping next to oxygen-blue alpine lakes that filled with pure runoff and emptied downhill toward larger creeks that met rivers far below.

The northern Cascades felt untouched and rare to our senses. Greener greens, bluer blues, a richness to the air that came in unexpected moments and filled the lungs with something exotic.

After five months in nature the reasons behind the motions within the greater cycles become apparent. Everything is in motion and I realized it's only in cities where we can simulate stasis for brief periods and frame it all with right angles and sidewalks; little rules and guidelines for cells of clustered people that have to live together somehow. I think we do alright as a species. That is, I'm not as pessimistic as I used to be, but nature...

Nature doesn't operate the way we do. It's never under control. It doesn't need to be. All animals and plants work within the seasons to bring more animals and plants forth into being. This seems to be the entire modus operandi of nature: to bring forth more life to live. To bear enough seeds. To pack the mountains with enough snow to melt and feed the lower valleys and leech down minerals from mountains that rise and fall endlessly according to tectonic dynamics all over the world. The planet we live on, as I have observed, isn't just a lucky outpost on the edge of a galaxy among billions of other galaxies. It may very well be, but whatever it is; this place that bears fruit and flower and lives and dies and feeds and nourishes with radiation smashing into it, tilted at 23 degrees...it boggles the mind and I've never felt it more apparent than out here. I've written about it before but never really understood, just witnessed over and over again until it made more sense.

And then we were in Holden standing in line to get the last slices of pizza from the great cafeteria where hikers, tourists and Lutherans all came together in the summer to get away from it all.

We talked with the volunteers and got some background on the property. It had been donated to the Lutherans by a mining company operating just a stone's throw from the road which ran less than a quarter mile and was dotted with a few inns, a supply store and cafeteria. The entire compound ran on hydro-electric power and there were signs urging us to be conservative with our hot water and electricity use. We stayed the night in a modest room that was decorated sometime in the late 70s and lined back up at the cafeteria for eggs and coffee in the morning.

We had to catch a bus to Chelan Lake about an hour later and then ferry to Stehekin, the last stop on the PCT before Canada.

We'd researched alternative routes the night before and come up with a decent plan. When the PCT got to Rainy Pass we'd move west to Ross Lake State Park and walk the East Bank Trail thirty miles north to the Canadian border. We didn't know if there was an official monument or marker there, or just a line of cleared foliage like most of the northern border but it sounded like our best bet. It turned out to be the preferred route of a few dozen other hikers as well, including T-bone, Stiina and Kristians who we hadn't seen since South Kennedy Meadows back in May. T-bone lost over forty pounds on the trail and had to start supplementing extra doses of protein. He was almost gaunt at one point but he figured it out. Now, he looked tough and sturdy with a great black beard and we leapfrogged each other for the remainder of the trip with Sunshine and four other Europeans.

Return to the Sierra
Letters Home #7

We drove south to Silverton to say hi to John and Kris again. They'd been incredibly helpful a month before and helped resupply our entire Washington stretch, sending boxes from Silverton to various remote places where we didn't have access to decent groceries.
    We met Kris at their home and drove up to the property they'd bought and had been working on for awhile and just sat with some deer and antelope burgers and cold IPAs sharing stories, information and some laughs before crashing hard back at their place. I didn't know if my body was quite sure of our trajectory at this point. It knew there were four full days off and it wanted to black out instead of drive hundreds of miles to South Lake Tahoe but we waved goodbye with many thanks in the morning, finished some laundry, got a big breakfast, and headed down I-5 toward Sacramento to grab the bear canisters that we'd sent to a friend of Hanne's a few months before. They were mandatory for most of Yosemite and cost around 70 bucks apiece so we found a key left under a bag of soil, went down into a dark basement, found everything and got back on the highway. We made it into South Lake Tahoe around 1am and crashed again.
    We were back. After five and a half months. After backtracking three days from Smedberg Lake in the snow and waist-high frozen creeks and hitching to Lee Vining and getting the news from my younger sister the moment I got online:
    "Can you get home any sooner?"
    Everything had changed since then...I'd returned to Donner Pass dazed, angry, helpless...determined to finish; to walk through all of it somehow.

In Chester I phoned home again and received the news. At Burney Falls Ranch I'd sent words home for the memorial. Words wholly inadequate to express the experience but there was solace there.

And now we were back. We resupplied and hitched to Echo Summit in the afternoon, walking around Echo Lake in the Tahoe Rim Trail behind little getaway cabins on the shore. Hanne said it reminded her of the tiny villages in Norway she'd seen.

Since we were now joined with the TRT we began passing scores of day hikers and others who were doing the 170-mile loo. Since we were going northbound in September no one assumed we were PCT hikers which was a little amusing. We got congratulated for making it over small hills, eating lunch by nice streams and making it into camp but it was also fun to share our story with people. The questions are endless and varied but there's answers for all of them.

"What do you eat mostly?"

"Ramen, anything with salt, anything with carbs, anything lightweight."

"What was your favorite part so far?"

"Sierras. Still the Sierras...also the Cascades are unreal."

"What are you going to do after this?"

"No idea. Probably look for another adventure and spend the next six months saving for it."

These answers are all dependent on the fact that we're here, wherever here is. We're acclimated and we think and speak PCT to each other most of the time.

We headed north. With the snow gone the trail stretched out for miles ahead of us. The days were becoming shorter and for the first time I could smell autumn approaching.

"You know, we'll have hiked in all four seasons as soon as we hit the equinox!"

"Whoa."

"On the 19th of September we will have been out here for six months. Half a year."

"Whoa."

There's a briskness to the air. Our bodies haven't slowed with the elevation gain. We're going from 3-7k to 8-12k although we already crossed the highest passes back in May.

When we reached Truckee five days later we came upon a ski resort offering showers for five dollars and affordable burgers. We talked to a couple locals and got back out on the trail, walking a quarter mile to a spot by Donner Pass Road.

In the morning we put our thumbs out to head back south to get back on at Echo Summit and become official SOBOs. Our goal was North Kennedy Meadows, a resort and pack station that hosted horse riders, hunters and hikers alike throughout the summer.

We knew the Donnel Fire had forced yet another closure for thirty miles along the PCT but it was 85 percent contained and as we passed through on the 8th Hanne got reception for a moment and we saw that it was officially open again. Phew. We'd been through so many fire detours and gotten lucky so many times, getting through stretches just before they were closed.

The days are now perceptibly cooler and locals are urging us to press on although most feel that October 1st is a perfectly reasonable time to get out at Kearsarge Pass.

The creeks are many feet lower, even completely gone in some places. The Deer's Ear plants, so soft and green when we came through last are yellow and withering and the Sierras are a bright mix of yellow, green, and red volcanic rock.

Last night we got to camp the exact same moment as a Russian section-hiker and we spent the night sharing info on NOBO/SOBO stretches. I gave him the last of my fishing equipment that I'd never ended up using because he was keen to catch some fish up north and he gave us some bacon because he was trying to unload any weight he could. Bacon is heavy as far as trail food goes. We took a picture of us three, all from different parts of the world and wished each other well. This stuck with me on the trail as we came toward Kennedy Meadows. That's what it's all about, right?

    At the trailhead we caught a ride into the pack station with Debbie, who was staying there to figure out some insurance details after her family cabin had just burned to the ground in the Donnel Fire. She showed us pics of the rubble. After the nails and metal had been scraped out it was nothing but ashes. Fortunately, they'd be able to rebuild. She'd lived in Berlin as a child like Hanne and we met again at dinner at the main lodge and shared some more stories.

    Laundry, showers, soft bed, cowboy breakfast. Next stop: Tuolumne Meadows, redoing thirty miles of a stretch we've already done twice when we had to abandon Yosemite.

    At the bottom of the Kearsarge Pass trail exiting into Independence, we will have finished the entire 2,650 mile Pacific Crest Trail. Two and a half more weeks until then and plenty of hairy passes and climbs in between.

Love,
Will

Journal
September 14, 2018
The Real Sierra

Got another cowboy breakfast at the pack station in Kennedy Meadows, grabbed a couple extra items and walked to the main road. Hardly any cars going toward Sonora Pass. Eventually a woman with a converted minivan / camper stopped as she was leaving. We hit the trail around 12:30 pm; a little late but only fourteen miles to go today. Instant climbing up to 11k. Spectacular views, rugged stretches of rocky barren trail, winds hitting 40-50 MPH on the passes and higher points. Wispy clouds. New fires in the distance where we'd just come through. Alpine lakes; all snow melt. Streams and creeks all receding and drying up. Passed a few hunters. Deer season starts tomorrow but I think we're generally further in than most people want to haul a deer out of. Thoughts of returning home. How tos. What ifs. It's going to be a process but it'll be fine. Made it to Walker River with a little bridge. Little more than a trickle now. Met two kids from Quebec. Scamper and Captain Fantastic I think were there names. All smiles. We'll maybe see them again but they're pretty fast. Four guys across the north side of a bridge. Hellos, etc. No other info. One might be a SOBO. Wonder how many we'll actually see on this stretch. Twenty miles tomorrow. Five more miles and we enter The Yosemite.
Love,
Will

Journal
September 15th, 2018
Bearanoia

Yes. I'd rather tangle with a cougar than a bear. Don't ask me why. Saw number five today two miles from camp coming down through some bushes. He looked at us and meandered off. We did the usual pole-clacking, speaking in loud voices to let it know we were coming though.

"Walking through the woods! Walking through the woods! Hey, Mr. Bear! Now, we're walking through the woods!"

Anyway, otherwise beautiful relaxed pace that took us up one or two steep steep sections. Officially in Yosemite. Various lakes dotting the sides of the trail. Grass now yellow next to the worn-in, six-inch groove cut by thousands of feet over the years. Lines on rocks where the water has receded multiple feet just this season. More deer. Three today. Two around noon and one that just wandered up to us in the darkness fifteen minutes ago while we ate. Higher energy in the Sierra. Not as sore. More awake in the morning. Maybe it was all the smoke we inhaled in OR & WA. Maybe it's the psychological aspect of being so close to Kearsarge and the familiarity of the terrain. Either way…beautiful. Tomorrow is Smedberg Lake. Going to be surreal to be back. 'Night.

Journal
September 16, 2018
There's Beauty All Around

    Back in early June around Burney Falls an Aussie fellow scoffed at our idea of returning to the Sierra.
"Just a bunch of rocks…better in winter anyway…"
    There is a sense of clarity and constant play of light and shadow on the sheer granite walls, stained by thousands of years of runoff. The half-moon arching over monuments of epic proportions. The golden afternoon sun dancing on Smedberg Lake when we finally got there. Yosemite becomes a paradise under the various conditions of light throughout the season. I'm glad we did it this way. Now here we are: A fourteen-mile day full of vertical switchbacks and stairs. We camped on the west side. In the morning we'll pass the spot where we turned around months ago. It was emotional, walking by the shore earlier. This entire journey - of footsteps, moments, memories and my mother. I keep having dreams that she's still alive and there's something I can do to help. One last thing to try. I dreamt we went to an indoor pool just to allow her to relax. As the months wear on out here my anger becomes quieter. There's nothing I can do. There's a finality to death. I can be an adult and accept it. It comes for us all…and I'm not sure I believe in "death" to begin with.
    Saw mama bear and two cubs today across a stream. They were curious but mama hauled them away up the hill. Beautiful day. 'Night.

Journal
September 18, 2018
Where Have We Really Been?

 4 pm. Tuolumne Meadows. A different world since we huddled under a frozen sky and found food left in a bear box from the year before. Today we made it over the old bridges and drying creeks we'd been so tepid about in late May. Caravans of mules and horses passed on their way to extract all the gear from the ranger stations five miles in. I've had a cold bug for the past 24 hours so even five miles into Tuolomne Meadows felt pretty laborious. A few SOBOS crowded and mingled with tourists. Employees looked like fresh high school grads happy to see the final days of their summer jobs. Assorted climbers repacking rope and gear outside their Vanagons, lounging on the picnic tables with us. We barely paid attention. Straight for double-bacon cheeseburger at the grill station / tent. Coffee. Resupply. You can always feel the stares but sometimes you can choose whether to put out a responsive vibe or not. Today I'm just a little under the weather.
 Up at the hiker sites with one or two other tents. Tomorrow we'll get a full breakfast and head out again. Only two days to Reds Meadow Resort and into Mammoth for a zero. Barely one hundred and fifty miles to go. Unreal…and this upcoming section looks like some pretty insane passes. Uncharted territory all the way to the bottom of Kearsarge. Tomorrow It'll be half a year doing this. I can't even quantify what it's going to feel like when its over, not that I'm in the slightest rush for that to happen.
 Tomorrow, we shoot for an easy sixteen miles due to health. I think I picked it up in Seattle. Distinct chill in the air now. Wore my gloves that I bought at Seattle REI the other night. Twelve

more days. Blue jays and squirrels trying to snatch our food already here.

Thus far, only plans upon returning are getting Hanne to the airport, finding a decent bike and getting my stuff out of Albuquerque for good. I want to be connecting with Aubrey, Randy and family as much as possible. Hope we can get everyone together for a big dinner at least when I get back. Randy's in Seattle with his son Josh and girlfriend Liz right now. This life. So profoundly short. I would have done the meaningful stuff sooner...

*"In a cool solitude of trees
Where leaves and birds a music spin,
Mind that was weary is at ease,
New rhythms in the soul begin."*

-William Kean Seymor

Journal
September 23, 2018
John Denver & Us

Hitched out of Agnew Meadows on the 19th with a couple locals. Dropped us at the Motel 6. Cold bug was coming on stronger. Figured we'd probably want to let it heal before hitting an eight-day stretch. Mexican dinner. Back to the motel to sleep. Woke up about the same...edgy, disagreements and misunderstandings blown out of proportion by both of us. Maybe the volcano was just ready...seemed to happen every two months or so but we figured it out.

Took the bus to Von's and resupplied eight days for under $100! Stayed an extra night at the Motel 6, then moved over to the Mammoth RV which was more our vibe. Just needed one more day and it was a good idea. We made a sort of Mediterranean / German dinner with wine by a campfire and woke up hearing John Denver coming from another site. My kind of morning. Bus to the village. Hitched back to Agnew Meadows with a nice couple and back on the trail at 2 pm. Did about ten miles. Seven more days until the end. It's coming up fast and I'm not sure what to think about it right now. There seems to be this window through all this, where I can make whatever I wish to happen come about. The will and vision are strong...but after 2,650 miles do I just need a breather? I don't know. I work better alone out in these woods than anywhere else it seems. The towns are such a drain...just go to Switzerland? What's my soul say? Need to listen quietly this next week. Either way...life happens.
Love,
Will

Journal
September 24, 2018
Last Full Moon

   Nestled below Silver Pass. Lots of section / JMT hikers today. The packs are heavy with seven days of food left in bear canisters and most available pockets. Slow going. Hanne exhausted right out of the gate. My exhaustion crept up and consumed me by lunchtime. Just trudged. All. Day. One foot after the other. Started getting some good views later on. Super-rugged scarred peaks lined up alongside each other after Virginia Lake. More switchbacks. More up and down. You'd think after 2,600 or so miles we'd be totally acclimated. Just depends where the body's at on any given day. Trying to eat the heaviest foods first; anything to lose an ounce or two.
   Last night coughing nonstop until a vision of gold...pure liquid gold surrounded my feet. Coughing stopped instantly...a voice said: "Remember, the universe does not distinguish thoughts from matter, whatever vibration you put out there is read by the conscious mind."
   Whoa.
   I've still wasted so much time feeling bitter...about what? I feel so free out here and shudder imagining a return to society and its crass conjecture. I must work to align my thoughts with the life I truly wish to have...

Journal
September 25, 2018
Still Beats Me Up

Today was climbs and descents...yes, like every single day on the PCT, however these were rough. Today was pretty much up, down, up, down, and slightly up. My shoulders, neck, hips, everything acted up today and I felt a twinge of leftover sickness in the stomach and neck when I swallowed. Just winded. Funny how you can still have relatively rough days after all this. Got to camp along a nice stream though. Views form Silver Pass pretty amazing. Three sixty with lakes and rugged Sierras all around. Four more days; tomorrow and the next being the most challenging. We're technically climbing *up* through the Sierras even though we're heading south. Hopefully this bear canister lightens up. Odd day psychologically. After lunch and Emergen-C packet felt totally disassociated and off until camp. It happens. Sun, hills, etc. Something in my stomach...what else is new. Hope tomorrow just feels a little easier and everything heals with this bug.

Journal
September 26, 2018
The Body Knows…

Nose running. Spitting and coughing up colorful amounts of phlegm. Throat sore-hard to swallow with that irritating dry spot in the back of the nasal cavity. Muscles sore from lack of healing while body is allocating resources somewhere else. Cramps in both shoulders…lazy floating rib on my right side now stabbing when I bend over. Doubled over in stomach pain last hour on the trail. Hanne made the tent while I moaned belly up with my head on a log.

Other than that, King's Canyon is a mythical autumn cathedral of yellow aspen, deep river pools, and great granite walls casting shadows across the valley. Less than seventy miles to go and it's still testing every last muscle and nerve at times. Whatever was killing my stomach came out after dinner. Sweet relief. Can't tell if sore throat or stiff / strained neck on left side. These last four days could be pretty ridiculous if everything doesn't clear up. I think my body is finally saying "Yeah, we're done here." Hopefully whatever left my stomach was the last of it! Please…

Journal
September 27, 2018
Beyond Words

I feel like I waited six months for this day. For these mountains. This light. Climbed slowly all day until rounding increasingly larger lakes and formations. Contrasted against the fall grass and shrubs. Crystal blue against the sky. Heights of scarred solid rock shooting into the heavens. Didn't know if I'd get that "moment" before the end. Today put everything in its proper perspective. Climbing above the trees. 10-13k pristine and rarefied. Felt mom's spirit, only in the most beautiful of places would she deign to appear. The photos will never do it justice. Maybe three or four good captures out of fifty shots. This is the "moment". The meeting of The Architect. No offering, whether song or literature or whatever we create down below will ever come close to what I saw today. Camped next to Helen Lake in a little spot guarded by rocks. Three more days and I think most of them are above 10k so hopefully some of the same.

Journal
September 28, 2018
My Timbers Are Shivered

Downhill most of the day. Good pace. Finally feeling less under the weather. Just lingering throat, but that felt better as well today. Followed Middle Fork Kings River then Palisade Creek Unforgiving switchbacks toward Mather Pass. A few hikers. Saw the two SOBO girls from Muir Pass once again. Bear can is finally manageable, not back-breaking. The Sierras are yellow, white, grey, black, some green and red. Aspens changing before our eyes and willows turning red as well. Yellow grasses and meadows with meandering creeks down the middle. Light clouds. Paradise. Tonight, we're at another beautiful lake (Palisade) in a valley, surrounded on all sides by sheer mountain walls and a tapestry of stars surrounding the great band of the Milky Way. Some philosophical talks after dinner about our place in the universe, relative scale and how silly chaos theory is. Two more full days. Hope tomorrow is equal in grandeur, but I'd be satisfied with what I've seen of the Sierras thus far. Unspeakable beauty. Feel so lucky to have finally witnessed it. Night, Night.
Will

Journal
September 29, 2018
Two Passes - Day 195

Got atop Mather Pass by 10:30 this morning. Brisk. Sunlight hitting our campsite early though. Wide views of full Sierra magic. We walked down the side in twenty minutes and came out on a long five-mile plain that went through rocks, fields, eventually back into woods where we had lunch at King Fork Creek before heading toward Pinchot Pass. Even more stunning when we got there. I truly feel that this is the best time for us to have come through. All the colors of autumn; warm enough to enjoy. All the snow has turned into streams and lakes but they're not overflowing. The trail is dry and the air is clear. Shadows from a low September sun are stark and bring out the full depth of the mountains. Small details in shadow and geological features from fifty miles away. Tomorrow is our last full day on the PCT. Only twelve miles. We'll go halfway up Glen Pass and camp, then make an early ascent in the morning and head up and over Kearsarge to the parking lot. Hoping to get a ride to Independence. As you can tell, none of the finality of this trail has hit me. It's just another day in a series of days on the trail. Am I ready for it to be over? No. I don't think so. I'm ready for a big hot breakfast at Bishop but that's as far as my heartstrings allow right now. It's beyond anything I could have imagined. Right now…I just don't have words.

Journal
September 30, 2018
4.9 More Miles

Today was slow. Easy. A little cold in the morning. No passes - just streams, rivers, autumn colors, lakes, a suspension bridge. A large group of Chinese hikers appearing around 11 am when we took our lunch break. We climbed. Hanne listened to an audiobook. I listened to the ramblings in my head. Wish I had an audiobook sometimes…but then we approached Rae Lakes and the trail wound right up between them with Glen Pass in the distance. We found a tentsite next to a big granite wall facing the lake and made an early dinner and talked about what the end of the PCT means. So many memories, beautiful people, beautiful towns and experiences. I feel new. Whatever that means. Who know what happens when I get back. I'm just glad I have these memories. They'll be with me forever. In the morning we walk over the pass, then three more to the Kearsarge Pass Trail where we got out in May with Freebird after Forester and Whitney. I still don't have words for this. It's been an honor.

One Day Was Day Two

I'm walking through parallel lines of fine white sand up a gradual slope bordered by green reeds of some kind...passing through a small iron gate and taking in the morning air. A couple dogs break out of the foliage at knee level barking madly, teeth bared. "Hey dogs. Good dogs..."
Their owner appears and we talk for a minute. He lives in the area and walks this section every day. I pass behind some houses and cross long slabs of granite, passing a group of three hikers. Two boys and a girl in their early twenties.
"Hey."
"Hey."
I move on. Stop below a concrete bridge and take out some trail mix. The kids pass me this time, walking single file with matching strides; moving with intent.
"Hey."
"Hey"
I walk under a bridge, over a paved road and into a low grassy field on the other side passing a family out for a stroll with their dog as well. It's difficult to mistake us. Overpacked, over-zealous, sun-burned, and probably limping a little from pushing too hard the day before.
"Hey!"
"Beautiful day!"
"Awesome day!"
"Good luck!"
"Enjoy!"
Moving on. Feeling good. Over a fetid stream with a tire submerged in the middle. I joke to myself about "my first water crossing". I step gingerly on the tire, pushing it down into the muck, soaking my foot and reaching for the branches of a

willow on the other side. The pack drags me backward and down toward the water but I hold on, arching myself under and swinging to the other side. A few minutes later I pass the kids again, taking a break under some trees.

"Hey."

"Hey."

I'd started with four liters of water from Campo but when I left camp there were only three bottles in my pack and I'd been working up a conspiracy that one of these kids has it. I'd seen them at the campground the night before…

"Who would do such a thing?" I seethed…

"No respect…none at all. I mean, that's *water*. That's my damn water we're talking about. What if three liters isn't enough today? I can see Smartwater bottles all over their packs just like mine…the nerve. I'll confront them sooner or later. Believe me…"

But we kept passing each other every half hour like this…

"Hey."

"Hey."

"I suppose I could be wrong. I mean really… who actually *steals* water bottles? I don't think anyone does. Is that a thing out here? You're not in Albuquerque, man. People don't just steal for the fun of it out here. What if I left it at Lake Morena? But I didn't even take them out except to refill this morning. Did I have three or four then? Wouldn't I notice a missing water bottle?"

After a few more leapfrogs they passed me for good and I purposely tried to slow my stride and look up more often, getting pictures here and there until I came upon a trailhead parking lot with a couple spigots and an outhouse. Under a tree at the end of gravel I saw a man lying on his back on a picnic table with his lunch spread out around him. Probably a good place to take a break and refill water…I walked over.

"Hey what's up?" I asked
"Ah man…ya know. Livin'."
"Yeah?"
"Cold chillin…"
"Right on."
　Something about this guy that told me he'd seen a trail or two before. Everything looked ultralight, streamlined, and barebones. He seemed right at home puffing on a massive joint, blowing billows into the air between long sighs and tapping it off to the side of the bench.
"Where you from man?" He asked.
"Albuquerque…my first thru-hike. What about you?"
"Virginia…did the AT last year. Gonna do this as long as I can."
"Nice…you did the Appalachian Trail?"
"Yep. Different trail for sure, but I'm digging this!"
"Can I see how heavy your pack is?" I was suddenly curious…
"Sure man, go for it."
　I lifted it up and was surprised that it wasn't much lighter than mine…but it *was* lighter.
"Huh…so any tips for a newcomer?"
He paused for a moment then shrugged:
"Ah man, in a month you'll be in the best shape of your life. Get enough food in town. You'll be golden"
I nodded silently…
"My shoulders are killing me already…"
"Gotta drop some weight or something. Make sure you've got enough weight on the hips. You'll figure it out man. Just takes awhile before you get your hiker legs under ya."
I nodded again.
"Cool…I'm gonna get some water. Do those spigots work?"
"Oh yeah. Fresh and clean."
"Cool. See ya."
"Peace."

He put his hat on his face and I turned around toward the spigots…Hanne was just coming over the hill into the parking lot.
"Hey!"
"Do you eat lunch here?" She asked.
"Yeah I guess so. My shoulders are killing me. When did you leave Lake Morena?"
"I don't know. I wake up and everyone is gone so I just start walking. My shoulders hurt a lot too."
We filled our bottles at the spigots and got our food bags out.
"I think someone stole one of my water bottles last night."
"No. You forgot it."
"I'm not so sure. I know I had all four when we came into camp."
"Yeah, but who steals a water bottle?"
"I don't know…people. Bad people."
"Just buy another in town."
"Yeah. I guess."
We ate lunch but didn't say much…I had the feeling all these little pains were growing into a much bigger pain that was going to manifest later in the week if I didn't take it easy but there were only a few more miles to go. We trudged on at a decent pace until we ran into the threesome again, having lunch in a wash by some broken crags. It was time for another break so we stopped and introduced ourselves. I'd given up the idea that there was a bottle thief on the trail by then and we all joked about the little injuries and sprains less than 48 hours into the trail. Blisters seemed to be the theme so far. Blisters and good old throbbing pain in the shoulders, hips, and knees.
"It gets better. I read that it all gets better."
"Yeah…might be rough for a few weeks till the body knows what's what."

"I just need to pop this blister on my heel when we get to camp…It's killing me!"
"What's that nerve under your foot? The long one under the heel that goes to the front?"
"It's not a nerve, it's a ligament called plantar fascia."
"Oh. That's the one I feel."
"Yeah, you need new shoes man. Those are gym shoes."
"Hanne thinks so too, but I'm the only one without blisters so far, right?"
"For now…"

I wasn't convinced. In fact, I thought I'd found a secret footwear solution and was going to stick to my guns as long as I didn't get any blisters…

Then we all got up and started walking in a larger train of five, spreading out and finding the right distance between each other, pushing over hills and winding back and forth through switchbacks for a few more hours. No one mentioned grouping up or vocalized anything about a destination. We were just a group that was suddenly hiking and taking breaks together. I didn't know if the kids knew each other or had met the night before or what. We just kept walking until the trail hit a junction with a quarter-mile dirt road leading down into a creekside campground and we all thought it was a great place to call it a day. It was about 5 pm again and my feet were killing me, but when I took off my shoes…no blisters. Victory.

The group dynamic was something I hadn't anticipated. I thought you didn't really see others on the PCT and secondly, I'd left nearly a month before most people, only because the other dates had been taken by the time I applied for a permit. March 19th had been the next available date so I just filled out the form and clicked "send".

It was only day two and our group of five suddenly became seven as two more exhausted faces appeared: The guy I'd met at the showers at Lake Morena introduced himself as Karson and another younger kid dressed in blue basketball shorts and a blue jersey with a big blue pack hobbled in.

We each set up our tents as fast as possible and gathered around the picnic table, digging into packs and pulling out bags of food. I was suddenly the only one without a propane system and my mouth watered uncontrollably as the smell of ramen and freeze-dried Chana-Marsala wafting through the air. I cut pieces of cheese and dried salami and pretended I was happy to gnaw on the same stuff I'd had the night before.

I tried to participate in the conversations, but I couldn't decide if I wanted to be around people at all just then. It felt like I was suddenly at risk of forfeiting something, but I didn't know what. Autonomy? My experience? Everything had been a quiet, calculated march toward Campo and I suddenly imagined we were all unconsciously sizing each other up with little reflexive social cues that we weren't in control of.

"Maybe this is just how people get to know each other. Maybe it's something that happens in nature…"

I'd read studies where people split into specific roles when they were forced to be around one another in isolation and I wondered if I'd unwittingly capitulate to some biological constraint; something that only happened on epic trails far away from the amenities that keep our wafer-thin identities intact. I'd get lost out here, quietly pandering to the whims of strangers until…

"Stop over-thinking everything and eat your cheese!"

At the beginning of these sorts of endeavors there's so little known and less *to* know than you think. The mind wants answers. It wants the available systems that plugged it into a tidy world full of normal expectations only days prior. It wouldn't occur to anyone in the first week of a thru-hike that they were already doing ninety percent of what the entire journey entailed. The rest would become details; the energy more refined. The complaints less useful. The purpose - evolving from a definable physical goal to an inward *sense* of things...a connection that simultaneously disconnecting from everything familiar. It would take months to understand this...but right now there were zero reference points. I was a music producer with a backpack but I wanted to own my energy instead of sharing it with "strangers".

    I went off to be alone down with my pen and notepad by a stream at the edge of the campground, sitting at a bench with the odd awareness of knowing that I knew nothing and had no sense of how that might affect me in the coming days. I couldn't imagine what I should expect to feel, I only felt something pressing against my heart. It felt well below the threshold of an open worry and I'd felt it before: The quiet knowledge that everything was in the midst of an evolution whether I was ready or not. My commitment to the trail was already overwhelming. I knew I wanted to be there despite anything I perceived as novel. I openly admitted that it *was* novel...in a good way. It was new. It was impossible to pin down and it made my heart race both ways. I laughed that I should complain about anything at all and shook my head and wrote in my pages...meandering ideas and abbreviated sentiments as my energy waned. The second night I came to appreciate one of the fundamental novelties of the trail that made its completion more likely: At the end of any day you're just too tired to care. You might wrestle with some minor motivational issues after breakfast and have a quiet tantrum over the pain in your ankles on an unforgiving downhill, but when you see that campsite and take that first bite of dinner...silent satisfaction. I watched the sun go down through the trees, sparkling in the water as it went. For a few more minutes I sat and listened and did little else.

Then I hobbled back to camp and made a small fire. A few of the others gathered round and we stared into the hypnotic flames.

Something about a good campfire makes people philosophical and we opened up a bit more to each other, asking in turn where we came from and why we were here. The youngest of the group appeared with a blue jacket covering his blue jersey and sat silently in the darkness a few feet out of the warmth of the flames.

"How about you?"

"Me?"

"Yeah...why'd you want to do the PCT?"

He shrugged with a gleam in his eye. He'd already heard some of our reasons...our conjecture and earnest poetics.

"Meh, I just felt like doing something stupid."

A series of uncomfortable chuckles followed. I'd done plenty of categorically stupid things by his age, but I was impressed by anyone who had conceived, planned, trained and showed up in Campo. People came from all over the world to test themselves and everyone seemed to have a reason ready to share when prompted. Of course, you need a reason and any reason will do...but it better be yours.

We watched the embers die out and took turns pouring water and stirring the coals until it was just another quiet part of the night. I leaned my solar charger against a stone where I thought it might catch the morning sun and snuck into the narrow tent.

"Day two...totally different than day one." I thought.

"I mean. the same but totally different...somehow."

And I fell deep asleep.

In Honor of The Howdies

I remember meeting John and Kris the day we came out of the Mojave River area...which was presently occupied with too many big black rattlesnakes. My choice in shoes was finally starting to disrupt my ability to saunter well although I was *still* the only person I knew without blisters. There just wasn't any support in them. The soles were almost nonexistent and I'd already had a couple hard elbows in the ice on San Jacinto because, among these issues, they had zero tread. I was being stubborn and I knew it. I just didn't know *how* bad they actually were. Hanne had said "Yeah, I wouldn't even wear these to walk around town...they are maybe for hanging out in a padded gym doing aerobics or something." And here I thought I'd had the whole thing beat.

Crossing the Mojave River canyon over bridges and wading a couple side streams brought us to our first and most magical trail magic involving a retired couple who had run into a couple of hikers the day before and had fallen in love with the idea so much that they went right out and bought a truckload of hot-dogs, fresh fruit, and sodas and posted up at the top of the first climb leading away from the river under a great Cottonwood tree.

When I say it's the little things on the trail, it's truly the little things. Even months afterward I shook my head in disbelief at just how many people it takes any given season to make the trail a reality for hundreds of hikers, many of whom never make it to Kennedy Meadows for a plethora of legitimate reasons...and the rest of the train who relied on Trail Angels, trail magic and water caches so regularly that it felt indispensable.

After the 10 am surprise second breakfast we went through a few long meandering stretches and came upon John and Kris in the shade by a tiny stream taking a break.

"Howdy Howdy!" Said John with enthusiasm. This was his trademark greeting which Hanne loved.

I tried to explain it was just an old western American "hello" that lots of people still used, but just then my legs were beginning to act awful funny. I welcomed the break and we shared a few moments with them.

They were taking on the PCT in sections and had been doing so for a few years. They hoped to make it to South Kennedy Meadows this year and tackle the rest of the Sierras and Northern California the following year. John was an engineer and Kris was a science teacher but they'd both been retired for some time and had taken to the trails and every other adventure they came across.

John carried traditional topo maps and we guessed together what the stretch after Lake Silverwood was going to look like.

After that I figured it was the last we'd see them, but after lunch Hanne started pulling away again and I resigned to my fate. Something just didn't feel right in my left hip. An hour later and my entire leg started seizing up. Then John and Kris passed me. Then I started to get really mad. I couldn't understand what was causing my entire left side to hang behind my right side, but now I was physically *dragging* half my weight behind me and the exhaustion was creeping like mad. I'd barely made it to the halfway point of the day, well before the great dam we'd be walking around just to get to the lake, and it felt like I was shutting down. At first, I took breaks and tried to stretch the hip, but I couldn't figure out a good way to do it. I tried drinking more water, eating more snacks. Then, I started chastising myself under my breath.

"This is ridiculous man. You're not that old. These two are in their sixties and they just blew past you. What is going *on* here? Get it together! It's all in your head!"

Things spiraled progressively downhill from there. At some point out of sheer desperation to protect my ego, it became my life's mission to catch John and Kris.

"Howdy howdy! How ya doing there?"

"Oh, I'm alright." I seethed.

"You know that pack's looking pretty full there. I can give you a few pointers later at the lake on how to lighten up if you're interested."

"No, no, no. I'm fine. I'm good! It's the sleeping bag. It's really puffy. Synthetic down. -18 Celsius. Takes up a lot of room."

"Alright well, we'll see you down there."

"Yep!"

I drug myself past, looking like a wounded animal with nothing left but his pride and it must have showed.

The last three miles into camp felt like an eternity. Silverwood Lake was actually a massive reservoir and the trail didn't lead directly to the closest shore. Instead, it hung to the bushy hills, overlooking everything and kept zigzagging with one false ending after another. Twenty minutes later a text came in: "Pizza down here!"

I was in a semi-delirious state, conducting an orchestra of small imaginary animals with a stalk of dry grass and the word "pizza" brought me back to earth long enough to stumble down into the parking lot and collapse next the open box and a warm bottle of root beer.

A few days later, after Hanne had shown me a miraculous stretching method for my hip and we made it to the Acton KOA outside Agua Dulce. I'll admit I've got a thing for those. It means a shower and clean socks and typically, a flat spot in the grass to pitch a tent. Hanne made it out of the mountains a good fifteen minutes before me that day. My legs worked, but not well. I had to tell myself to "Keep walking...just keep walking"

until the place came into view. I hopped off the trail across a field full of broken building materials and tires and glass and made my way toward Hanne who was sitting on a big swinging bench with her pack sitting against the front office.
"How are you doing?"
"Uhhh...tired. Hungry. Same as yesterday."
　Across the field a few giant teepees dominated the view. On the other side, a Swiss couple was getting ready to grill something up for dinner while their two kids played tag around a jungle gym, laughing as the shadows lengthened.
"Are we going to stay here tonight?"
"If it's cheap...might as well."
　We checked in and took a little spot in the middle of the field with our own little picnic table, staked the tents, set the food out, positioned the solar chargers, refilled the water and hung the sleeping bags over rocks to dry a little more. The Swiss donated a few drinks to the cause. It was a fine spread. People were genuinely interested in all the details and we'd inadvertently developed a sort of bullet-point response to the most common FAQs by this time. As they wandered down toward the laundry, we spotted John and Kris making their way into camp.
"Oh man...I didn't know we were ahead of them!"
We waved from across the field.
They waved back, tired but enthusiastic as ever.
"I'm gonna hit the showers. No. I'm going to take this glass of wine to the showers and stand there for fifteen minutes." I said.
"Ok. I want to go say hi to them."
"Cool...well, we're not going to drink all that beer...I bet they'd love some right about now."
"Yeah. Good idea!"
"I feel like I was rude the other day. I was just so wrecked."
"Oh, they don't care. I go make friends with them. Go take your shower."

"Ok, go make friends. See you in a bit."

I hobbled over clutching my titanium mug in my tiny REI towel and made my way up the wheelchair ramp. Something had to be done about my shoes. I knew Tehachapi was the next city with any sort of sporting goods store. It'd be just before Kennedy Meadows where I planned on switching over to hiking boots anyway, but I knew I wasn't going to last much longer. It was only by stopping to stretch my hip out every few miles that I'd been able to make it to Acton and I knew it'd be more of the same until I figured something out.

I stood there with my eyes closed and took long deep breaths. I'd be able to check back home in the morning and give an update. As expected, there was virtually no signal when we were deep in the mountains and I'd given up trying to check at each and every pass in order to get pictures through. My mom was a skilled botanist and local birdwatcher and guide on top of that, so I'd begun taking pictures of every flower I saw for a pop-quiz I planned after the trail.

All these thoughts. All these memories. All these moments. All these sunup-to-sundown days accumulating one after the other. I wanted to get off the trail and sit by her and say everything I'd never said and at the same time I wanted to keep sharing the trail. I knew it was where I was supposed to be. I knew it was the only way I was going to manage regardless of what happened. If I stayed home, I'd be in the way; micromanaging, compiling ever-more lists, demanding she try the next red ginseng extract brand to induce apoptosis in the irregular white cells that were crowding the red ones. I just knew I was supposed to be here. I slumped to the floor and let the hot water rinse the salt and dirt from my hair until the coins ran out.

Back at the camp Hanne told me that she and The Howdies had a long conversation and they'd been grateful for the cold beer.

There's no easy days and the past two had been sweltering from sunup to sundown. At night the temperatures would drop toward freezing and camping anywhere near water usually meant a good amount of frost in the morning. A good amount of frost meant wet bags and tents that we'd haul out during lunch and position on the sunniest boulders and logs for a direct solar hit that usually dried things in a few minutes.

The next time we saw them was a few days later at Hikertown before the equally infamous Los Angeles Aquaduct stretch. It meant packing as much water as we could carry and praying for shade beneath a Joshua tree or two before approaching the windmills. It's also one of the longest paved stretches and follows a wide canal until reaching an enormous steel water pipe that you can walk on for miles.

There was one lukewarm shower at Hikertown and we all took turns that night, before rummaging through an assortment of hiker boxes looking for shoes to switch out until Tehachapi. No dice. I compared a few discarded pairs and realized mine were more like pizza dough with laces than actual shoes. The shower and hiker boxes and a basic kitchen had all been built inside an old garage that doubled as a lounge with a couple big couches; currently occupied by Leo and Cherry from Taiwan and South Korea with whom we'd also leap-frogged since Lake Morena. Cherry stood about 5'1" and must have been in her late fifties. You honestly couldn't see her with her pack on, but she was tough as nails.

We left early to beat the worst of the sun. John and Kris had the same idea but left three hours earlier around 4 am to make it to a shaded bridge by the first reliable water.

When we finally caught up to them in mid-afternoon, they'd already had a nice break and were gearing up for the final stretch which would take us through the final windmills and back toward the mountains.

"Howdy howdy!" said John as we approached, in dire need of a break. We went over to their spot beneath the bridge and sat down with him and Kris while they packed up. We took out some snacks and talked about a potential campsite up ahead. It was about five miles which would put us somewhere around 25 for the day. We also met Vlado from Slovakia here. He was a former mountain climber in his mid-sixties with a thick eastern European accent. It was tough enough to get the right gear in his nick of the woods and he'd had to augment his entire outfit when he got to the San Diego REI. He'd had enough for the day though and was going to camp under the bridge. We'd run into him over three hundred miles later in Buck's Lake.

We ended up leaving within a few minutes of each other; passing through dozens more windmills. At the top of a steep stretch they realized I didn't have any trekking poles either. "Well, to each his own." John said. He was diplomatic, and it was dawning on me that I'd had some glaring blind-spots in my approach.

"Yeah...I don't know...I figured they'd just take up space but now I see everyone's got a pair. I don't know if I can afford a sweet pair of carbon poles though."

"Well, you don't need carbon." Kris said. "Just find a decent pair of aluminum poles like these and you're good to go!"

These things started to seem very matter-of-fact. Why *hadn't* I brought a pair of poles? Why *did* I think I'd get away with packing an extra ten pounds of food over longer stretches than I needed to? Why *did* I have two pairs of jeans? Why *was* I walking in gym shoes that didn't belong anywhere on a trail? I began to surmise that the romance outweighed the reality from the get-go, but I was willing to learn. I just needed to hear it from someone older and more experienced. I didn't want extra pain and hassle any more than the next hiker.

We split up somewhere around the rolling steps of the next mountain as Hanne and I climbed through fields of Golden Eye flowers and headed down into a gulch with a shallow stream full of grey silt coursing just below a sandy little bluff. We pitched the tents and started heating water for another ramen-noodle dinner. We waited for John and Kris but they never appeared. Must've called it a day at the top of the canyon instead.

Our next encounter was in Tehachapi at the bakery and then over a month later at Shelter Cove. They'd been off the trail for some time, having finished the Southern California section and pulled out at Kennedy Meadows. John met us at Shelter Cove in Oregon with a case full of Gatorade and fresh-cut melons before driving us back to the trailhead and inviting us to stop by their home in Silverton when we got further into Oregon. Their generosity was striking.

We weren't the first hikers they'd helped out but we felt grateful. We were both getting burnt out by the long dusty days in Oregon and took a couple zeros with Kris, cooking elk tacos and finding our way around Salem. Since the Washington locations were usually too remote for stores, Kris sent our boxes which made everything much easier to handle on our end.

When we finished the Ross Lake detour at the Canadian border and headed back south to finish the Sierra we stopped at their place again and had a relaxing night at their other property outside town which was in the process of becoming something a wildlife preserve. John has set up night-vision motion cameras at various points to catch animals crossing through and showed us all the recent pictures of deer, cougars, and bears. Amazing. We said goodbye to them one last time the next morning but stayed in contact as I made my way toward Switzerland and they geared up for their 2019 PCT adventure. The news from the forums was already coming in: 2019 was going to be tough. Snow, and lots of it; falling consistently on the next section they were planning to finish, but they are tenacious as ever and as I write they're regrouping for the final charge.

"On the first day of a thru, you know everything but you can't do anything. At the end you know nothing, without hesitation."

I'm the Reason Aren't You?

An old Chevy S-10 sat in the gravel driveway. Faded blue and grey with the white camper shell. We showed up on a hill in northern Arizona in 1991 with nothing more than a split-pine trailer on wheels one hundred feet of limestone to drill for a well. Lazy Lariat Lane wound up and over a short vertical climb to overlook the entire Verde Valley, sunsets and all. At night the stillness was so complete that the only sound would be the occasional hum of a lone semi-truck coursing past the exits a few miles away on I-17. A coyote here and there.

When it rained (which it rarely did until monsoon season) the air was thick with the smell of creosote bushes and dirt. When the monsoons came the thunderstorms rolled in from the north and shook the ground; great flashes of light silhouetting the sandstone monuments in the distance. The washes would fill with muddy water for an hour, drain into Beaver Creek and dry out the moment the sun returned.

When we went camping, the kids piled into the back of the truck. We'd laid down a thin sheet of outdoor rug on the floor and cut around the wheel wells but after a few miles chugging uphill, the bed became too hot and we'd put our shoes back on and perch with bowed heads, bracing ourselves along the frame.

One week it was Arches National Monument. The next, a starlit desert horizon deep in the Mojave. It was the Grand Canyon, Zion, San Juan, Yellowstone, Painted Desert, Wupatki, Meteor Crater, Silverton, Aspen, the Blue Bells, the Tetons, Moab, or Jackson Hole. At twelve I'd taken such a liking to Jackson Hole that when we returned, I immediately drew up an official "Run away to Jackson Hole blueprint" which I hid deep in my closet.

There was always movement from a young age, whether intended or necessary. It was the three of us: my two sisters and

I, while mom worked endlessly to provide and put herself through school.

Just two years before the quiet hilltop in Rimrock, we were parked in the ranger residence quarters at Lost Dutchman State Park outside Apache Junction directly in the shadow of the Superstition Mountains. At seven years of age, my only interest was uncovering pieces of obsidian, finding and exploring abandoned gold mines, and the gypsy girl with the great heap of unkept hair that lived down the road in a community called First Water.

A year before Lost Dutchman we lived in another ranger station (abandoned servant's quarters) at Oracle State Park as they began opening and renovating a turn-of-the-century mansion. My primary concern here was collecting minnows from the main cistern, luring mice into my live-trap and building a "museum" with Aubrey in the old barn comprised of broken china, horseshoes and fading apothecary bottles.

From time to time, we'd stay over at the Reevis Mountain School of Self Reliance in the hills north of Phoenix. Our friend Willy Whitefeather would show us how to find geodes and crystals, how to make fires from strings and sticks and we'd sleep in one of the yurpies with dirt floors somewhere on the property. My favorite memories from Reevis still revolve around the anticipation of the great bonfire we usually built after dinner. Every hand pitched in with harvesting, cooking, crafting and at the end of the long summer days around dusk we'd begin collecting wood. Guitars and harmonicas would accompany the flickering golden embers and I'd sit there, staring into the flames like I still do, listening to the various stories of the current tenants and volunteers.

In the fall of 1993, two months into my freshman year of high school, and already fed up with The System, I conspired once again to run away. I'd just finished a transcontinental bicycle ride and sitting behind a desk seemed like an act of deliberate sadism. I became a problem-student, lashing out at faculty and leaving the grounds regularly to spend my time alone in the county library reading about far-off places. The librarians seemed to understand. I was desperate to live out some great adventure somewhere somehow, no matter where it led me and I surmised the green rolling hills of rural England would be a good start. So, I crammed a suitcase full of everything I imagined I'd need, snuck it on the bus to school and snuck right back out during lunch.

At that time, mom was working at Red Rock State Park just down the road. My plan was to hitch down to Phoenix Sky Harbor, snare the sympathies of an elderly couple headed for England and hop aboard. If that didn't work I'd just empty the suitcase, climb inside, and somehow check myself onto a flight bound for The Shire. It honestly didn't sound too complicated...

Ten minutes later I was walking down 89-A, visibly preoccupied with the luggage, huffing along with determination, when Randy pulled up alongside and convinced me to put the whole idea on hold for a moment. I pretended to be put off by any suggestion that I was *not* prepared to carry out my plan but reluctantly agreed. I was young and full of the same wanderlust that follows me today. Ten minutes later we were at the ranger station. Busted.

Later, we traded the S-10 for a used maroon Dodge Caravan. It felt like a luxury yacht, with a working tape deck and reliable A/C compared to the faithful can that'd taken us up and down so many highways. We piled in and kept everything in the very back, wedged below seats, or strapped to the roof. We kept moving. Kept exploring. Kept living. As teenagers we were all forces of nature, breaking at the seams on a weekly basis, getting into trouble, falling down, dusting off, getting back up. In our latter days though, I was keen to let slip that she'd have to take a little credit for at least *some* of my adventures. I'd been raised on Whitman, Abbey, and Thoreau those old hardback covers glared at me from the bookshelves.

I'd been drawn to the northern steps east of Sedona one summer when I was twelve, convinced that something sacred and secret lie there waiting to be discovered by the right sort of person. I convinced my friend Spencer to pack his things immediately (including some cheese and water) and meet me behind his dad's property in an hour.

We set off in a beeline over the high desert and made it about four miles before Spencer lost sight of the Grand Vision and we ran out of cheese. To this day I wonder what drew me so viscerally to the lower Mogollon Rim. Sometimes you just have to find out. Sometimes you just start walking toward something.

Ambling back up Lazy Lariat Lane I turned around, watching wistfully as the afternoon sun lit up the ponderosa and creosote in a great wave of amber and green. I dropped the pack in my room, somewhat dejected and slunk over to the smell of dinner in the kitchen.

"Well, did you find what you were looking for?" Mom asked.
"I don't know. Yes and no." I replied with my face propped on my left hand. "There's something out there."

On our last hike we drove up through Jerome to a little spot on Mingus Mountain overlooking the valley again. She was already weak from the first rounds of chemotherapy, but we made it about a quarter-mile through the shrubs and pines and sat down amidst the rocks and sand while a few ravens circled the edge of a wide overlook.

"That's the trail down there." She pointed. "Remember that?"

"Yeah, we ran all the way down to Cottonwood! Randy laughed.

"We just decided out of the blue it'd be a good idea to run five miles down the mountain."

I was trying to picture myself doing this now. It was mid-October and I hadn't even heard of the Pacific Crest Trail yet. This seemed like a long-gone version of myself; running down mountains for the sheer joy of it...

Randy cut up some apples and handed them to us. We looked into the valley; like gazing through time. Almost every road, trail, and waterway out there we'd hiked, biked, swam, kayaked and otherwise explored. To the west, over at Dead Horse, we'd planted about 40,000 trees one summer in the hundred-degree sun, diverting flumes, collecting trimmings and sticking them in long, muddy rows. It was supposed to be a reforestation project but when the funding disappeared, they thinned it out with trails and large ponds; now a beautiful, quiet place where friends and families can walk and picnic.

On my last visit I drove to the park late in the afternoon and walked through slowly, listening to people laugh while little bugs danced on the water and dogs chased each other through the reeds. When the sun hit the top of Mingus Mountains a golf cart approached and a tired voice told me it was time to go.

I came back to the old split-pine on the hill, now a great sanctuary with additions, landscaped gardens, walkways, and bird feeders. Holiday pines planted and cared for in the front now towered thirty feet above the roof. The old redwood porch. The nails we set by hand. The prints we made in the cement foundations when the wheels finally came off.
"Does this mean it's a real house now?"

I crawled up on the deck railing and pulled myself onto the roof the same way I did as a teenager and walked quietly over to the south side and sat down on the edge facing southwest with my feet dangling and looked at the mountains until the stars began appearing one by one.

"And forget not that the earth delights to feel your bare feet and the winds long to play with your hair."

-Khalil Gibran

"What's my favorite song?"
"It has to be John Denver…Poems Prayers and Promises."
"You know! And what's my favorite bird?"
"Favorite bird? Oh man…I thought you loved all of them."
"I do, but I have an all-time favorite too."
"Ok…what is it?"
"The Mountain Bluebird."
"I was going to say Blue jay."
"No. They're much larger. You'll see plenty of them on the trail."

www.ingramcontent.com/pod-product-compliance
Lightning Source LLC
Chambersburg PA
CBHW051348290426
44108CB00015B/1925